# Understanding Sacramental Healing

## Anointing and Viaticum

John C. Kasza

**Hillenbrand** Books™

Chicago / Mundelein, Illinois

*Nihil Obstat*
Reverend Robert L. Tuzik, PHD
Censor Deputatus
October 31, 2006

*Imprimatur*
Reverend John F. Canary, STL, DMIN
Vicar General
Archdiocese of Chicago
November 1, 2006

UNDERSTANDING SACRAMENTAL HEALING: ANOINTING AND VIATICUM © 2007 Archdiocese of Chicago: Liturgy Training Publications, 3949 South Racine Avenue, Chicago IL 60609; 1-800-933-1800, fax 1-800-933-7094, e-mail orders@ltp.org. All rights reserved. See our website at www.LTP.org.

HillenbrandBooks™ is an imprint of Liturgy Training Publications (LTP) and the Liturgical Institute at the University of Saint Mary of the Lake (USML). The imprint is focused on contemporary and classical theological thought concerning the liturgy of the Catholic Church. Available at bookstores everywhere, or through LTP by calling 1-800-933-1800 or visiting www.ltp.org. Further information about the HillenbrandBooks™ publishing program is available from the University of Saint Mary of the Lake/Mundelein Seminary, 1000 East Maple Avenue, Mundelein, IL 60060 (847-837-4542), on the Web at www.usml.edu/liturgicalinstitute, or e-mail litinst@usml.edu.

Cover © The Crosiers/Gene Plaisted, OSC

19 18 17 16 15      3 4 5 6 7

Printed in the United States of America.

Library of Congress Control Number: 2006934427

ISBN 978-1-59525-009-4

HUSH

# Table of Contents

# *Preface*

The title of this book is *Understanding Sacramental Healing: Anointing and Viaticum*. While it was necessary to examine this topic from a historical perspective, it is clear from the research today, that the criteria for reception are much broader than they were in the past. As a result of the theological reflection done prior to the Second Vatican Council, it is no longer possible to restrict reception only to the *moribundi* (dying). Moreover, the shift in terminology from *Extreme Unction* to *sacrament of the sick* opened a window of opportunity for discussing the issue of serious illness.

While the Second Vatican Council accepted some of the suggestions of theologians and liturgists regarding the use of the sacrament, over the past 35 years, new illnesses (such as different types of cancers and AIDS) as well as the classification of conditions as diseases or disorders (such as alcoholism, addictions, and mental disorders) have prompted a need to reexamine the issue of serious illness. No longer can serious illness be solely classified as the moment of death *(articulum mortis)*; rather, a serious illness is that illness or condition, which left untreated, will lead a person to physical death *(magna infirmitas)*. A serious illness incapacitates or impairs a person to such a degree that he or she finds it almost impossible to function normally within society. A serious illness, like other illnesses but to a much greater degree, affects a person's relationship with himself, others, and God. Moreover, a serious illness has ramifications physically, psychologically, socially, and spiritually.

This research has shown that the Church should examine more carefully the issue of broadening her concept of serious illness in order to use the sacrament in a more effective manner. Specifically, more attention could be given to using the sacrament of the sick with those who suffer from mental disorders and alcohol, drug, sexual, and food addictions. Furthermore, perhaps there needs to be more careful preparation and liturgical catechesis regarding communal Anointing services. On the one hand, the sacrament could be used more inclusively. On the other hand, the sacramentality of Anointing must be preserved by not allowing it to be used indiscriminately. Finally, the Church could be more conscious of her pastoral ministry to all the sick, not just the seriously ill. Those who suffer from anxiety and depression (but not to the point of death) as well as those who have non life-threatening, but nonetheless serious, conditions could also benefit from a liturgical experience. The non-ordained minister often offers a unique perspective and can provide valuable assistance to both the patient and priest.

A second innovation of this study is its methodological approach. The historical-critical method of analysis was followed. However, in order to more fully determine the sacramental dimension of Anointing of the Sick, it was necessary to also examine the anthropological, sociological, medical, and theological underpinnings of both sickness and healing. In this day and age, it is imperative that the Church learns from other disciplines and uses what is beneficial in those fields of inquiry to more fully evangelize and catechize both the faithful and the world.

A third innovative aspect of this work is that because of the research and some of the questions we were able to raise, more inquiry may result. The issue of the use of the sacrament of the sick is not completely concretized. Perhaps the Church may wish to develop another rite of the sacrament for those who are not seriously ill. It may be necessary in the next millennium to formally create nonsacramental liturgies to accommodate illnesses that, although not life-threatening, nonetheless impair a person's functioning or outlook on life.

A fourth focus of the book is that of the minister of Anointing. While sacramental Anointing must be performed by a priest, in other cultures the healer-diviner was a charismatic figure renown for his or her healing abilities. Is there a need for the Church to return to a more charismatic[1] approach regarding her healing ministry? Would the inclusion of officially recognized healers[2] enhance the Church's credibility as an avenue for healing? Furthermore, non-ordained persons may sometimes be called upon in the absence of a priest to preside at liturgies for the sick, namely visitation (with or without Communion),

---

[1] Here charismatic is meant in the sense of *charismata*, meaning "gifted by the Holy Spirit," not in the sense of charismatic prayer groups.

[2] For example, there are some priests who already possess the gift of "healing" (see chapter 4). Could others who have similar gifts be invited to exercise their ministry in a more official capacity under the auspices of the Church? However, the question of allowing them to offer the sacrament of the sick would need to be addressed in a fuller way.

Viaticum, and assisting at the moment of death. In the weeks following an illness or death, non-ordained ministers can continue the process of healing by offering pastoral care to both the patient and the patient's family.

Finally, there needs to be a clearer articulation of the relationship between the sacrament of the sick and the forgiveness of sins.[3] As was noted in the exegesis of the Jacobean text, the phrase is in the conditional: "and *if* he has committed any sins . . . ." Does every illness require that a person be forgiven from sin? Moreover, what is the relationship between sickness and sin? This question needs to be addressed not only from a moral perspective, but from a sacramental and anthropological focus as well.

First, in writing this text, an interdisciplinary approach was utilized. Not only did I examine the historical, scriptural, and theological literature, I also used canon law, anthropology, and medical sources. This methodological approach enabled me to securely root the tradition of the sacrament within human experience. In sacramental theology, it is important that the sacraments are "grounded" in the everyday life experiences of those who celebrate them. All of our symbols—water, wine, bread, oil, sacramental touch, light, incense, etc.—flow from the lived experience and use by the people. The natural becomes the conduit to the supernatural. Furthermore, in using an interdisciplinary method of inquiry, the sacrament was situated within the broader dimension of human ritual and response. In other words, by examining medical and anthropological "rituals" of healing, it was seen that sacramental healing is connected to those rituals and yet surpasses them because in sacramental ritual, the human element comes into direct contact with the divine, responding to the deepest human need for immortality and relationship.

---

[3] Prior to the Second Vatican Council, some theologians and canonists briefly addressed this issue. See Stanislao J. Brzana, *Remains of Sin and Extreme Unction According to the Theologians After Trent* (Dissertation) Romae: Officium Libri Catholici-Catholic Book Agency, 1953; Adrian Jerome Kilker, *Extreme Unction: A Canonical Treatise Containing also a Consideration of the Dogmatic, Historical and Liturgical Aspects of the Sacrament.* St. Louis, MO: B. Herder Book Co. 1927; Henry S. Kryger, *The Doctrine of the Effects of Extreme Unction in Its Historical Development* (Dissertation), *The CUA Studies in Sacred Theology (Second Series)*, no. 33, Washington, D.C.: The Catholic University of America Press, 1949; and Charles George Renati, The Recipient of Extreme Unction, (Dissertation), Washington, D.C: The Catholic University of America Press, 1961. However, there has been little written on the topic since the Council.

I hope that this methodological study could be used by other students of theology in order to more concretely situate the sacraments within their human context. While anthropologists have studied human ritual from a scientific perspective, the reverse (theologians studying the sacraments and liturgical rites from an anthropological perspective) has not always been the case.[4]

From an anthropological perspective, I have seen the relationship between the patient, the community, and the Rite of Anointing. As stated throughout this work, sickness is alienating. The sacrament of the sick is designed to break through the alienation and bring the sick person back into the community. To accomplish this, the community of faith goes to the sick person, celebrates the rite and "re-incorporates" him or her back into the life of the Church. There is a "dialogue" that takes place between the patient and the assembled community. The patient, through suffering, imitates the sufferings of Christ. Moreover, the patient becomes a teacher of how God is active in his or her life even in sickness. The individual gives an impetus to the community to pray, to engage in pastoral care, and to minister in faith. In return, the community responds to the individual through acts of charity and kindness. More importantly, however, the community reminds the individual that he or she is not alone. The community has compassion (literally "suffers with") for the sick person. By their physical presence, the members of the community reflect the omnipotent presence of the crucified and risen Lord. Through their participation in the ritual of Anointing, the community of faith acts as healers and bearers of the mystery. Ultimately, in the sacrament of the sick the deepest longings of the patient are addressed and given meaning—the need for human contact, the need for a supportive and loving community, the need for touch, the need for immortality, and the need for the presence of God.

Theologically, we addressed a lacuna in the celebration of the sacrament: a clearer definition of *serious illness*. While the *praenotanda* (introduction) offers some suggestions for those who may avail themselves of the sacrament, it was written in 1972. Since that time

---

[4] There are a few European theological scholars who are noted for their anthropological studies of ritual and liturgy: Andrea Grillo, Silvano Maggiani, Giorgio Bonaccorso, Carlo Rocchetta, Crispino Valenziano, and Louis-Marie Chauvet. While some of Chauvet's work has been translated into English, the work of the other scholars remains relatively unknown outside of Europe.

many new diseases and disorders have arisen with which the sacrament of the sick, as well as nonsacramental celebrations, may be used.

The communal dimension of the sacramental celebration has been stressed by the Church. Unfortunately, despite the efforts of theologians and pastors, people still wait until the waning moments of a patient's life before inviting the Church to intervene. It is hoped that this book will encourage pastors to use the communal rite more often and with greater discrimination. Instead of inviting all present to receive the sacrament, perhaps some of the suggestions outlined could be employed.

Finally, this work has examined the nature of the Church as healer. The presence of the Church should be maintained from the very beginnings of a serious illness until the patient recovers or dies.[5] The Church's ministry to the sick should complement that of the physicians and nurses. On the one hand, the Church (in the person of the priest or members of the congregation) should act as an advocate to ensure that the patient is getting the best care possible (especially in the absence of a caring family). On the other hand, the Church can also assist physicians and nurses in their ministry of healing by supporting and working with them in a collaborative manner.

The Church, as well as the sick person, can exercise a catechizing function in the world. The Church can be a teacher of the wider ramifications of sickness and healing in the world today. The Church, in her ministry, can model appropriate responses to both sick persons and healing methods.

---

[5] The ministry of the Church should also be extended to the patient's family both during and after the patient's illness and death.

# Introduction

What role, if any, does the Church play in the art of healing? On one extreme, to some, the Church (or to be more inclusive, religion in general) has no purpose in the healing arts save that of serving as a placebo when the "real" medicine fails. On another extreme, to others, one's religious faith is part and parcel of the healing process, sometimes to the exclusion of all other forms of medicine. Perhaps the answer lies in the middle of these two extremes.

This study is concerned with the relationship between three areas: anthropology, medicine, and theology. The healing ministry of the Church must appeal to all three areas if it is to be viable and effective. In terms of anthropology, how society conceives of the human person will affect the way in which sick members of that society are treated. Furthermore, one must consider the relationship of the individual sick person to the community and the relationship of the community to that individual. Moreover, medicine (or to be more inclusive, healing) encompasses many dimensions: rational science, mythology, magic, faith, and a host of alternative therapies. Each has something to contribute to our understanding of how a person is healed, restored, or prepared for eternal life. In addition, healing involves relationships. These include the relationship of the sick persons within themselves, with their families, and with the community and vice versa. Finally, any discussion of healing from a Christian perspective cannot fail to include one's relationship with God. The theological dimension has been a part of the healing arts since the beginning of time. In examining the issue of the Church as sacramental healer, it is important to recognize how God heals and restores his people.

For the past two thousand years, Christianity (and specifically the Roman Catholic Church) has engaged in a love-hate relationship with the healing arts and medicine. In the early Church, for example, traditional medicinal remedies were eschewed as being pagan. The preference was to call for the elders of the community to pray over the sick person whose prayer of faith would save and raise him or her up (James 5:14–15). Furthermore, sickness was seen as having an intrinsic, yet often ambiguous connection to sin. This linkage of sickness and sin colored the Church's theological reflection on the manner in which God heals and how the Church saw herself as God's instrument of healing. As time went on, the theological tradition came to view the role of the Church as merely a preparation for eternal glory rather than as a method of healing *per se*.

This view prevailed until the twentieth century. As a result of advances in medical science, theologians reflected on the role that the Church could play in assisting the healing process. This major shift in thinking was most noticeable in the promulgation of the *Pastoral Care of the Sick* (PCS) in 1972. Yet, because of the ambiguity of the earlier tradition and the predominance of the medieval and Scholastic viewpoint, the sacrament of the sick still was seen as a preparation for death, rather than as a healing for continued life. Even today, the sacrament is more often seen as one received *in extremis* rather than *in infirmis*. This is especially true among certain ethnic populations and age groups. At the same time, however, there is a tendency among priests and pastoral care workers to allow (or even promote) reception of the sacrament to anyone who "feels sick." In many parishes in the United States, "healing Masses" are held in which all present are invited to come forward to receive the Anointing. Furthermore, even if a pastoral explanation is given as to who should receive the sacrament, some individuals who are mildly ill (if at all) come forward to receive Anointing as a "protection" or as "preventative medicine just in case something serious should happen" (à la the blessing of throats on St. Blase day).

In short, while much theological reflection has been done on the sacrament of the sick, the current state of the question is one of confusion, which leads to the above-mentioned laxity or rigorism. Moreover, perhaps due to the presence of "faith healers," the Church has downplayed her own role in the healing process. While not denying the effects of prayer in promoting health, the Church has allowed the medical arts to take preeminence. The Church, if her presence is felt at all, is usually seen in the last days of a person's life.

As a priest or minister to the sick, perhaps this is not the case in your experience. However, in my pastoral work, I have been called more often to administer the Anointing to an unconscious person in the dead of night without the presence of the family than I have when the recipient and family are fully, actively, and consciously participating. In an article written in 1989, Father Miguel Monge shared the results of a survey he conducted while serving as a hospital chaplain.[1] He noted that despite the change in the terminology of the sacrament and the desire of the Church that her seriously ill members receive sacramental Anointing early in their illnesses, "the pair Extreme Unction-death is still very much alive in the popular mind and in that of many pastors."[2]

In his survey conducted from 1984 to 1986, Father Monge found that families frequently resisted reception of the sacrament for their loved ones while the patients were usually open to receiving sacramental Anointing. As Monge notes, "There are always some who still intimately associate Anointing with the nearness of death. A generation will have to pass, and extensive catechesis will be needed (in families, schools, parishes, etc.) in order for this sacrament to be incorporated with normality into the health ministry."[3] Although Monge's data is from 1989, I have experienced a similar tendency in my own ministry as a parish priest since 1993. Moreover, Monge found that most Anointings were received "in the two or three days immediately preceding death."[4]

In the years since the Second Vatican Council, there have been many advances in the realm of medicine. People are living longer and healthier lives, several major diseases now have vaccines or even cures available, and several surgical procedures that were considered dangerous are now routinely performed in hospitals. Despite these advances in medical technology, new maladies threaten the well-being of the human race. Stress, a leading factor in heart attacks and strokes, is on the rise. New types of work-related injuries slow down productivity. Cancer and AIDS claim thousands of victims each day. Furthermore, advances in the areas of psychiatry and psychology draw our attention to the often-ignored problem of addictions and mental disorders within our society.

---

[1] Miguel Angel Monge, "Integral Care of the Sick: The Role of Spiritual Help," *Dolentium Hominum 11* (1989): 9–17.

[2] Monge, "Integral Care of the Sick," p. 15.

[3] Monge, "Integral Care of the Sick," p. 16.

[4] Monge, "Integral Care of the Sick," p. 16–17.

These advances in science, accompanied by the number of discoveries, need to be addressed by the Church in her official ministry to those who suffer.[5] While the revised rites of the sick and the prayers found in the revised *Book of Blessings* offer comfort and solace to those who use them, unfortunately, many people do not avail themselves of these pastoral resources due to ignorance of the Church's tradition. In short, it is my opinion that many individuals who could be comforted by the Church are not given consolation because of their own naiveté or that of their priest or minister.

Obviously, the theme of the recipient of the sacrament of the sick after Vatican II could on the one hand be reduced to a mere listing of the types of illnesses that would fall under the umbrella of Anointing. On the other hand, the topic could become unwieldy because of the necessity for explanation of the tradition and history which underlie the current theological approach. It is my task to navigate a *via media* between these two tendencies of the Scylla and Charybdis.

The *scope* of this book encompasses the nature of illness, how that illness affects the human person, and how the Church responds to the person with an illness in her official ministry. Even within this focus, certain parameters need to be set. The object of this investigation is to examine how the Church functions as healer in today's society. While some historical analysis is necessary to set the stage for the theological reflection of the current state of the question, it is the period of the Council leading up to the present day that will be the concern of this inquiry.

The *intent* of this book is to offer an anthropological, medical, and theological basis for broadening the use of the sacrament of the sick. In other words, the sacrament has a rich theological tradition that has been underutilized over the past several hundred years. Furthermore, the sacraments of Initiation and Penance have been the object of much theological debate and research in an effort to promote their practice among the faithful. In contrast, the Anointing of the Sick has not enjoyed the same promotional enthusiasm. It is hoped that through this research, individuals who have demurred from receiving sacramental Anointing may find an open invitation to participate more

---

[5] In addition, several conditions (alcoholism and mental illness, and to name a few) that were once classified as "moral disorders" are now viewed as addictions, or chemical imbalances. This subject will be pursued further in chapter 3.

fully in the Church's sacramental life and tradition. More importantly, the healing ministry of the Church cannot be reduced to reception of sacramental Anointing. Many individuals, deacons, religious, health care professionals, as well as family members and parishioners, participate in restoring the ill to health and assisting the dying on their final journey of faith. In short, all people play a vital role in bringing about healing. The intent of this book is to show how all people, both ordained and non-ordained, may better utilize their gifts in the healing process.

This study is *limited* by several factors. First, it is confined by the topic itself. This work is not intended to be a *chef d'oeuvre* or *magnum opus* of the literature. There is simply too much extant information to do justice to the topic of healing in the Church's tradition. Second, while other authors have written histories and theological reflections on the subject of healing in the Christian tradition, these are not strictly germane to this present discussion. A third limit is that of the scope and intent of this work. The primary focus is on the history and theological development after the Second Vatican Council. The theological tradition today relies heavily on that which has preceded it. While it is important to review the history of the sacrament, what is more pertinent to our investigation is how *current* issues (such as mental disorders, post-abortion healing, and addictions) fall within the tradition of sacramental healing and prayer.

The object of this research is not merely to duplicate the efforts of others. Rather, this present discussion is concerned with the anthropological, medical, and theological underpinnings of the sacrament of the sick. The purpose of this investigation is to develop criteria for the reception of this sacrament. Moreover, as in any inquiry, questions and issues will be raised for future consideration and research.

## Questions to Be Examined

When building a house, the builder first lays the foundation and then the framework is erected. Researching and writing follows a similar process. First I lay the foundation or the *raison d'être* of the topic which I then frame by the questions that I hope to answer in the course of the presentation. The answers are supported through the research much in the same way that the frame of a house is supported with plaster and nails.

The foundation of this study is rooted in the Church's long-standing practice of ministry to the sick. While the practice was not called "sacramental" until the Second Council of Lyons (1274), the custom of commending the sick to the care and mercy of God through the use of prayer and oil was part and parcel of the religious traditions of Christianity and Judaism. The New Testament scriptural basis for the tradition is of course Jesus' own ministry to the sick. However, the classic text is the letter of James:

> Is anyone among you suffering? He should pray. Is anyone in good spirits? He should sing praise. Is anyone among you sick? He should summon the presbyters of the church, and they should pray over him and anoint [him] with oil in the name of the Lord, and the prayer of faith will save the sick person, and the Lord will raise him up. If he has committed any sins, he will be forgiven. (James 5:13–15)

The text reveals several interesting distinctions that I will analyze during the course of the investigation. First, those who are sick should call for the presbyters who will pray over them and anoint them. Second, there is no discussion regarding the seriousness of the illness in question, nor to the person being near death. However, the fact that the presbyters were summoned to the bedside of the sick person suggests that the sickness was of a more serious nature. Third, it is the prayer made in faith that will save and raise the person up. Fourth, *if* there are any sins present, they will be forgiven. A fuller exegetical analysis of the text will be presented in the first chapter.

These preliminary distinctions, however, do give rise to several questions that will guide this discussion and analysis of how the sacrament may be used at the beginning of the third millennium. As we begin our study of the Church as healer, six questions will guide our discussion:

1. Who are the sick among us?
2. What constitutes "serious" illness? Perhaps the former distinction of "near death" no longer applies.
3. What is the relationship between sickness and sin? Does sickness always imply the presence of sinful behavior?
4. What are the effects of the sacrament of the sick? Is the sacrament primarily a sacrament of healing or of forgiveness? Is it both?

5. How is the sacrament being used currently? Is it underutilized or misused? How can the sacrament be used differently? How can nonsacramental celebrations also bring about healing and restoration?
6. Who are the ministers of healing in both sacramental and nonsacramental contexts?

## Who Are the Sick among Us?

There are many definitions of sickness and suffering. Some people restrict the term to those who are merely physically ill or incapacitated in some manner. Others take a more inclusive approach. As we will see in the first chapter, sickness has a variety of forms. A person may suffer physically, mentally, spiritually, morally, socially, and relationally. The suffering may be minor or serious; it may be acute or chronic; it may be a minor inconvenience or be incapacitating and debilitating.

However, as our study will show, you cannot see an illness or disorder as a separate entity. Our knowledge of the human person tells us that men and women are holistic beings. An illness affects all parts of one's being. Moreover, the sickness of one member of the community affects the whole community. As Saint Paul notes in his famous description of the body, "If [one] part suffers, all the parts suffer with it; if one part is honored, all the parts share its joy."[6] Any illness, no matter how inconsequential, has ramifications for affecting all of our human dimensions and relationships.

On the anthropological level, when a person is affected with disease or an illness, his or her relationship to self, to others, and even to God can change. Perhaps the patient will become withdrawn and reject any attempts to communicate. The patient may even become depressed or anxious, with thoughts turning to his or her own mortality. Often the patient not only feels physically ill; but the sickness affects his or her psychological, social, and religious dimensions as well. Because sickness has an alienating effect, the patient will often withdraw from society because he or she is unable to function in a usual manner. Sometimes, the patient is forced to withdraw from society because the illness is so severe that it requires hospitalization, surgery, or a longer recuperation process.

---

[6] 1 Corinthians 12:26.

Society has much to say about the sick person. Illness is taboo in many societies. It represents an abnormality or an aberration that must be healed or, if the disease cannot be cured, the patient, in many cases, is hidden from the public. In the United States, for example, in the past fifty years or so there has been a proliferation of convalescent centers and nursing homes as a means to care for those individuals whose families are unable to give them the care and attention they need. In prior generations, such individuals would have been cared for by their families and friends. In my own family, for example, my great-uncle Pete was considered "slow," or in common parlance "special need." Instead of placing him in an institution, however, his brothers and sisters kept him at home and taught him some basic skills. In contrast, my cousin Paula who has Down Syndrome was placed in an institution by the time she was 2 years old, because her family was unable to provide for the care she needed. Moreover, the euthanasia or assisted suicide movement is attracting quite a number of followers. In some countries, when individuals contract a debilitating disease or terminal illness, they choose to deliberately end their lives rather than living with the sickness. They are unable to see the value of redemptive suffering as enunciated by the Church.

This is not the case in all societies. Some traditional cultures still incorporate the sick person in societal functions and celebrate the healed person's return to full societal functioning with ceremonies and rituals. The family and the medical practitioner (often a diviner healer) take an active role in restoring the sick person to health. Even in sickness, the patient is still seen to have a function in society. He or she reminds the community of each person's mortality and becomes a symbol of the creative power to heal.

Unfortunately, in Western culture with its emphasis on health and beauty, there is distaste for sickness of any kind. Even when individuals are restored to health or wholeness, there is often a stigma that is attached to them. For example, if someone is hospitalized for a mental disorder such as depression, that person is still treated by others as if he or she still has the disease. If a person successfully completes cancer treatments, he or she lives under the constant specter that the cancer will return.

Theologically, sickness is seen as alienating; however, the alienation has been transformed by the Paschal Mystery. While the patient may still feel like he or she is separated from his or her person, from others, and from God because of the illness, within the separation there often is a realization that he or she is undergoing a process of transformation. All of the questions that arise from the experience of illness are answered in light of the suffering and death of Jesus. Sickness becomes a time for self-evaluation and analysis. It is an opportunity to assess one's relationships with others and with God. The patient may ask, What is God trying to tell me while I am temporarily incapacitated? What areas of my life is God inviting me to change or restore? If the person is restored to health and wholeness, the reflection that had taken place perhaps may be concretized in action. If the patient begins to decline further and moves closer to death, the meditation can perhaps lead him or her to a conversion in order to prepare for death.

In the theological sphere, a person can never be totally alone as a result of his or her illness. God is always present. Whether or not the person avails himself or herself of that knowledge and acts upon it depends upon that person's outlook on life. Furthermore, the community of faith commends to the suffering and risen Lord the sufferings of one of its members. On the ecclesial level, the community has the responsibility to ensure that its suffering members are not alienated from the faith community. Moreover, because God speaks in and through those who suffer, the community is called to hear the voice of God resounding in the atmosphere of sickness and even death.

The community needs to ask itself, What is God saying to us about life, death, sickness, suffering, and resurrection through the illness of this particular member? How does God want us to approach illness and death? What are we being taught by this particular illness? While the ritual of the sacrament of the sick may be utilized with only one person or several persons, the community of faith is always present in the person of the priest. However, because serious illness can be so alienating, liturgically it makes more sense to gather some of the faithful to celebrate the Church's commendation of the sick person to God and to ask for healing *as a community of faith*.

The ritual action of the laying on of hands and Anointing is performed on the sick person. However, in the rite, the communal aspect is also present. Moreover, the rite enables the community of faith to better attend to the needs of the sick person. Although the community may be very attentive in the area of visitation or sending prayer cards and flowers or even prayer, is that what the patient needs or wants? Participation in the Rite of Anointing by some of the faithful can help them to get a sense of who this person is. Moreover, the rite helps the community to come to terms with its own individual agendas and fears. The ritual of sacramental Anointing speaks to the deepest anxieties and hopes of the Christian person.

Ultimately, we do not know exactly what causes an illness. Some professionals say it is biological, others psychological. There are also some extreme positions which claim that sickness is the direct result of sin and that sickness is the result of God punishing evildoers with a plague or pestilence. However, not all sinners suffer illness—sometimes those who are the worst sinners are the healthiest people (at least in a physical sense), while those who are saintly are afflicted with terrible diseases.

What may be said is that all people at some point in their lives are affected by illness—either their own or that of a loved one. Today, many serious and life-threatening illnesses have been eradicated; however, new ones have arisen to take their place. Because of the work of psychologists and anthropologists, we now know that people suffer from ailments that are related to their relationships and their workplace environments. In the United States, for example, many adults and children are abused. Because of the pressures of the workplace, some employees have brought guns to work and opened fire. Because of new technology, more people are reporting work-related injuries, such as carpal-tunnel syndrome and eyestrain from the overuse of computers. In an effort to balance home, work, and school schedules for themselves and for their children, many parents become stressed out. In short, there are many kinds of illnesses, both biological and psychological, prevalent in the world today.

## What Is Serious Illness?

While everyone has an experience of illness, not all people suffer from a serious illness. As we will see through our historical analysis, the concept of *grave* or *serious* has changed over time. In the Church's mind, *serious* means "danger of death." To physicians and psychiatrists, *serious* takes on the connotation of an "incapacitation" which impairs the ability to function normally in society. A serious illness or disorder represents a severe dysfunction of the balance in one's psycho-physiological make-up. In today's society, many people suffer from this kind of dysfunction. Certainly, many physical ailments incapacitate a person or place the person in danger of death. However, many disorders also have both psychological as well as physical components. Addictions and mental disorders are two such examples. While persons with a mental disorder may appear to be physically fit, mentally and emotionally they are unable to function in society. Perhaps the mental condition is caused by a chemical imbalance or by a traumatic event (such as child abuse). Moreover, those who suffer from addictions may have a genetic or chemical attraction for the substance (such as food, alcohol, or drugs) which is compounded by the mental attractiveness or need for that same substance. When the physical and the psychic attractions interact, exacerbated by situations or events, the addictive cycle begins. Finally, a serious illness may be caused by a person's lifestyle. Again, many mitigating factors cause a person to contract a serious illness or disorder.

In the illnesses and disorders I discuss in this book, each patient was "in danger." He (or she) was in danger of incapacitation. He was in danger of physical death (however remote). He was in danger of psychological, spiritual, or moral death (however remote). He was in danger of doing physical or emotional harm to himself or to others. In short, when a person begins to be "in danger," then the illness or condition may be termed serious.

For a variety of reasons, the Church has not examined the possibility of admitting those with psychological illnesses or addictions to the sacrament of the sick. Moreover, there are some priests, even today, who would deny reception because of the moral nature of some psychological illness. For example, some priests may say that since this person contracted AIDS through illicit sexual contact, he or she should be denied the sacrament of Anointing unless he or she repents of sinful behavior. Others may see alcohol or drug addiction in a similar light.

However, as a Church that professes to follow in the healing footsteps of Christ, we cannot deny the sacrament of the sick to those who are ill, regardless of our own personal dislike of their lifestyle or actions. Moreover, when Christ healed, he restored the person to both physical and moral health. In many cases, the illness was addressed first, and only after healing was there a reference made to the person's sin. While there may be a connection between sin and sickness, one may not always presume that there is a direct connection. For example, a person who is sexually promiscuous may contract the HIV virus. In this sense, there is a direct connection between this person's sin of promiscuity and contracting AIDS. However, a baby born with the HIV virus is not guilty of sin per se, but we may say that as a result of original sin and the sin of his or her parents, this baby contracted the illness. This relationship between sickness and sin will be explored further through this book.

The seriously ill are those who suffer in mind, body, or spirit to such a degree that they become incapacitated as Christians or as human beings. The Church has the role of restoring people to health and wholeness in Christ Jesus.

## What Is the Relationship between Sickness and Sin?

In the first place, this relationship is complex. We cannot assume that there is a direct, proximally causal relation between sickness and sin. Nor can or should we assume that sickness is God's punishment for personal sinfulness. Perhaps these elements may be present; however, sickness, like sin, is part of the human condition. Because of the sin of our first parents, disorder entered the world. The disorder is found under many forms: sin, sickness, imbalance, disturbance, pestilence, geological phenomena, war, poverty, injustice, etc.

Despite the fallen (and some would say depraved) condition of humanity, God in his mercy sent Jesus to restore relationship and order in the world. Through his suffering, death, and Resurrection, Jesus Christ redeemed all of creation. The result of this redemption was transformation. No longer is death the end, but rather, the hope of eternal life. Sickness need not end in sorrow, but, when joined to the sufferings of Christ, becomes redemptive and transformative in itself. The human condition, once seen as an example of evil, now becomes an opportunity for doing good and restoring humanity to God. In short, because of the Paschal Mystery, human beings and God again have a relationship.

In this relationship, humans are charged with the task of fighting against both sin and sickness, in themselves, in their communities, and in society at large. Because of the redemption offered to us, we are called to share that redemption and good will with others. Sickness and sin, while related to one another, are not to be seen as punishments but as opportunities for growth. When we are alienated from self, others, or God through either sickness or sinfulness, it is an opportunity for us to participate in a life assessment. It is a time for us to examine our minds and hearts in an effort to determine what must change or be eliminated in order for us to grow in holiness and wholeness.

Sickness and sin, because of the Paschal Mystery, are beginnings rather than ends of existence. Both allow us to "start again" after "missing the mark" or after failing to live up to our potential as human beings. Ultimately, the goal in both sickness and sin is healing and growth in order to shape us more closely to the person of Christ.

## What Are the Effects of the Sacrament of the Sick?

There are several effects of the sacrament. For the first eight centuries, the primary effect was understood to be healing. In the following twelve centuries, the effect was preparation for death. As we enter the third millennium, all of the effects of the sacrament must be explored. Moreover, these effects must be seen in balance with one another. One effect is not more important than another; all have value and importance, although at times one effect may be more noticeable.

The first effect is *healing*. This may be physical, spiritual, psychological, moral, or social. The sacrament restores relationship. It restores a person to wholeness and balance. Perhaps this effect will not be apparent. However, because of the grace of the sacrament, the "whole person is helped and saved, sustained by trust in God, and strengthened against the temptations of the Evil One and against anxiety over death."[7]

A second effect is *strengthening* of the mind, body, and spirit. The person is given the necessary energy to "bear suffering bravely, but also to fight against it."[8] This strengthening allows the person to see value in his or her suffering. Moreover, this person is invited to join his or her sufferings to Christ; thus, is encouraged to fight against despair, depression, or anger. The sick person is called to work against the evil of sickness in order to be transformed.

---

[7] *Pastoral Care of the Sick: Rites of Anointing and Viaticum* (New York: Catholic Book Publishing Co., 1983), No. 6. Hereafter abbreviated as PCS.

[8] PCS, 6.

A third effect is *the forgiveness of sins*. All of us sin, but in the sacrament of the sick, the seriously ill are forgiven the sins that may have contributed to their disorder, and they are forgiven for the sins that may have arisen as a result of their illness. Forgiveness is recognition that all are on the road to wholeness and holiness. Through forgiveness of his or her sins, the sick person is restored to relationship with himself or herself, others, and God. The alienation that both sin and sickness cause is broken by the sacrament.

A fourth effect is *the preparation for eternal life*. Even if the sick person is not in the process of dying, because all sickness offers a glimpse of mortality, the sacrament counteracts despair by offering a glimpse of immortality and the eschatological reality of the resurrection. Sickness can be a time of conversion. The sacrament gives the reasons for converting.

A final effect is *the conjoining of the patient to the Paschal Mystery*. The patient is joined in his or her sufferings to the sufferings of Christ. In this, the patient shares an intimate connection with the crucified and risen Lord. The patient becomes "caught up" in the mystery of God. In some senses, the experience of sickness draws one closer to God. The celebration of the sacrament recognizes this special deep connection between those who suffer and the one who suffered. In the process, the patient is transformed, healed, and restored to new life. In sickness and in the celebration of the sacrament, the patient truly lives his or her faith. The celebration becomes "faith in action." Through the joining to the Paschal Mystery, the patient's faith is deepened and strengthened.

What is said about the sacrament of the sick may also be applied in an analogous way to the ministry of healing in general. Those who participate as healing ministers invite patients to experience the presence of God. Through their efforts, healing may occur. Moreover, by walking with the patient in his or her agony, the priest or minister can pave the way for the patient to seek out forgiveness and restoration of his or her relationship to God. Furthermore, ministers may be seen as bridge builders between the patient, family and friends, the Church, and even God. Sometimes, one who is not an "official" representative of the Church may be better received and can offer comfort in ways that a sacramental minister cannot. In short, all members of the Church need to work together so that those who are ill may come out of their alienation.

## How Can Ministry to the Sick Be Better Utilized?

There may be abuses in the celebration of the sacrament. Some of these abuses stem from a lack of understanding about the nature of and purpose for Anointing. Other abuses result from persons who want to "creatively" celebrate the sacrament by trying to be more inclusive. There are four areas that need to be addressed in order to provide for a better ministry to the sick.

1.    The first area is catechesis. Priests and ministers of the sick should acquaint themselves with all the documents associated with ministry to the sick. Moreover, they should try to gain an understanding of the anthropological, medical, pastoral, and theological bases for the sacrament of Anointing. Further, those who work with the sick should learn from them about the nature and functioning of illness in people's personal lives and in the world at large. Having accomplished this, priests and ministers should catechize their parishioners. This may be done through parish bulletin articles, workshops, and through carefully prepared and delivered homilies.

2.    A second area to assist in better celebration is personal prayer. Those who seek to minister to others should ground themselves in a relationship with Jesus Christ. Their own ministry should flow from their experience of being ministered to by Christ. Moreover, their own faith life needs to be nurtured by frequent meditation on the scriptures and the assiduous use of the sacraments of the Eucharist and Penance. Those who exercise a ministry of healing must themselves have recognition of the healing that God has done in their own lives or in the lives of those around them.

3.    Careful, prayerful preparation, whether it is individual or communal, is essential to a better utilization of the sacrament of the sick. This third area of concern flows from the other two. Good liturgy does not "just happen," it needs to be prepared by individuals who are well grounded in the tradition and in their own prayer life. Those who are charged with the arranging of liturgies for the sick should enlist the help of others in the parish to ensure that the celebrations will be prayerful, joy-filled, organic, and well executed.

4.    The fourth area of interest is that of the celebration itself. The sick persons should be made to feel welcome. Their alienation,

resulting from the sickness, should be diminished, not enhanced by the ritual. They should feel that the community desires their presence and truly wants to celebrate their restoration to health. Many individuals from the parish ought to be present to assist the sick and their caregivers. The presider (the priest in sacramental celebrations, another member of the community in nonsacramental celebrations) should be attentive to the generous use of symbols. Moreover, presiders should convey the presence of Christ not only in their actions, but in their attitudes, expressions, and body language as well. Finally, all of those who participate, both the sick and the healthy, should experience the healing touch of Christ through their participation in the ritual action, prayers, and song. Everyone should leave the celebration believing that real healing took place—both in the sick and in themselves.

## Who Are the Ministers of Healing in Both Sacramental and Nonsacramental Contexts?

In short, all people have a duty to participate in the healing process. As noted earlier in this Introduction, this duty flows from one's Baptism. The priest, because of his unique sacramental configuration, participates as Christ the healer. Through his ministry, he brings the sacramental consolation of the Church. The patient participates in the Passion of Christ on the cross and is encouraged to join his or her sufferings to Christ. In so doing, the patient's pain has the possibility of becoming salvific and transformative.

The underlying theme of this book is that the sacrament of the sick and the rites found in *Pastoral Care of the Sick* could be more fully employed as part of the healing process. While much historical research on Anointing has been already been done, there is a lack of analysis as to how the data may be applied in a modern context. Moreover, the disciplines of anthropology and medicine can further our understanding of how a ritual action may engender healing, not only of the individual, but of the community as well. Furthermore, there is a need for more positive collaboration between medical science and religion in the art of healing. It is hoped that the fruits of this endeavor will contribute to furthering this rapport.

# Chapter 1

# The Relationship between Sickness and Sin

## INTRODUCTION

At certain points in history, especially in the ancient world and during the Middle Ages, it was believed that there was a direct correlation between the onset of illness and moral behavior. At other junctures in history, there was a more tenuous link between sickness and personal sin. This bond between illness and iniquity has implications for sacramental celebrations. Indeed, the way in which the sacrament of the sick has been viewed for the past two thousand years is the result of the interpretation of the Jacobean text. Therefore, we need to examine closely the text itself as well as the definition of *sickness* as preparation for the discussion of contemporary use of the sacrament of the sick.

In an effort to establish the relationship between sickness and sin, we should examine the extant scriptural and ecclesial texts, which refer to this association. To this end, it will be helpful to analyze the classic "proof" text associated with the sacrament of the sick, namely, James 5:14–15. It is important to remember that this text must not be taken in isolation from the theological and cultural milieu in which it was written, and because our current beliefs are conditioned by the past, we will need to examine the theme of sickness within the various epochs. So that we might develop an understanding of the historic relationship of sickness to sin, we will analyze the texts of the Hebrew Scriptures (Old Testament), the Christian Scriptures (New Testament), the Middle Ages, and the Modern period in order to establish

- A definition of sickness in that period,
- The cause or reason given for the sickness, and
- The method of healing or curing the illness.

To assist in this analysis, I will use the disciplines of moral theology, psychology, anthropology, and philosophy. Finally, I will draw some preliminary conclusions and implications for the sacrament.

## Exegesis of James 5:14–15

Let us consider the following questions when examining the letter of James (5:14–15). Who is to be anointed? What is the criteria for "sickness" as envisaged by the author of the letter? What is the connection between sickness and sin?

> Is anyone among you sick? He should summon the presbyters of the church, and they should pray over him and anoint [him] with oil in the name of the Lord, and the prayer of faith will save the sick person, and the Lord will raise him up. If he has committed any sins, he will be forgiven.

### Who Is to Be Anointed?

The first phrase concerns the subject of Anointing, in other words, the sick person. In Greek, the term used is *asthenei*. The term may be translated as either "to be weak [or] to be sick."[1] Some commentators feel that *asthenei* refers only to physical sickness,[2] while others place the term under the general heading of "suffering."[3] Balz and Schneider note that the word group from which *asthenei* derives, signifies "weakness or powerlessness of various kinds." These weaknesses include bodily weakness, sicknesses, and weakness in the capacity to understand, ethical-religious weakness, and the economically weak, the poor.[4] Finally, Gerhard Kittel offers this explanation of the term and its

---

[1] Fritz Rienecker, *A Linguistic Key to the Greek New Testament,* Translated and revised by Cleon L. Rogers, Jr. (Grand Rapids, MI: Zondervan Publishing House, 1980), p. 395.

[2] Clifton J. Allen, et al., *The Broadman Bible Commentary,* Volume 12: *Hebrews-Revelation General Articles* (Nashville, TN: Broadman Press, 1972), p. 137.

[3] George Arthur Buttrick, ed., *The Interpreter's Bible,* Volume XII (New York: Abingdon Press, 1957), p. 70.

[4] Horst Balz and Gerhard Schneider, *Exegetical Dictionary of the New Testament,* Volume I (Grand Rapids, MI: William B. Eerdmans Publishing Company, 1990), pp. 170–71.

cognates: "In the [New Testament] the words are hardly ever used of a purely physical weakness, but frequently in the comprehensive sense of the whole man."[5] According to Dudley and Rowell, "the word used for 'sick' in verse 14 *(astheneo)* is neutral; it is sometimes used in the New Testament to refer to mortal sickness, but it may also have the quite general sense of 'being ill'."[6] However, the word used to refer to the sick person in verse 15 *(kamnonta)* has a much stronger meaning. "Its fundamental sense is that of physical exhaustion or debility, but it was also widely used to mean 'sick beyond hope, withering away,' and it may even mean 'dead'."[7] Finally, it is worthwhile to note that some ambiguity still exists among commentators on this passage. Most agree that the term *asthenei* seems to suggest that the person is "sick enough to be confined to bed, but not yet in extremis."[8] Yet, the use of the stronger term in verse 15 precludes a definitive ruling.

In his monumental work on the sacrament of the sick, Carlos G. Alvarez Gutierrez notes the difference in the two terms used to designate the sick person: *asthenei* refers to *periculoso morbo laborare* (one who is suffering and is in danger of death) while *kamnein* is concerned with *morti propinquum esse* (one who is at the point of death).[9] In his excellent exegesis of the Jacobean passage, Gutierrez summarizes the thinking of major commentators. He notes that there is some disagreement among scholars, yet the key to understanding the passage is that the subject is a "believer of the Christian community."[10] Within this context, the subject of Anointing is joined to the community by an individual's Baptism as a Christian. The Anointing for healing is a clear demonstrative action that refers to one's baptismal Anointing. The sickness need not be mortal or grave, yet all sickness in some way

---

[5] Gerhard Kittel, ed., *Theological Dictionary of the New Testament,* Translated and edited by Geoffrey W. Bromiley, Volume I (Grand Rapids, MI: William B. Eerdmans Publishing Company, 1964), p. 491.

[6] Jeffery John, "Anointing in the New Testament," In Martin Dudley and Geoffrey Rowell, eds. *The Oil of Gladness: Anointing in the Christian Tradition* (London: SPCK/Collegeville: Liturgical Press, 1993), p. 58.

[7] Dudley and Rowell, *The Oil of Gladness*, p. 58.

[8] *Jerome Biblical Commentary,* section 35 (CD-ROM: Logos Library System 2.0).

[9] Carlos G. Alvarez Gutierrez, *El Sentido Teologico de la Uncion de los Enfermos en la Teologia Contemporanea* (1940–1980), (Bogota: Typis Pontificiae Universitatis Xaverianae, 1982), p. 29.

[10] Gutierrez, *El Sentido Teologico de la Uncion de los Enfermos en la Teologia Contemporanea,* p. 95. "Donde si hay conformidad es en la afirmacion de que el sujeto de la Uncion es un creyente de la comunidad cristiana." (Translation by author.)

refers to the perspective of one's eventual death.[11] In short, we see from the evidence that ambiguity exists regarding the subject of Anointing. What this text indicates is that the subject is an ill, baptized member of the Christian community.

## What Is the Criteria for Sickness?

What is the severity of the illness in question? The scriptures do not offer a medical diagnosis for every sick person other than to briefly indicate that he or she is suffering. Most commentators see in the letter from James an implicit (but strong) indication that the subject is seriously ill and unable to go to the presbyters; hence, they (the elders) need to visit the sick person.[12] Yet the Jacobean text does not indicate that the person is close to death if confined to bed or if mobility is difficult. This is an important point for future consideration: Clearly, the author of the letter has in mind a person who is dangerously ill, not someone who merely has a cold. Furthermore, the term, as defined above, may also refer to those who suffer from psychological or emotional illnesses as well.

In his exegesis of James, Ambroise Verheul notes that there are five points to the passage that should be considered:

1. The elders (presbyters) pray over the sick person (v. 14a and b);
2. In the name of the Lord (v. 14b);
3. They anoint him with oil (v. 14b);
4. The prayer of faith will save the sick person (v. 15a);
5. The Lord will raise him up (v. 15b).[13]

Concerning sickness, Verheul does not mention the degree to which one is ill (in fact, the text itself merely states, "when someone is ill . . ."). However, he does offer the following observation: "For

---

[11] Gutierrez, *El Sentido Teologico de la Uncion de los Enfermos en la Teologia Contemporanea*, p. 219: ". . . un creyente enfermo que se halla sufriendo y posiblemente esta en cama. Pero no se refiere a una enfermedad mortal y grave, porque siempre que el Nuevo Testamento quiere especificar esto, agrega un calificativo. Mucho menos, por consiguiente, se refiere a la perspectiva de la muerte. Ahora bien, este enfermo debe ser 'ungido en el nombre del Senor.' Esta espresion es profundamente cristiana y reclama el Bautismo. Indica el uso y la forma de orar propia de los creyentes a partir del Bautismo el el nombre de Jesus." (Translation by author.)

[12] Dudley and Rowell, *The Oil of Gladness*, p. 58.

[13] Ambroise Verheul, "The Paschal Character of the Sacrament of the Sick: Exegesis of James 5:14–15 and the New Rite for the Sacrament of the Sick," in *Temple of the Holy Spirit*, Translated by Matthew J. O'Connell (New York: Pueblo Publishing Company, 1983), p. 249.

James and Mark (6:7–13), however, the purpose of the Anointing of the Sick is not purely medicinal; it is salvific as well. The letter of James speaks of 'saving' and 'raising up.' In Mark, the anointing is connected with the expulsion of demons and the coming of the kingdom of God."[14] When this anointing is connected with the word *sosei* (v. 15 "save") in the passage, Verheul says, "I think we can conclude that the religious and eschatological meaning is intended, although not, of course, to the exclusion of the medical and physical."[15] In short, one could make a case that the author of James is recommending Anointing only for those who are seriously ill and possibly in danger of death.[16]

To quickly survey Verheul's commentary, he notes that in order to be "saved" (i.e., "healed"), one must believe: "the *prayer of faith* will save the sick person." Therefore, it is prayer to the Lord, connected with belief in the Lord's healing power that will restore the sick person to health. In examining the healing passages, even those in which "the most obvious meaning is medical and physical, we find that an eschatological meaning as well is often to be glimpsed."[17] Furthermore, as Dudley and Rowell have suggested, the passage is ambiguous enough to support this interpretation: "The prayer of faith will save the mortally ill/dead man and the Lord will resurrect him."[18] In other words, while the intent of the passage is to heal the ill person, the reality that the patient could die loomed in the background. Moreover, "it is not the anointing as such nor the prayer as such that effects the cure or *raising up*, but the risen Lord who in virtue of a prayer inspired by faith and trust is present, sanctifies, and heals."[19] In the final analysis, the passage accounts for both the possibilities of healing the sick person from the illness and preparing the mortally ill person for entrance into God's kingdom.

## What Is the Connection between Sickness and Sin?

The third part to the exegesis of this passage is the connection between sickness and sin. As noted earlier, the link between sickness and sin is a conditional, rather than causal, one. In Greek, *kan* (in Latin *et si*)

---

[14] Verheul, "The Paschal Character of the Sacrament of the Sick," p. 251.

[15] Verheul, "The Paschal Character of the Sacrament of the Sick," p. 252.

[16] See the discussion in Dudley and Rowell, *The Oil of Gladness*, pp. 57–58.

[17] Verheul, "The Paschal Character of the Sacrament of the Sick," p. 252.

[18] Dudley and Rowell, The Oil of Gladness, p. 58.

[19] Verheul, "The Paschal Character of the Sacrament of the Sick," p. 253.

is used to begin the conditional phrase. *Kan* is a contraction of the two words *kai* and *ean*, which is translated "and if," further heightening the conditional nature of the phrase that follows. However, one commentator suggests that there is a connection between *kan* and *hamartias* in that *hamartias* refers to "sins which have occasioned the sickness."[20] He cites numerous passages where this seems to be the case.[21] Furthermore, there is a strong association between sickness and sin in the Jewish tradition. Yet, in his ministry Jesus heals both physical sickness and moral deficiency. There is some ambiguity as to the connection between the two.[22] In many healing *pericopés,* sickness was associated with sin and when Jesus healed, it was done in the context of forgiving sins. "In order to terminate a sickness it was necessary to confess one's sins and to receive forgiveness for them."[23] However, in the Fourth Gospel, "Jesus rejects the view that all sickness springs from sin (see John 9:3)."[24]

Needless to say, because sickness was attributed to sin, it posed a particular problem for the early Church community.[25] As Jeffrey John notes, "perhaps aware of the difficulties involved, James makes the connection a tentative one: '*if* he has committed sins, he will be forgiven.' The causation is admitted as possible, but not inevitable."[26] The use of the perfect participle "implies a past act of which the effect remains."[27] He suggests that this sentence could be paraphrased thus: "If he is in the state of having committed sins, the effect of which remains, he will be forgiven. It is probable that only serious sins are meant, the kind which might be expected to entail disease."[28] As

---

[20] James Hardy Ropes, *A Critical and Exegetical Commentary on the Epistle of St. James* (Edinburgh: T. & T. Clark, 1916, 1973), p. 308.

[21] Ropes, *A Critical and Exegetical Commentary on the Epistle of St. James,* p. 308. For example, Mark 2:5ff., John 9:2f., John 5:14, 1 Corinthians 11:30, Deuteronomy 28:22, 27, Psalm 38, Isaiah 38:17.

[22] Jeffrey John, *A Critical and Exegetical Commentary on the Epistle of St. James,* p. 56.

[23] Bo Reicke, *The Epistles of James, Peter, and Jude: Introduction, Translation and Notes.* (Garden City, NY: Doubleday & Company, Inc., 1964), p. 60.

[24] R. R. Williams. *The Letters of John and James* (Cambridge: Cambridge University Press, 1965), p. 139.

[25] Reicke, *The Epistles of James, Peter, and Jude,* p. 59.

[26] John, *A Critical and Exegetical Commentary on the Epistle of St. James,* p. 56.

[27] John, *A Critical and Exegetical Commentary on the Epistle of St. James,* p. 56.

[28] John, *A Critical and Exegetical Commentary on the Epistle of St. James,* p. 56. Thomas W. Leahy in chapter 58 of *The New Jerome Biblical Commentary* indicates that in view of James 3:2, the sins referred to in this passage "are apparently something more than the unavoidable faults committed by all" (p. 916).

another commentator has written, "This association is stated here only as a condition: *if* the illness was a punishment for sins, then the cause as well as its effect will be removed."[29] In short, the writer of James retained the ambiguous connection between sickness and sin in order to show that the Lord both heals *and* forgives. The epistle is a reminder that in sickness, one should depend on God.[30] In other words,

> The important point—then as now—is to realize that God desires the health and well being of the whole man, body and soul. God's will is not always done, and death and disease have to be accepted as having some place in God's ordering of things. But the Church follows Jesus and his apostles in praying hopefully and faithfully for physical health and spiritual restoration.[31]

In short, "the act of healing and the act of forgiving are indistinguishable in James's thinking here; and presumably the 'prayer of faith' would have included a request for both."[32]

## Summary Conclusions to the Exegesis of Saint James

As the above exegesis has shown, the subject of Anointing is a believer of the Christian community who has fallen into sickness. While the sickness is neither defined nor given parameters (mortally ill, seriously ill, dangerously ill, etc.), the presumption is that the person is so ill as to be unable to go to the presbyters of the community; hence, they visit the patient. The acts of healing, forgiving, and raising up the one who is sick are considered simultaneous actions in the mind of the writer of the epistle. If one is ill, presumably he or she has committed a sin for which the sickness is a punishment or consequence. However, even if the sickness is not a result of sin (hence the use of the conditional *if*), the person is still offered forgiveness and raising up. Furthermore, because it is the Lord who offers healing, forgiveness, and eternal life, the action of praying over the person in faith will offer restoration either in this world or the next. While the author of James clearly tries

---

[29] Martin Dibelius, *James: A Commentary on the Epistle of James* (Philadelphia: Fortress Press, 1976), p. 255.

[30] Clifton J. Allen, et al., *The Broadman Bible Commentary.* Volume 12 *Hebrews–Revelation, General Articles* (Nashville, TN: Broadman Press, 1972), p. 137.

[31] Williams, *The Letters of John and James,* p. 139.

[32] John, *A Critical and Exegetical Commentary on the Epistle of St. James,* p. 57.

to balance the tension between sickness and sin and does not wish to link the two causally, throughout the Church's history, the balance has not been so easily maintained. As will be seen in this chapter, the tendency during the time of the letter of Saint James has been to equate sickness with sin or at least to view sickness as somehow being a consequence of sinful behavior. It is not until the age of the Enlightenment and the dawn of modern medicine that this causality is diminished. However, even today, some individuals still attempt to equate sickness with sin.

## Sickness: Changing Definitions over Time

While the common designation for the scriptural texts prior to the time of Christ is "the Old Testament" and those of the Christian era, "the New Testament," some scholars generally prefer to use the terms *Hebrew Scriptures* and *Christian Scriptures* to distinguish between these two bodies of biblical literature. Furthermore, the extra-biblical literature, which is extant in these two periods, is phenomenal.[33] In short, there are numerous sources of information from which to derive a sense of ancient medical practices.[34] In addition, due to the development and documentation of the scientific method and advances in medicine and research in the Middle Ages and the modern period, we are able to piece together a synthesis of the practice of medicine over the past two to four thousand years.[35] However, this is not our primary intent or purpose.

While there is a connection between sickness and sin, it is not necessarily causal. Furthermore, the theology, anthropology, and psychology significantly influence this relationship in each generation. Because the Church of the twentieth-first century has inherited over three millennia of history and reflection, it is important to survey the major ideas of these historical epochs which have influenced our

---

[33] See James B. Pritchard, *Ancient Near Eastern Texts Relating to the Old Testament* (Princeton, NJ: Princeton University Press, 1955).

[34] For example, one may examine the literature of the Akkadians, Sumerians, Babylonians, and other ancient peoples. See Pritchard for a basic bibliography.

[35] For more information, the reader is invited to consult the works of the following authors and the bibliographies contained therein: Hector Avalos, Romeo Cavedo, André-Marie Dubarle, Christian-J. Guyonvarc'h, Howard Clark Kee, Roy Porter, Simon S. Levin, Richard Broxton Onians, and James B. Pritchard.

current understanding of medicine and healing. As will be seen in chapters 3 and 4, how the Church defines sickness and healing has a great impact on how the Church determines the way in which she will minister to those whom she considers marginalized by sickness.

## Sickness in the Hebrew Scriptures

As Christians, we are "spiritual Semites" as Pope Pius XI so aptly noted.[36] We are inheritors of not only the covenant made with our Israelite forebears; and as we will see, we have somewhat appropriated their attitudes toward sickness and healing as well. How did the Israelites define sickness? What did they see as the causes of illness? How did they heal those who were so afflicted?

Given the limits of space and time, I will not attempt to answer the question, From whence comes evil? Nor will I try to answer the query, Why do good people suffer? Rather, this section is purely a fact-finding mission to ascertain the kinds of sickness that predominate in the Hebrew Scriptures.

For obvious reasons, not all the references to illness and healing can be cited. Furthermore, several excellent studies have been compiled in this area.[37] However, it is important to realize that in the Hebrew mindset, one did not compartmentalize nature. Rather, the Hebrews saw life as a unity and in holistic terms. In order to understand the Hebrew anthropology of sickness and healing, it is necessary to explore the Israelite concept of the body.

In his excellent summary of "the Jewish tradition," Elliot N. Dorff writes a succinct analysis of the Jewish attitudes toward life and death. He notes that "God created bodies as well as minds, emotions, and wills." "Because the body was God's creation, it was right to enjoy its legitimate pleasures and wrong to deny them to oneself." However, the human body was God's property, and therefore no one had the

---

[36] See Georges Passelecq and Bernard Suchecky, *The Hidden Encyclical of Pius XI*, Translated by Steven Rendall, (New York: Harcourt Brace & Company, 1997), p. xviii-xix ". . . in his famous 1938 address to Belgian pilgrims, he read Saint Paul's reference to "our patriarch Abraham." The pope said that "we are the spiritual offspring of Abraham. . . . We are spiritually Semites." See also *Lumen gentium* 2, 11 and *Nostra Aetate*, 4.

[37] See for example the work of Hector Avalos, George Gordon Dawson, Morton Kelsey, Simon S. Levin, Ronald L. Numbers, and Darrel W. Amundsen, Klaus Seybold, and Ulrich B. Mueller listed in the bibliography.

right to destroy or abuse it.[38] Furthermore, one has the responsibility to care for the body by proper diet and exercise in order to maintain one's health. Yet, as Dorff correctly notes, "Jewish views on diet, hygiene, exercise, and protection of the body have distinctively religious roots apart from any pragmatic results they may foster. God gave life to be enjoyed, but pleasure must yield to health as a value because health is necessary for one to *function as the servant of God.*[39]

Since God had created human beings, they were God's servants. More importantly, their servanthood was based upon a special, intimate relationship with God that was rooted in the covenant. Faithfulness to the covenant precepts determined one's status before God. Those who adhered to the precepts were "blessed" while those who disobeyed God's commands were liable to punishment. Because God created everything, according to the writers of the Hebrew Scriptures "he is ultimately the author of health and disease: 'I deal death and give life; I wounded, and I will heal; none can deliver from My hand' (Deuteronomy 32:39)."[40] In the words of Morton Kelsey, "God, the giver of all good things, was seen equally as the dispenser of misfortune and pain, including sicknesses of all kinds."[41] The biblical authors paint a strict, legalistic image of God in which illness is visited upon people "as punishment for sins and as a means of expiation."[42] Furthermore, because of a lack of belief in an afterlife (until very late in Judaism), God's rewards and punishments had to be dispensed during one's lifetime. Hence, "health and wealth are the rewards of God, and sickness, poverty, and misfortune were divine punishments."[43]

While adherence to the Mosaic covenant was thought to guarantee health and well-being and disobedience brought about sickness and poverty, there were some changes in the attitude that sickness was a result of sin. Most notable was the book of Job in which God's role in causing sickness was questioned.[44] Instead, malevolent agents—

---

[38] Elliot N. Dorff, "The Jewish Tradition," in Ronald L. Numbers and Darrell W. Amudsen, eds., *Caring and Curing* (Baltimore and London: The Johns Hopkins University Press, 1986, 1998), p. 9.

[39] Dorff, "The Jewish Tradition," p. 13 (emphasis added).

[40] Dorff, "The Jewish Tradition," p. 13.

[41] Morton Kelsey, *Healing and Christianity*, (Minneapolis: Augsburg, 1995), p. 27.

[42] Dorff, "The Jewish Tradition," p. 13.

[43] Kelsey, *Healing and Christianity*, p. 27.

[44] Simon S. Levin, *Adam's Rib: Essays on Biblical Medicine* (Los Altos, CA: Geron-X, Inc., 1970), see pp. 54–56.

demons—are blamed for causing illness and misfortune. As Simon S. Levin notes, "the Babylonians and the Persians had a particularly well systematized demonology, which penetrated Hebrew thought espe- cially during the 500 years following their Babylonian exile. Prior to this period demons played little part in the causation of illness."[45] Yet, there is some ambiguity regarding the power that the demons pos- sessed. At some points, scripture agrees with their presence; at others, denies a dualistic outlook.[46]

In addition to God and demons being the source of illness, natural phenomenon and matter could also exert their influence on health. Changes in the seasons, solar or lunar eclipses, and even water (presumably due to the bacteria present) affected the well-being of the inhabitants of Israel. Furthermore, ever-present superstitions about magic, sorcery, and curses had a psychological effect on the ancients much more than they do today. This psychic phenomenon often mani- fested itself in physical effects as well.[47] The Hebraic value of the holistic nature of the human body also extended to societal relationships as well. Anthropologically, the Hebrews viewed the human person as a holistic entity possessing unity of body and soul. Just as one could not separate the mind from the body or the emotions from the soul, one could not separate the individual from the community without dire consequences.

Yet it is against this backdrop of unity and community that illness becomes so jarring. Illness was particularly insidious because it had repercussions for both the individual and the community. Hector Avalos points to infertility as one such example. An infertile woman could not fulfill her societal role as mother. While she herself did not die because of this condition, it did lead to the "death" of her lineage.[48] Furthermore, agrarian, theocratic societies such as those of the Middle East regarded children as a commodity that allowed the tribe to continue.

---

[45] Levin, *Adam's Rib: Essays on Biblical Medicine*, pp. 56–57.

[46] See for example Isaiah 34:14: "Wildcats shall meet with desert beasts, satyrs shall call to one another; there shall the lilith [female demon] repose, and find for herself a place to rest." As compared to Isaiah 45:6–7: "so that toward the rising and the setting of the sun men may know that there is none besides me. I am the Lord, there is no other; I form the light, and create the darkness, I make well-being and create woe; I, the Lord, do all these things."

[47] See Levin, *Adam's Rib*, pp. 60–61.

[48] Avalos, Hector, *Illness and Health Care in the Ancient Near East: The Role of the Temple in Greece, Mesopotamia and Israel* (Atlanta, GA: Scholars Press, 1995), p. 249.

In summary, illness is any condition that, regardless of physical danger as defined by modern Western medicine, renders a person physically or mentally unfit to execute a social role defined as "normal" by the society at issue, here ancient Israel . . . . It should be noted that any non-human entity that could not execute the role assigned to it was also deemed to be sick. This is the reason why the land (cf. 2 Chronicles 7:14) or a nation could be described as ill.[49]

What were the conditions that the Hebrews classified as sicknesses? According to Hans Walter Wolff, the Hebrew root *hlh* "almost always designates a state of weakness—of slackness and exhaustion; that is to say, vital power that has somehow been sapped."[50] He notes that this could mean injury through an accident, unusual illnesses, the aging process, as well as abnormal mental conditions. When the root *dwh* occurs, this "reflects the mental effects of weakness—anxiety and a feeling of indisposition, such as are typical of a woman's menstrual periods."[51] In addition, the Hebrew Scriptures mention a variety of skin diseases—leprosy, ulcers, inflammation, eczema, and scabies. The Hebrew Scriptures also mention diseases of the eye including blindness. Wolff also notes the presence of mental illness under the headings of madness and confusion of the mind mentioned in Deuteronomy.[52]

Leviticus 21:16–23 indicates the kinds of irregularities (illness and deformities) that prevent one from participating in the cultic activity of Israel:

The Lord said to Moses, "Speak to Aaron and tell him: None of your descendants, of whatever generation, who has any defect shall come forward to offer up the food of his God. Therefore, he who has any of the following defects may not come forward: he who is blind, or lame, or who has any disfigurement or malformation, or a crippled foot or hand, or who is humpbacked, weakly, or walleyed, or who is afflicted with eczema, ringworm or hernia. No descendant of Aaron the priest who has any such defect may draw near to offer up the oblations of the Lord; on account of his defect he may not draw near to offer up the food of his God. He may, however, partake of the food of his God; of what is most

---

[49] Ibid., p. 250.

[50] Hans Walter Wolff, *Anthropology of the Old Testament*, Translated by Margaret Kohl (London: SCM Press LTD, 1974), p. 143.

[51] Wolff, *Anthropology of the Old Testament*, p. 143.

[52] Wolff, *Anthropology of the Old Testament*, p. 144.

sacred as well as of what is sacred. Only, he may not approach the veil nor go up to the altar on account of his defect; he shall not profane these things that are sacred to me, for it is I, the Lord, who make them sacred.

It is interesting to note that many of the "defects" mentioned would not be considered "illnesses" in the modern sense of the word. However, these limitations do render someone "impure" to participate in the Israelite cultic practices. Moreover, in many cases the symptoms of illness overlap those of impurity, making it difficult to discern who was "ill" or merely "impure."[53]

In summary, we may discern several different types of illness in the Hebrew Scriptures: infertility, leprosy, "terminal illnesses," depression, and physical ailments. It appears that illness of any type is considered "impure," which creates a barrier between God and human beings. Furthermore, illness is often seen as a punishment for sinful behavior as well as a kind of "gift" from God.[54] Given the issues of impurity, punishment, and general capriciousness, the question of healing becomes convoluted. If a person is ill due to punishment for sin, how can one be sure of being healed? What about chronic illnesses? Are they signs that a person is in a perpetual state of sin? Can one ever be healed in this case? Given the Hebrew mindset of God as his or her Lord, judge, healer, and Savior, why would one turn to a healer or sorcerer when he or she became sick? Would not that somehow violate the covenant that person had with God?

Is this to say, however, that the ancient Hebrews did not use any medical techniques known to them? To the contrary, they used medicines and herbs to alleviate pain and cure sickness, as did their counterparts in the Middle East. However, in conjunction with medical techniques, they also relied heavily on prayer. With regard to illness in the Hebrew mentality it may be said that

1. God had exclusive responsibility for both the sickness and the healing of that sickness.

---

[53] Cf. Avalos, *Illness and Health Care*, pp. 249–50.

[54] Consider for example, the difficult text of Job. While he did not commit sin, somehow God was punishing him perhaps out of general principle or just to show Job who was God. This is not the place to analyze the problem of evil or to debate the Job text; however, if one posits, as the Hebrews did, that God is the author of sin—and makes people ill out of capriciousness—the issue of sickness and its origins becomes problematic.

2. God had total power over life and to that extent "traces all sickness directly back to Yahweh's intervention."

3. All life has perpetual dependency upon God because life "hangs in the balance between God's actions toward life and God's actions toward death. . . ."[55]

In the literature of the Hebrew Scriptures (especially in the Psalms), there is recognition on this total dependence upon God as the healer of body and soul: "the sick person or the one in danger of death turns to God for protection. He asks unceasingly not to go down into the pit or into Sheol. When he is cured or rescued, he thanks God for having been brought back from death."[56]

In short, "natural and miraculous healings are not distinguished from one another fundamentally. Whether human prescriptions and applications also help or not, what is always essential is that the invalid in his sickness and the convalescent in his recovery should encounter the God who indirectly or directly sends both sickness and healing."[57] It is through the experiences of sickness and healing that one is able to more fully experience the action of God. This occurs not only for the individual, but for the community as well.

"Just as it can lead to an examination of what is past, sickness can also lead to meditation on what is to come."[58] Sickness often encourages people to ponder on where their life is going as well as if they should change behaviors. This is also true for the community. Illness can be an occasion for warning and educating not just the invalid, but those who function as caregivers as well. It can also invite whole peoples to change their ways and return to the path set forth for them by God.[59]

Furthermore, sickness puts the dialogue that humans should have with God into sharper relief. Outside of God, there is no future. As Wolff posits, "To remain closed up within oneself in a monologue, or to seek other healers *in place of Yahweh* (2 Chronicles:16:12), where

---

[55] Seybold, Klaus, and Ulrich B. Mueller. *Sickness and Healing,* Translated by Douglas W. Scott (Nashville: Abingdon, 1981), pp. 66–67.

[56] André-Marie Dubarle, "Sickness and Death in the Old Testament," In O'Connell, *Temple of the Holy Spirit,* p. 58.

[57] Wolff, *Anthropology of the Old Testament,* p. 147.

[58] Wolff, *Anthropology of the Old Testament,* p. 148.

[59] Cf. Elihu's speech in Job 33:19ff. and the healing of the bite of the fiery serpents in Numbers 21:4–9. Also the making of the waters of Marah sweet (Exodus 15:23–25). The impact of sickness upon a whole community can exhort them to conversion and repentance.

they ought at most, according to Ecclesiasticus, to be consulted *because* of Yahweh, shows a hopeless misunderstanding of man."[60] Yet, in the Hebrew Scriptures, one finds several methods of healing open to the sick person. Hector Avalos notes that the home is the "main locus of therapy."[61] Within this structure, the family provided the means of healing or relief through the use of care in the home, herbal remedies *(materia medica)*, and direct prayer by the patient and the family (see Psalms 38, 39, and 88).[62] A second avenue open to the sick person was to consult a prophet who would act as an intermediary between the patient and God, especially when the patient's own prayers had not been answered.[63] Two other "healers" mentioned in Scripture were midwives who assisted at childbirth (Exodus 1:15ff., Genesis 35:17, and 1 Samuel 4:20) and musicians (1 Samuel 16:14ff.). Of midwives, Avalos notes, "although the precise statistics are not available, the midwife may have been one of the most ubiquitous health care consultants in the ancient Near East."[64]

However, by the fourth century BC, physicians were well established in the daily life of Israel.[65] A least one commentator notes that prophets such as Moses, Elijah, and Elisha were "physicians" in their own right. Indeed, the Hebrew word for a physician is *rofeh*, derived from "a root meaning to ease, to assuage."[66] In later Judaism (in contrast to the negative attitude toward physicians in Chronicles), Sirach writes:

> Hold the physician in honor, for he is essential to you, and God it was who established his profession. From God the doctor has his wisdom, and the king provides for his sustenance. . . . My son, when you are ill, delay not, but pray to God, who will heal you: Flee wickedness, let your hands be just, cleanse your heart of every sin. . . . Then give the doctor his place lest he leave; for you need him too. There are times that give him an advantage, and he too beseeches God that his diagnosis may be correct and his treatment

---

[60] Wolff, *Anthropology of the Old Testament*, p. 148.

[61] See Avalos, *Illness and Health Care*, pp. 251-58.

[62] See Levin, pp. 61–63 for a brief synopsis of homeopathic remedies. For example, olive oil (plentiful in the Middle East) was used for soothing bruises. Pomegranates symbolized fertility and rendered one immune to demons. Wormwood was thought to cure worms and fever.

[63] A well-known story is that of the prophet Elisha and Naaman who was afflicted with leprosy (2 Kings 5).

[64] Avalos, p. 280.

[65] Simon S. Levin, *Adam's Rib*, p. 46.

[66] Levin, *Adam's Rib*, p. 45.

bring about a cure. He who is a sinner toward his Maker will be defiant toward the doctor. (Sirach 38:1–2, 9–10, 12–15)

It is the temple and the various shrines, however, which provided a special role as health care consultants. While the constraints of space prevent a thorough discussion, it is sufficient to note that the temple provided a "long-distance" therapeutic role.[67] It was there that petitions were made for fertility (cf. Hannah's prayer in 1 Samuel 1) and other maladies (2 Kings 18:4). It was also the place to which those cured of leprosy and other diseases were declared "clean" (cf. Leviticus 13). Finally, the temple was also the locus where one made a prayer of thanksgiving for deliverance from disease or death.

In summary, in ancient Israel, the one who was sick had both "legitimate" and "illegitimate" options concerning healing. Legitimate options included seeking the advice or prayer of a prophet, the use of a midwife to assist in childbirth, direct prayer to God himself, and making a pilgrimage to the temple or a shrine such as at Shiloh. Illegitimate options to be avoided were consulting sorcerers or diviners of other religions and visiting a "non-yahwistic" temple or place of healing.[68] However, above all, healing is from God, whether directly or using a mediator as mentioned above. God's power is ultimate and unlimited. God is both God of the living and the dead. God chooses to give life or take it away. God alone is able to heal and restore. It is in this vein that the prophet Ezekiel describes the scene of the valley of dry bones (Ezekiel 37), prompting one commentator to write:

---

[67] See the discussion in Avalos, *Illness and Health Care,* pp. 299–397. "Although the main locus of health care was probably in the home, the temple may have been a viable petitionary or therapeutic locus prior to the full implementation of P. [Editor's note: Literary analysis of the Torah shows that it was not written by one person, but derives from a variety of source material. Commonly called the Documentary Hypothesis, the four sources are Jahwist (J), Elohist (E), Deuteronomist (D), and Priestly (P). The priestly source put the Torah into its final form around the time of the Exile. In the priestly writing, the focus is on geneology, the priesthood, and worship.] Indirect evidence for the existence of these functions comes from P itself. The very fact that P commands people not to come to the temple when they are ill suggests that people might have done so in prior times, but one usually does not prohibit a behavior which has never been practiced. Furthermore, Israelites certainly knew that temples were used as petitionary and/or therapeutic loci in some pagan societies (e.g., the temple at Ekron), and the biblical texts themselves attest to the fact that Israelites were prone to follow pagan cultic practices (p. 378). Yet the experience of the bronze serpent and the prayer of Solomon (1 Kings 8) points to the use of the temple as a petitionary and therapeutic center prior to the eighth century BC. After that time, however, the temple assumed the primary role of being the locus of thanksgiving to which those healed of sickness came to be "officially" recognized as cured. In this context, the priests became the "guardians of purity" who determined those persons who could have access to God.

[68] See the chart on p. 405 in Avalos.

The imagery of the psalms and the emotional picture painted by a vision-ary were remotely preparing hearts to accept belief in the resurrection. In the healing of sick persons whom all had abandoned and in the reestab-lishment of the community of believers at Jerusalem after their return from deportation, the important thing was not the concrete incident with its limited empirical dimensions, but the gift of God's goodness and power which they had enjoyed in an extreme situation. This experience, which was of the religious order, justified a still greater hope. Human beings had, as it were, touched the very reality of Yahweh and could depend on him to escape death.

In this way the Old Testament serves as a prelude to the text in James 5:15 with its ambiguous tonality. The term *egeirein*, "to awaken, to lift or raise up," here refers directly to the healing and restoration of the sick person, but it can also be understood as connoting the resurrection, since the New Testament uses it in both senses. Bodily healing is an image and promise of the resurrection for James 5:15, just as it had represented for the psalmists a return from the dwelling place of the dead.[69]

In conclusion, we have seen how the Hebrew Scriptures con-ceived of illness as being that which separates a person from the com-munity. Sickness is intimately connected with impurity and thus renders a person unable to fulfill his or her societal and cultic functions. Furthermore, sickness afflicts not only the individual, but society as well, in that the sick person diminishes the daily ordered functioning of the community. The cause of sickness is varied. However, in the Hebrew mindset, ultimately sickness, like everything else, is attributed to God. The reasons that God would afflict a person in this manner range from personal sinfulness to God's testing of his people to a sim-ple act of God's own will. Healing, then, is also from God. A person could consult a prophet or seer to seek out the reason for the ailment or to ask for a prayer of intercession, but the restoration to health was linked directly to God's will and desire. It was not until the ministry of Jesus of Nazareth that a shift begins to occur in how sickness and healing was viewed. In the next section, we will explore the attitudes of the early Christians regarding sickness and healing, both during the time of Jesus and in the period known as the Early Church.

---

[69] Dubarle, "Sickness and Death in the Old Testament," pp. 58–59.

## The Christian Scriptures

In the exilic and post-exilic periods of Jewish history, the Israelites encountered a variety of healing practices that were exclusive of the temple cult. First, they encountered the Hellenizing influence of the ancient Greeks that combined empirical medicine with homeo-pathic remedies. In other words, the ancient Greek physicians sought to explain the causes of illness and effect a cure through a thorough examination of the human body. Moreover, in the view of the Greeks, a true physician should not only be a scientist but a philosopher as well. An essential characteristic of Greek medicine is "the association of empirical inquiry with a natural-philosophical interpretation of individual phenomenon within the framework of a total view of the cosmos."[70] Here we see the anthropological basis of the Greek system: the Greeks viewed the individual not only as unique but also in *relation to* the rest of the world.

In addition to physicians, there were cultic healing places— temples and sanctuaries dedicated to the gods of healing, especially Aesculapius and Apollo. I do not have the space or time to describe the Greek healing practices here, but suffice it to say, when the physicians' art failed to heal, many people (especially the poor) turned toward the gods for assistance. Nevertheless, even within the cultic healing places, the Greek physicians worked alongside the priests. "Sickness is here a quantity, within the framework of popular-magical thinking that cannot simply be healed by means of empirical diagnosis and therapy; it needs rather the miraculous power of the god."[71]

A third means of treating illness in the Hellenic world was the art of magic. Although not always condoned by the state or government, many ill people turned to magic in times of societal unrest, especially among the lower classes; since the Greeks viewed sickness as the result of demonic activity and therefore the magician or conjurer may combat this threat by knowing efficacious words and materials.[72] Due to the connection between sickness and demons, the art of exorcism belonged to the realm of magic. Furthermore, the Greeks believed that epilepsy

---

[70] Klaus Seybold and Ulrich B. Mueller, *Sickness and Healing,* Translated by Douglas W. Stott, Nashville: Abingdon, 1981, p. 100.

[71] Seybold and Mueller, *Sickness and Healing,* p. 102.

and many forms of mental illness were particularly dangerous because they were forms of demonic possession.[73]

The beliefs of ancient Judaism, influenced by their contact with the Greco-Roman culture, continued into the Christian era. While rationalism seemed to eclipse superstition (especially with the growth of folk medicine), belief in demons and transgressions of the law continued to be considered the primary cause for illness and misfortune. Rabbinical Judaism promulgated the idea that there was a close connection between sin and sickness. As such, when one was afflicted, it was easy to ascertain what sin had been committed. For example, incontinence is the reason for dropsy, epileptic children are the result of engaging in intercourse under the light of a lamp, and idolatry, thievery, or slander causes leprosy. It was for this reason that healing needed to be preceded by a forgiveness of sins.[74]

It was into this world of tempered rationalism and superstitious practices that Jesus came preaching the kingdom of God. According to Morton Kelsey, there are 41 *distinct* instances of physical and mental healing recorded in the four Gospel accounts.[75] In his book *Healing and Christianity*, Kelsey attempts to analyze the accounts of Jesus' healing practice according to modern clinical diagnoses. He notes that "probably the most common ailment healed was mental illness, generally described in New Testament times as demon possession."[76] Kelsey sees three broad categories of illness, which Jesus healed:

> First, there is organic disease in which the structure or tissue of the body is damaged in some way. Second are the functional disorders, in which sickness results because one organ or part of the body is not working properly. Third is psychic or mental illness, which shows up as a disturbance of the personality. Brain damage is usually included here, although there is some question as to how much ordinary mental illness can be attributed to it.[77]

---

[72] Seybold and Mueller, *Sickness and Healing*, p. 103.

[73] Seybold and Mueller, *Sickness and Healing*, p. 103. Demonic possession was a continual theme in the Christian Scriptures as was the close connection between sickness and sin.

[74] Seybold and Mueller, *Sickness and Healing*, p. 113.

[75] Kelsey, *Healing and Christianity*, pp. 43–45. Kelsey summarizes the work of Percy Dearmer and notes the kind of healing, where the account is found, and the method used to heal the sick person.

[76] Kelsey, *Healing and Christianity*, p. 55.

[77] Kelsey, *Healing and Christianity*, p. 58.

Like his Jewish contemporaries, Jesus saw that illness separated a person from the community. Because of sickness, one was unable to participate in cultic worship. Sickness marginalized one from family, from society, and from religion. When he healed, Jesus invited the restored person to begin again and continue living in the world. Sometimes, the sick person was admonished to refrain from sinning as a guarantee that "some greater sickness would not befall" him or her (cf. John 5:14).

The Christian Scriptures are ambiguous as to the reason for sickness. On the one hand, it is suggested that sin is the cause of sickness, on the other, it is quite clear that the reason for the sickness and the subsequent healing was to show God's glory. In short, the cause of sickness could be specific sin (i.e., this person engaged in a sinful activity and is now being punished for it) or generic sin which is a consequence of being a member of the human race. In other words, sickness is part of our post-lapsarian state of being.

While sickness is a part of the human condition, through his healing ministry, Jesus showed the immanent presence of God's reign. According to George Gordon Dawson, "Christ's method was to energize the sufferer's desire for health by a quick command, the helping hand or healing touch of a personality unique and awe-inspiring, and the potency of the will of His perfect Nature."[78] This is not the place to discuss whether Jesus' cures violated the laws of nature to effect healing, yet it is important to recognize that healing activity continued into the apostolic and sub-apostolic age. It is should be remembered that whether Jesus healed demonic possession, blindness, leprosy, or paralysis, the purpose was always for a greater good; namely, that God's grace should be made manifest. It is in the same vein that the Church continues the healing mission of Christ.[79]

In examining scriptural evidence, it is important to note the distinction between disease and illness. John J. Pilch states that the word *disease* reflects "a biomedical perspective that sees abnormalities

---

[78] George Gordon Dawson, *Healing: Pagan and Christian* (London: Society for Promoting Christian Knowledge, 1935), pp. 122–23.

[79] Seybold and Mueller offer an analysis of the various healing accounts in the Gospels (pp. 130–71). They point out that the purpose in healing is to show Christ as merciful (cf. Matthew 14:14; 20:34). In healing, God is glorified (cf. John 11:4). Through the miracles, faith is bolstered and revelation takes place (cf. John 8:12). Yet, "faith and prayer are the fundamental prerequisites of miraculous deeds (Mark 11:23ff.). . . . In the final analysis this is the conviction that only the plea or prayer of the person seeking help makes the healing possible" (p. 184).

in the structure or function of organ systems. . . . As such, a disease affects individuals and only individuals are treated."[80] Furthermore, in first-century Palestine, society was radically group oriented. The individual existed only in relation to the group to which he or she belonged. This perspective was a result of the tribal experience and culture of the Israelite people.

Moreover, according to Pilch, "the concept and word 'illness' reflect a sociocultural perspective that depends entirely upon social and personal perception of certain socially disvalued states including but not necessarily restricted to what modern Western science would recognize as a disease."[81] As we saw in the above discussion of the Hebraic concept of sickness, any illness or dysfunction that marginalized the sick person from cultic activity also separated him or her from society. What is operative in first-century Palestine is a continuation of that which had begun in the post-exilic period of Judaism regarding sickness and healing.[82]

In conclusion, the Christian Scriptures offer a continuation of Judaic thought regarding sickness and healing. As was seen in the Hebrew Scriptures, sickness separated a person from society because it rendered one impure to fulfill cultic functions. Furthermore, sickness afflicted not just the patient, but his or her family and extended family ("kin") as well. Because of the influence of Greek philosophy and Greco-Roman medical practices, physicians played a more prominent role in healing. In addition, magicians and cultic centers of healing assisted in

---

[80] John J. Pilch, "Sickness and Healing in Luke-Acts," In *The Social World of Luke-Acts: Models for Interpretation,* Jerome H. Neyrey, ed., pp. 181–209 (Peabody, MA: Hendrickson Publishers, 1991), p. 191.

[81] Pilch, "Sickness and Healing in Luke-Acts," p. 191.

[82] Pilch notes that there were three parts to the "health care system" in Jesus' day: a professional sector, a popular sector, and a folk sector. By *professional,* he means the use of a physician. As Pilch notes, "neither in the Gospel nor Acts is there any direct and explicit information about the professional sector or the health care sector. Yet the key word that belongs to that sector offers insight into the community's understanding of the role of a healer and the nature of illness. In the Gospel, Jesus adopts the image of a healing prophet, or prophet-healer. A central function of his healing ministry is to lead those whose lives have lost cultural meaning back to the proper purpose and direction in life. That is, the prophet-healer preaches repentance, change of heart, transformation of horizons, broadening of perspectives" (p. 194). In the popular sector, illness affects both the individual and his or her family. The concept of "kin" was very strong in Mediterranean culture (and still is today). "In all cultures, no sick person suffers alone; kin are always affected and involved in all the stages of the illness" (p. 195). Furthermore, social networks and community beliefs and practices also operate in how the sick person conceives of himself or herself and how others treat him or her. Specifically, Pilch notes that the biblical concepts of *hesed* and *zedekah* factored in how beggars and cripples were treated. As seen above, the biblical worldview was

the treatment of illnesses of every type. While folk medicine and homeo-
pathic remedies became more prevalent, superstition and a belief in
demonology continued to influence daily life.

It was in this milieu that Jesus did his ministry. He was a
product of his age, and while his methods were often characterized as
"miraculous," he was completely in the tradition of other prophet-
healers. Like others of his religious background, Jesus saw illness as
the work of the devil. Very often in his own healing ministry, he made
the connection between sickness and sin. However, there is a great
degree of ambiguity as to how strong this connection was. Clearly,
Jesus saw his ministry as ushering in the reign of God. As Edouard
Cothenet notes, from the very beginning of Jesus' ministry (cf. Luke
4:18–19), access to God's reign is through liberation from anything
that prevents one from coming close to God (which included sickness,
slavery to a person or to the Law, and ignorance of the Good News as
well as sin). Yet,

> liberation (aphesis) does involve the forgiveness of sins, but it cannot
> simply be isolated from all the concrete elements referred to in the
> proclamation of the great Jubilee. God, the author of life and the source
> of light, establishes his reign by raising up the supreme prophet. By means
> of his message and his deeds, the latter restores sight to those plunged in
> the darkness of death, and freedom to those who experience the chains
> of slavery in body and soul.[83]

The healing events are not merely signs of God's reign; rather, they are
invitations to conversion and transformation of hearts and lives. The

---

heavily under the influence of demons and malevolent powers. This attitude came to play heavily
in the folk sector. "Within this scheme, the healing enterprise is concerned with diagnosing the
problem, prognosing outcomes, and applying suitable therapies. Another way of viewing this
process is that the healing enterprise seeks to explain, predict, and control reality" (p. 198). Pilch
notes the following common characteristics of all folk healers: 1) The folk healer shares significant elements of the predominant worldview and health concepts. 2) The folk healer views everything that is presented as of equal importance. 3) The client of the folk healer is treated as an
"outpatient" in which the healing is done in a public fashion so as to validate the folk healer's honor
and reputation. 4) The folk healer takes the patient's view of the illness at face value. 5) The folk
healer does not use technical terminology to describe the illness; rather, he or she employs the
language, experience, and belief system of his or her patients. 6) In order to maintain connection
with the community, the folk healer makes special use of the historical and social context of every
illness (see pp. 198–200).

[83] Edouard Cothenet, "Healing as a Sign of the Kingdom, and the Anointing of the Sick,"
In *Temple of the Holy Spirit: Sickness and Death of the Christian in the Liturgy,* Trans. Matthew J.
O'Connell, 33–51 (New York: Pueblo Publishing Company, 1983), p. 36.

Gospel is a call to participation in God's own life. By healing those who were in the slavery of sickness or sin, Jesus indicated that every person is invited into God's sanctuary.

Conversion is the clarion call of the Gospel message. Indeed, a period of sickness and convalescence is often the occasion for just such a process. During this period, religious conversion and renewal can take place. An illness can also bring intellectual reflection about the meaning of life. One's own sufferings can evoke compassion for those whose sufferings and pains are even more severe. Furthermore, various types of illness can have a transforming effect on society as well.[84]

In his work, Donald L. Gelpi offers a succinct analysis of the different types of healing done in the four Gospel accounts.[85] While each one has a slightly different nuance, the overarching theme is clear: "Jesus' ministry of healing endows his proclamation of the kingdom with sacramental significance by transforming it into a manifestation of divine authority and power."[86] However, it is only through the eyes of faith that one is able to perceive the full meaning of Jesus' signs and wonders, which are ultimately rooted in his Resurrection. In the Gospels, physical healing symbolizes the salvation that Jesus brings through his preaching and presence.

## QUESTIONS FOR DISCUSSION

1. Given this brief historical background, do both an exegesis and an eisegesis of the Jacobean text based on your experience of healing.
2. What are the anthropological, spiritual, psychological, and physical effects of a minor illness? Of a serious illness?
3. What is the goal of any kind of healing service?

---

[84] Donald L. Gelpi, *Committed Worship: A Sacramental Theology for Converting Christians.* Volume II: The Sacraments of Ongoing Conversion (Collegeville, MN: The Liturgical Press. 1993), p. 173.

[85] See Gelpi, *Committed Worship,* pp. 173–81.

[86] Gelpi, *Committed Worship,* p. 181.

# Chapter 2

# Christian Healing: From the Apostolic Period to the Reformation

## INTRODUCTION

This chapter is a brief historical study of the healing ministry in the Church. Please note that other authors have made a great contribution in this area. Most notably, Charles Gusmer in his work *And You Visited Me* offers a thorough treatment of the history of sacramental Anointing. John Pilch's *Healing in the New Testament* and *Visions and Healing in the Acts of the Apostles* offer an insight into the healing ministry of the Apostolic and Post–Apostolic ages. Finally, *Recovering the Riches of Anointing*, edited by Genevieve Glen, provides a series of articles relating to the healing ministry.[1]

In the next three chapters, I will present a brief survey of how the Church has exercised healing, both sacramentally and nonsacramentally, over the past two thousand years as a means by which the ill, the elderly, and the dying encountered God. For a more in-depth analysis, consult the works mentioned above.

This chapter will cover the period from the Apostolic Age through the fifteenth century, just prior to the period commonly known as the Reformation. We will see how the healing ministry became more professionalized and more localized in the person of the ordained priest.

---

[1] Charles W. Gusmer, *And You Visited Me: Sacramental Ministry to the Sick and Dying* (Collegeville, MN: The Liturgical Press, 1990; John J. Pilch, *Healing in the New Testament*, Minneapolis, MN: Fortress Press, 2000; John J. Pilch, *Visions and Healing in the Acts of the Apostles*, Collegeville, MN: The Liturgical Press, 2004; Genevieve Glen, ed., *Recovering the Riches of Anointing*, Collegeville, MN: The Liturgical Press.

This had later ramifications for the tensions that often existed between the priest and the medical practitioner as well as contributing to the restriction of the healing ministry to the moments just prior to death.

## The Early Church

In the Apostolic Age, the apostles and disciples of Jesus continued his healing ministry. The Church participated in the art of healing in three ways: sacramental, superstitious, and scientific.[2] Initially, the apostles carried on the ministry of healing through miracles as recorded in the Acts of the Apostles.[3] Gradually, as it became apparent that the Parousia or Second Coming was not immanent, the Church established a sacramental system for healing. The epistle of James[4] became the model for healing activity. As George Dawson notes, "from the first, the healing ministry was considered as much an integral part of the Church's work as preaching the word and administering the sacraments. The attempt was made to fulfill the commission to preach, to teach and to heal which Jesus gave to his followers."[5] Healing was considered such an important function of the primitive Church that the Bishop prayed for the charism of healing be given to candidates for orders.[6] Healing in the early Church was aimed toward restoration of the sick person to complete health of mind, body, and spirit.

It is difficult to determine how exactly illness was defined in the early Church, yet many inexplicable cases (due to a lack of understanding of medicine) were attributed to demonic possession. As such, mental cases, obsessions, phobias were treated by exorcism. In fact, there is evidence that the "energumens" (as the mentally disordered and demonically possessed were usually called) were exorcised on a daily basis, frequently in church.[7]

In his work on the Anointing of the Sick, Andrew Cuschieri notes the following:

---

[2] Dawson, George Gordon, *Healing: Pagan and Christian* (London: Society for Promoting Christian Knowledge, 1935), p. 145.

[3] For example see Acts 3:1–10; 4:23–37; 5:12–16; 8:4–8; and 9:32–43.

[4] See the discussion of the letter of Saint James in chapter 1 of this book.

[5] Dawson, Healing: *Pagan and Christian*, p. 146.

[6] Cf. Canons 17 and 39 of Hippolytus and the *Apostolic Constitutions* book 8, chapter 16.

[7] Dawson, *Healing: Pagan and Christian,* p.148.

*Energumeni* used to be anointed. Pope Benedict XV does not deny the historical evidence of this custom in the Church. With due respect to this learned pope, however, one is bound to confront his allegation that the diabolically possessed were anointed with the oil of the lamp. Venerabilis Bede, Theodulfus Aurelianensis, Jonas Aurelianensis all vouch that the Sacrament of the Anointing of the Sick was administered also in the case of diabolical possession. The point in discussion here is not whether the diabolical possessions of the mediaeval times were indeed genuine or rather emotional, psychological disturbances. The fact is that the Sacrament was administered in the belief that the person was possessed by the devil. It appears from this custom that the theology of the Anointing of the Sick, at least down to the ninth century, took into perspective the text of Saint James as well as that of Saint Mark: ". . . . they cast out many devils, and anointed many sick people with oil and cured them." This custom also insinuates the belief in the devil as being the cause of both the spiritual and physical sickness, and the close relation between the two.[8]

Therefore, although evidence is scant regarding the Anointing of the mentally ill, it appears that until the ninth century or so, those who were afflicted with any kind of illness (physical, psychological, or diabolical) were anointed. Furthermore, the prayers of blessing over the oil suggest that all the sick could benefit from the Anointing. The extant liturgical prayers clearly indicate that the specific purpose of the Rite of Anointing was to strengthen the sick person and restore him or her to health. From the *Apostolic Tradition* (ca. 215), there is the following formula:

> O God, who sanctifiest this oil, as Thou dost grant unto all who are anointed and receive of it the hallowing wherewith Thou didst anoint kings, priests and prophets, so [grant that] it may give strength to all that taste of it and health to all that use it.[9]

In the *Euchologion* of Serapion of Thmuis (ca. 350) there is a more developed and detailed prayer over the oil of the sick:

---

[8] Andrew Cuschieri, *Anointing of the Sick: A Theological and Canonical Study* (Lanham, MD: University Press of America, Inc., 1993), p. 133.

[9] Cited in Paul F. Palmer, "The Purpose of the Anointing of the Sick: A Reappraisal," *Theological Studies* 19 (1958): 314. "Oleum hoc sanctificans das, Deus (sanitatem) utentibus et pereipientibus, unde unexisti reges, sacerdotes et prophetas, omnibus gustantibus confortationem et sanitatem utentibus illud praebeat." (Cited in Antoine Chavasse, *Étude sur l'onction des infirmes dans l'église latine du IIIe au XIe siècle*, Tome I: *Du IIIe siècle à la réforme carolingienne* [thèse de doctorat], [Lyons: La Faculté de Théologie de Lyon, 1942], p. 34.)

We invoke Thee, who hast all power and might, Saviour of all men, Father of our Lord and Saviour Jesus Christ, and we pray Thee to send down from the heavens of Thy Only-begotten a curative power upon this oil, in order that to those who are anointed with these Thy creatures or who receive them, it may become a means of removing "every disease and every sickness" [Matthew 4:23], of warding off every demon, of putting to flight every unclean spirit, of keeping at a distance every evil spirit, of banishing all fever, all chill, and all weariness; a means of grace and goodness and the remission of sins; a medicament of life and salvation, unto health and soundness of soul and body and spirit, unto perfect well-being.[10]

While the mentally ill are not specifically mentioned in the prayer, one may presume that they are included under the phrases "every disease and every sickness" as well as "unto health and soundness of soul and body and spirit, unto perfect well-being." Again, it is seen that in the ancient world, the human person is conceived as being a unity of soul, body, mind, and spirit.

## The Early Middle Ages

Mental illness has its first mention in the prayer of the Gelasian and Gregorian Sacramentaries (seventh–ninth centuries). Palmer suggests that the following prayer "may well represent the formula used in the Roman Church from the fifth century:"[11]

Send down from heaven, we beseech Thee, Lord, the Holy Spirit, the Paraclete, upon the richness of this oil, which Thou hast deigned to bring forth from the green tree for refreshment of mind and body. And may Thy blessing be to all who anoint, taste and touch a protection for body, soul and spirit, for dispelling all sufferings, all sickness, all illness of mind and body. . . .[12]

Finally, Palmer notes that Gallican-Visigoth formula from the pre–Carolingian period is instructive on the purpose of the oil of the sick:

---

[10] Palmer, "The Purpose of the Anointing of the Sick: A Reappraisal," p. 315.

[11] Ibid., p. 315.

[12] Ibid., p. 315. "Emitte quaesumus Domine Spiritum sanctum paraclitum de coelis in hanc pinguedinem olei, quam de viridi ligno producere dignatus es ad refectionem mentis et corporis. Et tua sancta benedictio sit omni ungenti, gustanti, tangenti, tutamentum corporis animae et spiritus, ad evacuandos omnes dolores . . . , etc." (Cited in Chavasse, pp. 54–55).

Prayer is made that the oil "may be of profit to those who are troubled with fever and dysentery," that it may be of help to "paralytics, the lame, the blind and others similarly afflicted." Hope is expressed that the use of the oil "may drive out the quartan, tertian and daily chill of fever; that it may loosen the lips of the dumb, cool and refresh feverish members of the body, restore to knowing the mind that is demented." In a word, the oil of the sick is regarded as a panacea for every disease and infirmity.[13]

It is clear from the above examples that the primary purpose for the oil of the sick is for the physical cure of all sickness and infirmity. While the letter of James refers to the forgiveness of sins, the early Church focused on the importance of the curative effects of the oil and Anointing. Furthermore, there is nothing to suggest in the literature of the early Church that the sacrament of Anointing should be considered a sacrament to be administered in preparation for death.[14]

It is not until the period of the Carolingian reform that the first traces of Unction being used as a sacrament of the dying are detected. Yet, as Palmer notes, Unction is still regarded as a sacrament of the sick and not principally of the dying.[15] In his article, Palmer cites a Carolingian rite for the visitation of the sick in which the following prayer is said:

> . . . . cure, we beseech Thee, our Redeemer, by the grace of the Holy Spirit, the weakness of this sick man; heal his wounds, and forgive his sins; drive out from him all pains of body and mind, mercifully restore him to full health, both inwardly and outwardly; that recovered and healed by the help of Thy mercy, he may be strengthened to take up his former duties of piety to Thee. Through . . . .[16]

Once again the psychosomatic unity is a feature of this prayer as seen in the references to "mind" and "inwardly."

In short, there does not seem to be a distinction made with regard to the recipient of the sacrament of the sick in the earlier prayers. What is clear is that they are seriously ill. There is some connection between the person's illness and sin, but not necessarily a causal one. Furthermore, the sickness, while presumably of a physical

---

[13] Ibid., p. 316.
[14] Ibid., p. 321.
[15] Ibid., p. 325.
[16] Ibid., p. 324.

nature, could be an emotional or mental ailment as well. What is asked for in the prayers is a restoration to health in order that the patient may once again resume his or her position within society.

Moreover, as Placid Murray notes (citing Chavasse),

> The evidence of the first period (before AD 800) may be fairly taken to show that the Anointing was in fact administered to the sick who were not in danger of death and that of the three effects expected from the Anointing—bodily health, spiritual well-being and forgiveness of sins— the earliest sources seem to place bodily health *first* in order, sometimes even referring to it alone.[17]

While this earlier period focused on bodily restoration, in subsequent years a shift occurred which placed the emphasis on spiritual healing and preparation for death.

## The Late Middle Ages

In terms of Church legislation, the work *Mental Affliction and Church Law* by R. Colin Pickett offers a historical analysis of the use of the sacrament from a legal perspective. He notes, however,

> We cannot say with certainty whether the insane were considered capable of receiving Extreme Unction or not in the early Church. The question is still a matter of obscurity as of the time of the *Decretals*. There is evidence that would lead us to believe that they were not. We have seen authoritative texts giving them the right to be baptized, absolved, confirmed and even given the Eucharist. Since most of these refer to the occasion of danger of death, it is very significant that none of them mentioned that Extreme Unction was also to be conferred.[18]

Pickett further gives evidence of the lacuna regarding the use of Extreme Unction with the mentally ill found in the writings of Saint Raymond of Pennafort and the legislation at the Synod of Nimes in 1284. Pickett says that the Synod

---

[17] Placid Murray, "The Liturgical History of Extreme Unction," In *Studies in Pastoral Liturgy*, Volume Two, Vincent Ryan, ed. (Dublin: The Furrow Trust, 1963), p. 36 (emphasis added).

[18] R. Colin Pickett, *Mental Affliction and Church Law: An Historical Synopsis of Roman and Ecclesiastical Law and a Canonical Commentary* (Ottawa, Ontario: The University of Ottawa Press, 1952), p. 57.

. . . . authorized the priest to absolve the insane penitent in danger of death. . . . yet no mention was made in the decree of conferring the Sacrament of Extreme Unction. Such a significant omission can by no means be attributed to mere distraction or oversight on the part of the legislators. Had they intended or believed that Extreme Unction should be administered in such a case, they would certainly have included legislation that it would be.[19]

In his book *The Origins of European Thought*, Richard Broxton Onians examines the term *mind* as found in the Middle Ages and its antecedents. He notes that from the earliest times, the head (and presumably that which is contained therein) is honored or holy because it is the seat of life. In some cultures, it was believed that the head also contained the soul (or psyche).[20] The psyche is very close in meaning to the Hebrew *nephesh*, which has been associated with *breath, exhalation,* and *spirit.*[21] These concepts came into the Latin under the terms *anima* and *animus.*[22] While their original meanings are obscured in history, Onians suggests that the term *mens* is "secondary and belongs to *animus.*"[23] In the liturgical literature, *mentis* and *animae* are used in references to the mind. When referring to the insane, *amentia* is used.

It is clear from the linguistic evidence that in ancient times as well as in the Middle Ages, the head (containing the mental capacities as well as the soul) was considered a sacred place. Therefore, when diseases attacked the head or when the mind ceased to function properly, the whole person was thought to be imperiled. Furthermore, as seen above, prayers were addressed to God for the healing of both body and mind in order that the person may not lose his soul as a result of the experience of sickness. Gradually, however, theologians began to focus on the distinction between body and soul echoing the flesh-spirit dualism found in the writing of Paul and Augustine. The early Scholastics, namely Hugh of St. Victor and Peter Lombard, reflected on the effect of the remission of sins with regard to Anointing of the Sick. As Palmer notes, "sometime before the year 1200 the Rite

---

[19] Pickett, *Mental Affliction and Church Law,* p. 58.

[20] Richard Broxton Onians, *The Origins of European Thought: About the Body, the Mind, the Soul, the World, Time and Fate* (London: Cambridge at the University Press, 1951), p. 97.

[21] Ibid., p. 481.

[22] Ibid., pp. 168–73.

[23] Ibid., p. 172, n. 4.

of Anointing the senses as the organs of sin was accompanied by the prayer that the Lord would remit all sins committed through these various organs of the body."[24] This led to the practice of Anointing only those who were capable of sinning, namely those who were of the age of reason and capable of using it. Therefore, children and those who had lost the use of reason (the insane and frenetics) were excluded from receiving the sacrament of the sick. Furthermore, the concern of the theologians of the pre–Scholastic period was regarding the effect of the Anointing of the Sick. In other words, many theologians considered the healing of the soul (remission of sins) as the primary effect of the sacrament while bodily healing is "conditional on whether it is really beneficial for the sick man."[25] Moreover, scholastic discussion centered on Unction as a sacrament for "the elimination of all obstacles to entrance to heavenly glory, and saw in it the consummation of the efforts of the Church for the salvation of the soul."[26] The sacrament had devolved from being one of healing to being a necessary preparation for death eliminating all sin. These attitudes, along with some superstitious beliefs among the faithful, led to delaying reception of the sacrament until the last possible moment before death.[27] However, and this is an important distinction, the official legislation of the Church (from the beginnings to the Council of Trent) never mentions danger of death as a condition for the reception of the sacrament. In fact, the Second Council of Lyons (1274) states in the profession of faith of Michael Paleologus:

> The same holy Roman Church holds and teaches as well that there are seven sacraments of the Church; . . . another is extreme unction, which, according to the instruction of Blessed James, is used for the sick.[28]

---

[24] Palmer, "The Purpose of the Anointing of the Sick," pp. 325–26.

[25] Bernhard Poschmann, *Penance and Anointing of the Sick.* Translated and revised by Francis Courtney, SJ (New York: Herder and Herder, 1964), p. 252.

[26] Poschmann, *Penance and Anointing of the Sick,* p. 253.

[27] See Palmer's thesis, "The Purpose of the Anointing of the Sick: A Reappraisal," pp. 330–36. Some superstitions included the belief that because a person was anointed on the feet, he or she could not walk around barefoot, and nor could a person marry or resume marital relations after having received Anointing. In fact, theologians such as Albert the Great, Duns Scotus, and Thomas Aquinas saw in Anointing the "last remedy" which the Church could offer, and as such can be given only to those who were in a state of departure from this life.

[28] ". . .extrema unctio, quae secundum doctrinam beati Iacobi infirmantibus adhibetur."— Mansi, XXIV, 71. Op. cit. Charles George Renati, *The Recipient of Extreme Unction* (Dissertation), (Washington, D.C.: The Catholic University of America Press, 1961), p. 27.

Therefore, despite the theological reflection surrounding the sacrament and the change in the pastoral practice,[29] the Church in its official teaching considered Unction to be a sacrament for the sick.

## THE SCHOLASTIC PERIOD AND THE REFORMATION

Given this milieu, theologians of the period sought to clarify and explicate the many distinctions surrounding the recipient of Extreme Unction. Given its close association with Penance and the remission of sins, the question arose as to whether those who were incapable of sinning were permitted to receive the sacrament. In the *Summa Theologica* (ST III, QQ. 29–33), Thomas Aquinas examines the sacrament of Extreme Unction. In Q. 32, he notes that it is to be given to those who are sick:

> I answer that, This sacrament is a spiritual healing, as stated above (Q. 30, AA 1, 2), and is signified by way of a healing of the body. Hence this sacrament should not be conferred on those who are not subjects for bodily healing, those namely, who are in good health.
>
> Reply Obj. 1. Although spiritual health is the principal effect of this sacrament, yet this same spiritual healing needs to be signified by a healing of the body, although bodily health may not actually ensue. Consequently spiritual health can be conferred by this sacrament on those alone who are competent to receive bodily healing, viz. the sick; even as he alone can receive Baptism who is capable of a bodily washing, and not a child yet in its mother's womb.
>
> Reply Obj. 2. Even those who are entering into life can not receive Baptism unless they are capable of a bodily washing. And so those who are departing this life cannot receive this sacrament, unless they be subjects for a bodily healing.[30]

---

[29] See Palmer, "The Purpose of the Anointing of the Sick," pp. 330–31. As the author notes, "Up until the close of the twelfth century the normal order of the rites of the dying was reconciliation, anointing, and viaticum. When the great Scholastic period opened, however, the sacrament of viaticum had yielded its climatic position to the sacrament of extreme unction. Up to this time viaticum had been regarded as the Church's last or parting gift, as food for the journey, as an antidote against evil, and as a preparation for eternal life. . . . But as extreme unction became in point of administration the last sacrament, it is not surprising that theologians, faced with a new sacrament of the dying, should ascribe to unction what had formerly been ascribed to viaticum, and that they should insist that unction as a preparation for glory should be received only upon departure from this life."

[30] Thomas Aquinas, *Summa Theologica*. First Complete American Edition in Three Volumes. Literally translated by Fathers of the English Dominican Province. Volume Three (New York: Benziger Brothers, Inc., 1948), p. 2675.

It is interesting to note that while Thomas admits that spiritual health is the primary effect of the sacrament, the possibility of a bodily healing must be present (even if it may not actually occur). Furthermore, given the Platonic and Aristotelian mind-body dualism, the emphasis given to bodily (rather than emotional or mental) healing is to be expected.

In the second article, Thomas posits that "any sickness can cause death, if it be aggravated . . . [therefore] there is none in which this sacrament cannot be given. . . ."[31] However, he notes that "if we consider the degree and the stage of the complaint, this sacrament should not be given to every sick person."[32] In short, Thomas is arguing that the sacrament should be reserved to those whose illness is of "such a nature as to cause death."[33]

In the Fourth Article, Thomas offers a further stipulation to the criteria for reception: the causal relation between sickness and sin. As he notes in his Reply Obj. 1: " Children's infirmities are not caused by actual sin, as in adults, and this sacrament is given chiefly as a remedy for infirmities that result from sins, being the remnants of sin, as it were."[34] In a sense, Thomas "consecrates" the presumed relationship between sickness and sin. Since children could not "sin" because they lacked the use of reason, so too, they were excluded from receiving Extreme Unction.

What of those who were of the age of reason but were somehow mentally incapacitated; could they receive the sacrament? In Q. 32, Art. 3, Thomas answers the question of whether this sacrament ought to be given to madmen and imbeciles. His answer is in the negative; yet for purposes of this study, it is useful to quote the response in its entirety:

We proceed thus to the Third Article:—

Objection 1. It would seem that this sacrament should be given to madmen and imbeciles. For these diseases are full of danger and cause death quickly. Now when there is danger it is the time to apply the remedy. Therefore this sacrament, which was intended as a remedy to human weakness, should be given to such people.

---

[31] Aquinas, ST III Q. 32, A2 Reply Obj. 1., p. 2675.

[32] Aquinas, ibid.

[33] Aquinas, ST III Q. 32, A2, I answer that, p. 2675.

[34] Aquinas, ST III Q. 32, A4, p. 2676.

Obj. 2. Further, Baptism is a greater sacrament than this. Now Baptism is conferred on mad people as stated above (P. III, Q. 68, A. 12). Therefore this sacrament should also be given to them.

On the contrary, this sacrament should be given to none but such as acknowledge it. Now this does not apply to madmen and imbeciles. Therefore it should not be given to them.

I answer that, The devotion of the recipient, the personal merit of the minister, and the general merits of the whole Church, are of great account towards the reception of the effect of this sacrament. This is evident from the fact that the form of this sacrament is pronounced by way of a prayer. Hence it should not be given those who cannot acknowledge it, and especially to madmen and imbeciles, who might dishonor the sacrament by their offensive conduct, unless they have lucid intervals, when they would be capable of acknowledging the sacrament, for then the sacrament should be given to children the same in that state.

Reply Obj. 1. Although such people are sometimes in danger of death, yet the remedy cannot be applied to them, on account of their lack of devotion. Hence it should not be given to them.

Reply Obj. 2. Baptism does not require a movement of the free-will, because it is given chiefly as a remedy for original sin, which, in us, is not taken away by a movement of the free-will. On the other hand this sacrament requires a movement of the free-will; wherefore the comparison fails. Moreover Baptism is a necessary sacrament, while Extreme Unction is not.[35]

By way of commentary, it is interesting to note that Thomas admits that the mentally ill "are sometimes in danger of death." Yet, he denies the sacrament to them because they "might dishonor the sacrament by their offensive conduct." However, he offers a window of opportunity, as it were, with the following phrase: "unless they have lucid intervals, when they would be capable of acknowledging the sacrament, for then the sacrament should be given . . . ." As Bernhard Poschmann notes, "by this St. Thomas means actual devotion, not just habitual devotion. In the latter case the sacrament could be efficacious by reason of a previous act of devotion consciously elicited."[36] For Thomas, it appears that the main concern is that the sacrament not be subjected to misuse or dishonor. Because it is a sacred action, both

---

[35] Thomas Aquinas, ST III, Q. 32, A3, pp. 2675–76.

[36] Poschmann, *Penance and Anointing of the Sick*, (New York: Herder & Herder, 1964) p. 255.

the minister and recipient must be predisposed to a proper and just celebration in order to bring about the true effects of the sacrament.

With the publication of the *Summa Theologica,* there is a "canonization" of the theological shift of the sacrament from being administered "for the sick" to one that was administered in order to prepare a person for death. For the next 800 years, the use of the sacrament seemed to be restricted to persons "in extremis." Yet the tension still remained, both theologically and canonically, of viewing the sacrament as both healing of illness and preparation for eternal glory. For the most part, however, the sacrament of the sick came to be seen in practice as well as in name as an "extreme unction."

Through the influence of Thomas Aquinas and the other Scholastics, the subject for Anointing was restricted to one who was near death. Furthermore, he or she must be of the age of reason, thereby excluding children and the mentally disordered from reception. In addition, the Anointing *in extremis* replaced Viaticum as the "last sacrament." Thomistic thought influenced later Church legislation regarding the recipient and effects of the sacrament of Extreme Unction as it came to be known. Pickett notes in his historical analysis that the Ritual of Benedict XIV (ca. 1757) contains a text that had been ascribed to the sixth Council of Benevento in 1374:

> Frenetics and the insane, especially those who could show irreverence to the Sacrament through some indecency, are not to be given this Sacrament, unless they have lucid intervals during which they can appreciate the Sacrament [. . . .], for, in order that this Sacrament be fruitful, a certain interior devotion is necessary, which insane and similarly afflicted souls cannot have.[37]

In the General Council of Florence, Decree for the Armenians (1439) we see a further influence of Thomas:

> The fifth sacrament is extreme unction. Its matter is olive oil blessed by the bishop. This sacrament may not be given except to a sick person whose life is feared for. He is to be anointed on these parts: on the eyes on account of sight, on the ears on account of hearing, on the nostrils on account of smelling, on the mouth on account of taste and speech, on the hands on

---

[37] Pickett, *Mental Affliction and Church Law,* p. 59.

account of touch, on the feet on account of movement, on the loins on account of the lust seated there.[38]

Note that the sacrament is to be given only to those in danger of death. However, in the following paragraph the Council also affirms that Extreme Unction is also a sacrament for the sick:

> The minister of the sacrament is the priest. The effect is the healing of the mind and, as far as it is good for the soul, of the body as well. Of this sacrament blessed James the apostle says: "Is any among you sick? . . ." (James 5:14f.).[39]

It is also worthy to note that the Council refers to the healing of the mind as one of the effects of the sacrament. While the legislation is borrowed heavily from Thomas, there is still a recognition that the primary reason for the sacrament is for the benefit of the sick person (albeit a spiritual effect), not as a preparation for death.

In the years prior to the Reformation, the Church struggled with the meaning of the sacraments. In 1215, the Fourth Lateran Council had established the number and order of the sacramental system and had enshrined the priest as the dispenser of God's grace. Yet the winds of change were in the air. Governments were being established, kingdoms were solidified, and science was once again regaining its place albeit slowly. In the age of exploration and experimentation, not to mention a renewal in interest of philosophy and theology, questions were being raised not just by theologians, but by ordinary people as well.

The Council of Trent, responding to Luther's attacks against the sacrament, issued the Doctrine on the Sacrament of Extreme Unction in 1551. As Neuner and Depuis note in their commentary on this document, "the Council still continues the Scholastic tradition which had made the Anointing the 'extreme' unction, but mitigates

---

[38] Josef Neuner and Jacques Depuis, eds., *The Christian Faith: Doctrinal Documents of the Catholic Church*, fifth revised and enlarged edition (New York: Alba House, 1990), p. 499. "Quintum sacramentum est extrema unctio, cuius materia est oleum olivae per episcopum benedictum. Hoc sacramentum nisi infirmo, de cuius morte timetur, dari non debet; qui in his locis ungendus est: in oculis propter visum, in auribus propter auditum, in naribus propter odoratum, in ore propter gustum vel locutionem, in manibus propter tactum, in pedibus propter gressum, in renibus propter delectationem ibidem vigentuem" (Denzinger-Schönmetzer, n. 1324).

[39] Neuner and Depuis (ND), *The Christian Faith: Doctrinal Documents of the Catholic Church*, p. 499. "Minister huius sacramenti est sacerdos. Effectus vero est mentis sanatio et, in quantum animae expedit, ipsius etiam corporis. De hoc sacramento inquit beatus Iacoubus Apostolus: 'Infirmatur quis in vobis? . . .'" (Denzinger-Schönmetzer, n. 1325).

the scholastic stand by extending the sacrament to those 'dangerously ill' and by including among its effects psychological and physical relief."[40] Despite this more positive approach, Henry Kryger notes that the sacrament

> . . . . is to be the completion and consummation "not only of penance but of the whole Christian life, which ought to be a continual penance." This statement agrees more with the thought and expression of Thomas Aquinas.
>
> In regard to the effects, the chapter lists four: 1. remission of sin; 2. removal of the consequences of sin; 3. alleviation of the soul; and 4. restoration of health to the body, when useful for the welfare of the soul.[41]

However, those with mental afflictions are governed by even stricter legislation. In the *Catechism of the Council of Trent*, there is this instruction:

> All who lack the use of reason are not fit to receive this Sacrament, nor are children who commit no sins from the remains of which they would have occasion to be healed by the remedial efficacy of the Sacrament, nor *fools and madmen* also, unless they have lucid intervals and then, in particular, give signs of piety and ask to be anointed with the sacred oil; for a sick person insane from his very birth is not to be anointed; but if a sick person, whilst yet in full possession of his faculties, had expressed a wish to be made partaker of this Sacrament and subsequently becomes insane and delirious, he is to be anointed.[42]

It appeared that the Scholastic position had won the day.[43] Opinions regarding the position of the insane followed the above line of logic.[44] Charles George Renati suggests that after the Council of Trent a shift

---

[40] Neuner and Depuis, p. 509.

[41] Henry S. Kryger, *The Doctrine of the Effects of Extreme Unction in Its Historical Development* (Dissertation), The CUA Studies in Sacred Theology (Second Series), No. 33 (Washington, D.C.: The Catholic University of America Press, 1949), p. 21.

[42] Pickett, *Mental Affliction and Church Law*, p. 82. "Omnes praeterea, qui rationis usu carent, ad hoc Sacramentum suscipiendum apti non sunt, et pueri, qui nulla peccata admittunt, quorum reliquias sanare huius Sacramenti remedio opus sit: amentes item, et furiosi, nisi interdum rationis usum haberent, et eo potissimum tempore pii animi significationem darent, peterentque, ut sacro oleo ungerentur. Nam, qui ab ipso ortu nunquam mentis, et rationis compos fuit, ungendus non est: secus vero, si aegrotus, cum mente adhuc integra huius Sacramenti particeps fieri voluisset, postea in insaniam, et furorem incidit" *(Catechismus Romanus ex decreto Sacrosancti Concilii Tridentini, Romae: Typis Sacrae Congregationis de Propaganda Fide, 1796)*, p. 304.

[43] Charles George Renati, *The Recipient of Extreme Unction* (Dissertation), (Washington, D.C.: The Catholic University of America Press, 1961), p. 37.

[44] See Pickett, *Mental Affliction and Church Law*, pp. 82–83. He notes in particular the work of Charles Borromeo, the Provincial Council of Cambrai, and the *Roman Ritual of Paul V* (which he cites as being more lenient in matters regarding the insane).

in focus took place. He notes that "the law of particular synods began to urge pastors to anoint the sick in good time rather than wait until the last moments as had once been thought most opportune."[45] However, this indicates that pastors were *not* doing what Trent had asked, for if they were, there would have been no need to remind them of their duty to anoint earlier. For all intents and purposes then, from 1215 to 1545 pastoral practice focused on administering the sacrament very close to death (and sometimes immediately after as well). Furthermore, the faithful continued to call the priest only at the last possible moment, desiring not Viaticum as food for the journey, but the Anointing and last blessing for the remission of sins.[46]

## QUESTIONS FOR DISCUSSION

1. According to Saint Thomas, what are the effects of the sacrament of Extreme Unction?
2. What is the relationship between Viaticum and Extreme Unction? What is its relationship today?
3. Describe the matter, form, minister, recipient, and effects of Extreme Unction prior to the Council of Trent.

---

[45] Renati, *The Recipient of Extreme Unction,* p. 37.

[46] See Palmer, "The Purpose of the Anointing of the Sick: A Reappraisal," p. 343.

# Chapter 3

# Christian Healing: From Trent to the Second Vatican Council

## INTRODUCTION

In chapter 2 we established the historical antecedents of the recipient of sacramental Anointing. The Church moved from viewing healing as an ecclesial activity with a quasi-charismatic dimension to an action contained in an officially recognized sacrament performed by an ordained minister. Over a period of time, the Church shifted its focus from healing the sick to preparing the dying person for eternal glory. The sacrament, while retaining its healing function, became a last Anointing which "sealed" and "signed" the person as a member of the Body of Christ as he or she left this world for eternal life.

In the face of the Reformation, in which some reformers challenged the value of Extreme Unction as a sacrament, the Church, during the Council of Trent, continued to uphold the long tradition of the sacrament as being both for healing the sick and strengthening the dying. Yet in pastoral practice, the primary emphasis was the value of the sacrament for the dying person. Thus, while the theology proclaimed the need to minister to the sick, the ritual was most often used with those who were dying. This practice has caused some confusion that still exists to this day.

We have also examined the theme of sickness and healing from the perspectives of history, theology, and anthropology. In answering the question, Who was the sick person and how was he healed? we observed that the responses varied over time. From the perspective of social history, we saw that the definition of *sickness* has changed over time. In the ancient world, any disease or malaise that separated one from the community, either physically or ritually, was classified as *illness* that needed healing. The reasons for the illness varied from the weather to poor diet to demons to the capriciousness of the gods. Illness rendered a person "weak" and unable to fulfill his or her individual as well as social duties and obligations. As such, the sick person was alienated from family and society. Therefore, the sick person needed to be reintegrated into society. The curing of illness was undertaken by diviners, sorcerers, priests, and physicians as well as by family members.

## THE AGE OF ENLIGHTENMENT TO THE MODERN ERA

Since the Enlightenment, the medical profession has enjoyed a privileged place in exercising the art of healing. While other forms of curative treatment are not excluded, the majority of illnesses, both physical and mental, are treated by individuals trained in a medical profession.[1] This has led to a tendency to compartmentalize the human person. In other words, the area of illness is localized from the whole individual. A person who has a broken leg, then, is treated as if no other part of his or her being is affected. Yet recently, there has been a return to the holistic view of the person in which sickness affects the whole individual, not only a specific part of his or her body.

Theologically, there is a connection between sickness and sin. At times, this link is quite strong. For several thousand years, in a variety of cultures, sickness was viewed as the result of a person's disobedience to God. With the growing awareness of how disease works, however, there is more of a tendency to ascribe illness to microbes and bacteria rather than to an angry god. Yet, the belief that God somehow "causes" illness is still prevalent in our society. One may easily remember in the earlier stages of the AIDS crisis when some preachers and ministers said that HIV was God's punishment. While not going toward either extreme, there is a connection between sickness and sinfulness.

---

[1] This is especially true in the so-called "developed" nations. While other cultures may employ the use of shamans, medicine men, or religious leaders to effect healing, in the developed nations there is a recognition that a particular class of persons is responsible for healing and curing within a given society.

Perhaps the connection is not directly causal, but nonetheless, it is present.

Sin is a kind of sickness—a sickness of the soul—which needs healing as does any disease or malady. Physical, mental, or emotional illnesses are a result of the human condition, which has been touched by original, as well as individual and social sin. The role of the Church today is to steer a *via media* between those who would deny any theological reasoning for sickness and those who see one's personal sinful behavior behind every illness and disease. Yet, it is important to see that all sickness, whether of a moral or physical nature, initially can alienate one from God. When a particular malady or condition is given value because the person is joined to the sufferings of Christ, he or she is once again connected to God and the community.

In the anthropological realm, the definition of the human person underwent some changes during the period of the Enlightenment. In the ancient world, the human being was seen as a whole comprising many aspects. With the onset of Platonic and Aristotelian philosophy and its canonization in the Medieval world, the human person was divided into body and soul, the soul being far superior. Emphasis was placed on the final destiny of the human person rather than on his or her present life. Furthermore, the body-soul dualism was partly responsible for the compartmentalization of the human body into different components. It is only in this century that a holistic approach to the human person is once again finding favor.

Anthropology sees sickness as affecting both the individual and the community. When someone is ill, it affects his or her internal relationship as well as relationships with others. Not only is that individual alienated from the community, he or she is also alienated from himself or herself. Sickness has far-reaching ramifications for how the human person is seen in society. One major area in which this is most prevalent is that of health care. In the ancient world, the family was the primary caregiver. Today, the sick and dying are often sent to hospitals or clinics, shifting the caregiver responsibility to strangers in the antiseptic environment of these institutions. In some cases, they even deny access to family members for fear of "contamination." However, this attitude toward health care is slowly changing for the better.

## Antecedents to the Second Vatican Council

From this brief history of the sacrament of the sick, as well as from the perspective of social history, three broad aspects emerge which comprise the state of the question in the years immediately preceding the Second Vatican Council. These three aspects helped to shape the current attitudes and research into the use of the sacrament of the sick.

First, many changes in society emerged around the world following years of economic and social upheaval. Since 1900, there has been a major world depression, two major world wars, several skirmishes of a lesser magnitude, the genocide of various peoples, and the advent of many technological advances. These radical and sometimes catastrophic changes prompted a need to examine the nature of humanity. Furthermore, due to these changes, many often questioned the role of religion in contemporary society.

Second, new advances in medicine and psychology that caused a re-appreciation of the holistic dimension of the human person furthered this examination of the nature of humanity. No longer were human beings seen as being disconnected from each other; instead there was the recognition that all humans were interrelated. Moreover, the parts of the human person were seen as working together in concert. The human person was said to be a composition of physical, mental, psychological, social, and spiritual needs and aspects. When one need or aspect was alienated or diseased, the whole human person suffered.

Third, in terms of Roman Catholicism, the social changes and the recognition of the holistic approach to the human person led to a call for the rejuvenation of the Church's liturgical life, specifically in the area of sacramental theology. More and more theologians were examining the nature and effect of the sacraments.[2] They recognized that the sacrament of Extreme Unction in particular was in need of restructuring. While the theology said one thing (a sacrament for the sick to offer healing and comfort), the practice said another (a final Anointing to prepare one for death and forgive one's sins). In short, the

---

[2] This was especially true in the early twentieth century with the development of the liturgical movement. The reader is invited to consult the work of Bernard Botte, Antoine Chauvasse, the work of theologians at the Vanves Conference, and various articles found in the early editions of the periodical *La Maison-Dieu*. Also, The subsequent footnotes in this chapter provide more detailed publication information.

faithful (and many pastors as well) were receiving mixed signals regarding the use of this sacrament. In the end, more questions than answers were arising out of the theological reflection that was taking place.

In the period following the Council of Trent in 1551, theologians reflected on the ways in which sins could be remitted by the sacrament rather than the ways in which the sacrament could have a healing effect upon the recipient.[3] In this way, theologians viewed Extreme Unction as a true complement to the sacrament of Penance. In other words, in the period following Trent, the rituals focused on three issues concerning the recipient of Extreme Unction. First, the recipient must have once had the use of reason, even for a short time. Second, the recipient must have been capable of sin. In other words, he or she must be capable of being tempted and of resisting temptation. Third, the recipient must be open to receiving the sacrament with devotion and trust in God.

These conditions had great impact for the use of Extreme Unction with those who were mentally ill. First, regarding the use of reason, George Renati notes: "Those, on the other hand, who have never attained even the temporary use of reason, no matter what their age, are ineligible *(incapax)* to receive Extreme Unction. Such are the perpetually insane and infants."[4] Yet, if a person had once had the use of reason and subsequently lost it, he or she was capable of reception. "The actual use of reason at the time of reception is not necessary. It is only necessary to have once had it."[5]

Concerning the second condition, that of capacity for sin, Renati offers this pastoral explanation:

---

[3] See Kryger's dissertation, especially pp. 90–96. (Henry S. Kryger, "The Doctrine of the Effects of Extreme Unction in Its Historical Development" [Dissertation], *The CUA Studies in Sacred Theology* [Second Series], No. 33, Washington, D.C.: The Catholic University of America Press, 1949). As he notes in the concluding paragraph of his study: "Extreme Unction, as all sacraments, works toward the spiritual good of the subject and will produce its effects as they are necessary and advantageous to the soul. Accordingly, its sacramental grace will bring about the health of the soul through the remission of sin and its consequences and through an alleviation and comfort granted it; and *if it is necessary for the welfare of the soul, it will restore health to the body* (p. 96) (italics mine). Also examine Stanislao J. Brzana, *Remains of Sin and Extreme Unction According to Theologians After Trent* (Dissertation), (Romae: Officium Libri Catholici—Catholic Book Agency, 1953), pp. 80–111.

[4] Charles George Renati, "The Recipient of Extreme" Unction (Dissertation), Washington, D.C.: The Catholic University of America Press, 1961, p. 104.

[5] Ibid., p. 105.

The importance of conferring Extreme Unction on the insane is magnified when one remembers the words, "And if he be in sins, they shall be forgiven him." These people are no longer capable of using the sacrament of Penance. Yet, if they went insane in the state of mortal sin and before making an act of perfect contrition, Extreme Unction is the only certain means available to extricate them from sin and its consequences of eternal damnation. For them, the *ex opere operato* effect of this sacrament seems the only hope of salvation.[6]

Again, one sees the close interplay between forgiveness of sin and sickness. Extreme Unction could be given to the mentally ill, not so much to heal them, but to forgive them of any sins they may have committed before going insane. Of course, they would not be culpable for sinful activities committed while they were insane because one needs reason in order to commit sin: By its common understanding, insanity implies a lack of reason; therefore, no sin can be committed.

The third condition of devotional reception caused some problems. Thomas Aquinas had already decreed that one needed personal devotion to receive Extreme Unction. Other theologians had followed his reasoning by declaring that one needed the actual use of reason when one received Extreme Unction.[7] The *Rituale Romanum* of 1614 said that it is fitting and proper that one receive the sacrament with devotion, but this is not necessary for validity. However, the *Rituale* also said that "if in his delirium or insanity the recipient was thought likely to act in a manner disrespectful to the sacrament he should not be anointed unless all such danger was completely obviated."[8] Renati notes that this prohibition has been revoked through its deletion from the *Rituale* after the promulgation of the Code of Canon Law (1917). Yet despite its revocation there are those who still held the position that "those who are raving and delirious cannot be anointed except in lucid intervals, or only in times of the most urgent crisis, if there is no danger of irreverence to the sacrament."[9]

In the early eighteenth century, Clericatus (1633–1717) presented a comprehensive (for its day) and pastorally sensitive treatment

---

[6] Ibid., p. 105.

[7] Including Bonaventure, Scotus, and Gerson. See Renati, p. 106.

[8] Renati, "The Recipient of Extreme Unction," p. 105.

[9] Renati, "The Recipient of Extreme Unction," p. 107.

of the question of Anointing the mentally ill in his work entitled *Decisiones de Sacramentis*. As Pickett notes:

> He distinguished no less than eighteen different types of mental derangement which the priest is liable to encounter in his ministry, and, after presenting the arguments against the anointing of the insane, he concludes very forcefully that they should be anointed if they have ever had the use of reason and have at least virtually shown, while sane, a desire for the Sacraments of the dying. He adds that it would be seldom, indeed, that any insane adult would be found who had certainly never enjoyed any use of reason whatever. Therefore, in practically all cases, the Sacrament could be given, although not, of course, to one who *certainly* never had enjoyed the use of reason.[10]

From the time of Clericatus until the Code of Canon Law (CIC 1917), numerous authors defended the use of the sacrament of Extreme Unction with the mentally ill. In addition, various provincial and local councils urged that the insane be anointed.[11]

The Code of Canon Law (CIC 1917) further delineates the conditions under which a person may receive Extreme Unction: 1917 CIC, 940§1. "Extreme unction can be administered only to one of the faithful who, after attaining the use of reason, is in danger of death through sickness or old age."[12] Some commentators on this canon note that the recipient need not possess the use of reason at the time of administration; however, "probable danger of death, subjectively conceived in the mind of the physician, the minister, or the sick person suffices for the valid administration of the sacrament and thus imposes on the ordinary minister the obligation of conferring it."[13] 1917 CIC, 940§2: "This sacrament cannot be administered a second time during the same illness, but only if the sick person has recovered after he was anointed, and then fell again into the danger of death."[14] Here again

---

[10] Pickett, *Mental Affliction and Church Law*, p. 83.

[11] Pickett cites the work of Benedict XIV, St. Alphonsus, Schmalzgrueber and Lehmkuhl, and the Provincial Councils of Naples (1699), Westminster (1852), Quebec (1854), and Baltimore (1866) as examples of legislative action. See p. 83, nn. 42–46.

[12] C. 940 § 1 "Extrema unctio praeberi non potest nisi fideli, qui post adeptum usum rationis ob infirmitatem vel senium in periculo mortis versetur."

[13] John A. Abbo and Jerome D. Hannan, *The Sacred Canons: A Concise Presentation of the Current Disciplinary Norms of the Church*, Volume II (Canons 870–2414), Revised edition, (St. Louis, MO: B. Herder Book Co. 1957), p. 62.

[14] C. 940 § 2 "In eadem infirmitate hoc sacramentum iterari non potest, nisi infirmus post susceptam unctionem convaluerit et in aliud vitae discrimen inciderit."

the concern of the canons is that danger of death be present before one receives Extreme Unction. Furthermore, 1917 CIC, 941–943 stipulate that "when there is a doubt whether the sick person has attained the use of reason, whether he is truly in danger of death, or whether he is dead, this sacrament is to be conferred conditionally."[15] Moreover, 1917 CIC, 943 states that "this sacrament, however, is to be conferred without any condition on those sick persons who, while they were conscious, desired it or very likely would have desired it at least implicitly, even though thereafter they say have become unconscious or have lost the use of reason."[16] In other words, if the person, previous to his incapacity, had not refused the sacraments, could now in his incapacity receive Extreme Unction with the presumption being that he would want to receive the comfort of the Church. By the promulgation of the 1917 Code, the reversal regarding the effects of the sacrament, begun in the Middle Ages, was complete. Whereas healing had been primary in the letter to James and forgiveness of sins only seen as a conditional secondary effect, now forgiveness of sins in preparation for death is the primary (and for perhaps some theologians, the only) reason for administering the sacrament.

In short, the CIC 1917 focuses on administering Extreme Unction to those who are mentally ill and are dying as opposed to merely suffering from some mental affliction. The commentaries on the Code seem to suggest that mentally ill persons may be anointed at least conditionally (if there is a doubt as to whether they had ever enjoyed the use of reason). Yet the strong connection between sickness and sin is maintained. The implied reason for administering the sacrament of Extreme Unction clearly is focused on its primary effect of forgiving sins in preparation for eternal life, not on the secondary effect of physical healing. Furthermore, "although it may be argued that internal unmanifested contrition cannot be elicited by an insane person because his mind is not rationally engaged at all, nevertheless, there is always the possibility that contrition was elicited in the last *moments* of sanity."[17]

---

[15] Abbo and Hannan, *The Sacred Canons,* p. 63.

[16] Abbo and Hannan, *The Sacred Canons,* p. 64. C. 943 "Infirmis autem qui, cum suae mentis compotes essent, illud saltem implicite petierunt aut verisimiliter petiissent, etiamsi deinde sensus vel usum rationis amiserint, nihilominus absolute praebeatur."

[17] Pickett, *Mental Affliction and Church Law,* p. 137.

It is clear through this brief historical survey that the sacrament of the sick or Extreme Unction has followed a twisted path. Initially, Anointing was given to those who were sick and suffering, the *asthenei* in Greek. While this term usually refers to physical afflictions, secondary definitions suggest that the term could also encompass those who are emotionally or psychologically ill as well. The scriptural evidence suggests that sickness is closely related to sinfulness, and healing is a sign of God's victory over the demonic powers that have caused the illness.

As the Church became more public in its ministry and worship, Sacramentaries and ritual books began to be disseminated throughout the ecclesial world. The extant prayers of Anointing or blessing of the oil of the sick state that the use of the oil was for healing of not only physical ailments, but those of the mind as well. In the ancient world, as well as in the early centuries of the Church's existence, there is a clear emphasis on the psychosomatic unity of the human person.

As Church administration became more codified and structured, and as theologians developed more precision in their investigations and definitions, Church life became increasingly more compartmentalized, especially with regard to the reception of the sacraments. Gradually, the Church moved away from a charismatic expression of the Gospel and God's grace toward a more legalistic one defined by norms and procedures. This is especially seen in the exclusion of certain kinds of individuals from the reception of the sacrament of the sick. Colin Pickett strongly suggests in his analysis that the mentally ill was one of those groups that was denied Anointing. Despite what was written in the ritual books and eventually in the 1917 Code of Canon Law, mentally disordered persons and children were often prevented from receiving the sacrament.

While the legislation had become more lenient with regard to anointing all persons, in practice, the faithful continued to wait until the last moments before calling a priest to come and anoint their loved one. Very often, the presence of a priest offering the comfort of the sacraments at an early stage of a person's illness induced fear and anxiety rather than solace and assurance. In the popular mind, "calling the priest" was a clear sign that "the end was near." Because of a general fear of death on the part of both patient and family members, an attempt was made to forestall the final moment of death as long as possible.

As a result, many individuals were denied the prayerful and sacramental support of the Church while they were still conscious and alert.

Today, because of the advances in medicine, individuals are living longer and healthier lives. Yet, there is still a fear of death. Because of the Church's long history of associating sacramental Anointing with immanent death, some people are afraid to seek out a priest until the last moments of life. There is also a temptation to put too much faith in the medical profession and too little faith in the efforts of spiritual and sacramental healing. There is a rupture between the physical and spiritual components of a person's life. However, with increased knowledge of other cultures and systems of belief, there is a gradual movement toward seeing the human person as a whole comprising physical, mental, emotional, and spiritual components. These aspects must work together in concert in order to create a healthy human being. If one aspect is "diseased" or "wounded," the whole human person is affected.

## OFFICIAL CHURCH TEACHING

As noted in the last section, the Church continued to profess what had been promulgated by the Council of Trent in 1551. With the promulgation of the Code of Canon Law in 1917, the Church more clearly indicated the subject for reception of the sacrament. The 1917 CIC canons 940–944 concern both strict and conditional reception of Extreme Unction; 1917 CIC, 940 notes that "extreme unction can be administered only to one of the faithful who, after attaining the use of reason, is in danger of death through sickness or old age."[18] Furthermore, "this sacrament cannot be administered a second time during the same illness, but only if the sick person has recovered after he was anointed, and then fell again into the danger of death."[19] In short, the subject for Anointing was a person who was in danger of death due to old age or sickness, yet possessed reason. If there was doubt as to whether the person had attained the use of reason, was in danger of death, or whether he was dead, then the sacrament was to be

---

[18] John A. Abbo and Jerome D. Hannan, *The Sacred Canons,* p. 62.
[19] Ibid., p. 63.

administered conditionally.[20] In addition, the sacrament was denied to those who remained "impenitent in manifest mortal sin." However, if there was some doubt in this regard, the sacrament was to be conferred conditionally.[21] Also indicated in 1917 CIC, 943 is that those who were unconscious or had lost the use of reason were to be anointed without condition, provided that they would have at least implicitly desired to receive the sacrament when they were in full possession of their faculties.[22] Finally, while the sacrament is not necessary for salvation, "thoughtful and assiduous care must be taken that the sick may receive it while they are fully in possession of their senses."[23]

In summary, the canons note that the subject for anointing is a person who is in danger of death due to illness or old age. In this sense, the illness must be serious. Furthermore, the presumption for reception is in favor of the sick person. If the subject is unconscious or has lost the use of reason and is presumed to have desired to receive Extreme Unction, he or she is to be anointed, at least conditionally.

Despite the broad parameters given in the canons, Benedict XV, through his apostolic letter *Sodalitatem Nostrae Dominae* in 1921, again reminded priests of their duty to anoint earlier. Those who care for the dying

> should make every effort in order that those who are in their last crisis may not delay the reception of the viaticum and the extreme unction till they are about to lose their consciousness. On the contrary, according to the teaching and the precepts of the Church, they should be strengthened by these sacraments as soon as their condition worsens and one may prudently judge that there is danger of death.[24]

In essence, Pope Benedict highlighted the fact that the sacrament of Extreme Uunction was intended for the living and, more importantly, for those who could participate in the ritual.

In 1923, Pius XI issued his Apostolic Letter *Explorata res* in which he further clarified Benedict's statement:

---

[20] Ibid., p. 63. See also canons 941, 943.

[21] Ibid., p. 63. See also canon 942.

[22] Ibid., p. 64.

[23] Ibid., p. 65. See also canon 944.

[24] Benedict XV Apostolic Letter *Sodalitatem Nostrae Dominae* (1921) in Neuner and Dupuis, n. 1661, p. 642.

For it is not necessary either for the validity or the liceity of the sacrament that death be feared as something proximate; rather, it is enough that there be a prudent or probable judgment of danger. And if in such conditions unction ought to be given, in the same conditions it surely can be given.[25]

As Paul F. Palmer further explicates, "the degree of sickness does not affect the validity of the sacrament of Unction, although a prudent judgment of danger of death, whether proximate or *remote,* is required on the part of the priest to administer the sacrament licitly."[26]

## Theological and Canonical Interpretation

In this section, we will discuss the theological and canonical opinions offered by leading scholars regarding the sacrament of Extreme Unction. As noted in the last section, the criteria for reception of the last Anointing was that the subject be a baptized Catholic in danger of death. Yet, because of significant theological studies, notably the work of Antoine Chavasse, more attention was given to the sacrament's use with those who were sick and not merely dying.

One of the first theses regarding Extreme Unction was written by Adrian Jerome Kilker in 1926 as part of his doctoral work in canon law.[27] While the nature of the dissertation is juridical, Kilker presents an excellent history of the use of the sacrament, citing major theological and canonical opinions of the past. In Chapter V, he explores the requisites for administration of the sacrament and the subject of Anointing. Kilker notes that in canon 840 of the 1917 Code of Canon Law, the subject must possess the following qualifications to be admitted to the sacrament:

1. He must be a *"fidelis."*
2. He must have acquired the use of reason.
3. He must be in danger of death from sickness or old age.

---

[25] AAS 15, 105. Cited in Paul F. Palmer, "The Purpose of Anointing the Sick: A Reappraisal," *Theological Studies* 19 (September 1958): 341.

[26] Palmer, "The Purpose of Anointing the Sick," p. 341. Emphasis added. The concept "remote danger of death" will be further explored in subsequent chapters.

[27] Adrian Jerome Kilker, "Extreme Unction: A Canonical Treatise Containing Also a Consideration of the Dogmatic, Historical and Liturgical Aspects of the Sacrament" (Dissertation), (Washington, D.C.: The Catholic University of America, 1926).

All three must be verified before administration can be validly made.[28]

> Given the tenor of his argument, Kilker's focus is on valid reception and the distinctions between validity and liceity. Hence, he examines cases in which a person may validly and licitly receive the sacrament of extreme unction.[29]

The significance of Kilker's thesis is that he attempted to offer criteria for reception from both theological (using history) and canonical perspectives. He notes that the subject of Extreme Unction must "1) be afflicted with a serious disease which is putting him in danger of death, but 2) not necessarily to such an extent that he is outside the pale of recovery."[30] In short, Kilker states,

> Hence the subject must be sick, and in danger of death from the sickness. Neither without the other is sufficient. Canon 523 shows that the Code recognizes a state of serious sickness that does not place the patient in danger of death. Nor is danger of death without sickness enough. It is absolutely required that the danger come *ex intrinseco*, from the patient himself.[31]

The canonical examination of Kilker revealed a further criterion for reception of Extreme Unction: the danger of death must be intrinsic

---

[28] Kilker, "Extreme Unction," p. 123.

[29] Without pursuing Kilker's canonical argumentation, it is interesting to note some of the legal machinations pursuant to whether one may receive Anointing or not. He explores the following contingencies that may arise: 1. "If the disease is a slight one, even though there is a fear that it will subsequently become dangerous, Extreme Unction cannot be administered. Such a subject has not the depression of soul which the primary effect of the sacrament is ordained to remove. . . . 2. If a man is but lightly affected by a disease itself, but is nevertheless placed thereby in peril of sudden death, he is a valid and licit subject of the sacrament. Though severe bodily pains and depressions are to a great extent absent, nevertheless there are present all the needs for sacramental alleviation. The condition of the patient, not his symptoms, is to be considered. Cases of this kind happen frequently when persons are afflicted with cardiac conditions. It is in this way also, that the unction of old people is justified. 3. If a man is seriously affected by a disease, which is of its nature dangerous, but which has not as yet placed the life of the patient in danger (because in the judgment of a skilled physician it is pursuing its normal course), Kern thinks that the Unction can be validly and licitly bestowed. Vermeersch heartily agrees with him in this belief . . . . 4. If a sick man is gravely afflicted by a disease whose nature and gravity is not yet apparent, he can be validly and licitly anointed, according to Kern. . . . 5. If the disease brings with it a remote yet certain danger of death, the sacrament can be validly given. The subject in such a case is actually in danger of death" (pp. 170–172). Kilker goes on to examine the cases of women in parturition and people before a surgical operation (pp. 173ff.).

[30] Kilker, "Extreme Unction," p. 164.

[31] Kilker, "Extreme Unction," pp. 164–65. In other words, those about to be executed, soldiers entering battle, passengers on a sinking ship, and martyrs would not be candidates for Anointing because the cause of their death is extrinsic to their person (p. 165).

to the person. In other words, the person's own body must be the cause of the illness that is leading toward death.

In a theological conference held at Vanves, France, in April 1948, participants reflected on the liturgy of the sick. The papers and discussions were compiled in an issue of *La Maison-Dieu* published later that year.[32] The topics included visitation of the sick, the sacrament of the sick, Viaticum, and the death of a Christian. Clearly, there was a recognition that the sacrament of Extreme Unction was not merely for those who were dying. Moreover, the Church was mandated in her mission from Christ to visit the sick and be a source of comfort and assistance to them.

As noted in the introductory article of that issue of *La Maison-Dieu*, there are three purposes of pastoral liturgy: community of faith, community of worship, and community of charity. These correspond to three pastoral activities: the proclamation of the Good News, the celebration of worship, and the practice of charity.[33] In visiting the sick, the Church offers the Good News and celebrates God's presence in liturgical rites and actions flowing from the universal call to charity.

While the focus of discussion was the pastoral care and visitation of the sick, some attention was drawn to the need for a broader use of the sacrament with those who were sick. In his article on the Anointing of the Sick, Bernard Botte offered several practical resolutions to his own research. First, he noted that the terminology should be changed from *extreme unction* to *sacrament of the sick* or *unction of the sick*.[34] Second, he notes that there should be a return to the ancient order of Anointing followed by Communion, restoring Viaticum to its proper place as the last sacrament. Third, he proposed that "danger of death" be interpreted in a broader sense in order that those who were sick could indeed hope for a cure. Finally, he noted that "anointing is not a magic remedy which infallibly produces healing. . . ." Nevertheless, it is important to believe in the "efficacy of prayer."[35]

---

[32] *La Maison Dieu 15* (1948).

[33] C. Rauch, "La visite des malades, action liturgique," *La Maison-Dieu* 15 (1948): 11.

[34] Bernard Botte, "L'onction des malades," *La Maison-Dieu* 15 (1948): 105.

[35] Botte, "L'onction des malades," p. 106. "Ce n'est pas que l'onction soit un remède magique qui doit produire infailliblement la guérison. Mais puisque nous croyons à l'efficacité de la prière. . . ."

In the discussion regarding the Anointing of the Sick, the participants reflected on the themes of the corporal effects of Anointing, the time to give the Anointing, the symbolism of Anointing, and whether Anointing may be refused.[36] In his response to the question, When must Anointing be given? Aimé Georges Martimort offered this observation:

> When we administer a sacrament, it is the subject that interests us. But the sacrament is a social act: it is a public witness that the Church gives to itself.[37]

In a sense, because the sacrament is a public act of witness, the Church should make every effort to ensure that it is witnessing to the truth. The sacrament is not an act of magic, but offers both spiritual consolation and sanctification of the body.[38] Furthermore, the sacrament is for the sick, not primarily for the dying. As Lambert Beauduin noted in his article on Viaticum, "the real danger of death, that is the essential and indispensable condition [for Viaticum]. Sickness is not a requisite; . . . on the contrary, Extreme Unction requires the state of illness."[39]

At the end of the Vanves Conference, the following conclusions were reached regarding the sacrament of Extreme Unction and the subject for Anointing:

> 1. Extreme Unction (the texts and prayers of the Ritual as witness) is a remedy not only for the soul, but for the body *(coelestis medicina, non animae solum sed etiam corpori salutaris)*. It is not the sacrament of the last instant of life.
>
> 2. In that which concerns bodily health, it [the sacrament] does not act as a miracle which snatches a cadaver from death, but *per modum medicinae*, when sickness is still capable of being taken care of and healed. That is why it is necessary to wish that one renounce the faulty and relatively recent word Extreme Unction to revisit the traditional expression of Anointing of the Sick.

---

[36] Various participants, "L'onction des malades," *La Maison-Dieu* 15 (1948): 108–16.

[37] Ibid., p. 109. "Quand nous administrons un sacrement, il y a le sujet qui nous intéresse. Mais le sacrement est un fait social: il y a un témoignage public que l'Église se rend à elle-même."

[38] Ibid., p. 110.

[39] Lambert Beauduin, "Le viatique," *La Maison-Dieu* 15 (1948): 118. "Le réel danger de mort, tel est la condition essentielle et indispensable. La maladie n'est donc pas requise. . . . Au contraire, l'Extrême-Onction requiert l'état de maladie."

3. The Anointing of the Sick is not the sacrament of agony, that which closes the sanctifying action of the Church. It is viaticum which is the last comfort of the dying and the pledge of resurrection. That is why it should be hoped that one could, as in the ancient Ritual, administer the Anointing of the Sick prior to giving viaticum.

4. One wishes that the pastors of souls would make of this sacrament a wide usage, conforming to the faith of the directives of the Church and to the sense of the prayers.[40]

As is seen in these conclusions, the concern of theologians and liturgists was that the sacrament of the sick be restored to its ancient usage and interpretation. This restoration included not only a name change, but also more importantly a stress on the usage with those who were sick, not merely dying. In fact, in subsequent years, theologians looked to the use of Viaticum with the dying as more in keeping with the ancient tradition of the Church.[41]

In a little known article entitled "Anthropologie de l'âme et du corps devant la mort," René Le Trocquer offered the following observation:

The soul and the body will be reunited; man, marked by time, triumphing over death. That is the man total and concrete, and not only the human soul, that Christianity defines destiny, the soul confers to his body its perfection and its immortality. . . .[42]

---

[40] Anonymous, "Conclusions de la session d'études de Vanves 1948," *La Maison-Dieu* 15 (1948): 169–70. "1.—L'Extrême-Onction (les textes et les prières du Rituel en témoignent) est un remède non seulement pour l'âme, mais pour le corps (coelestis medicina, non animae solum sed etiam corpori salutaris). Elle n'est pas le sacrement du dernier instant de la vie. 2.—En ce qui concerne la santé corporelle, elle agit non pas comme un miracle qui arrache un cadavre à la mort, mais per modum mdeicinae, quand le malade est encore capable d'être soigné et de guérir. C'est pourquoi il faut souhaiter qu'on renonce au vocable fautif et relativement récent d'Extrême-Onction pour revenir à l'expression traditionnelle d'Onction des Malades. 3.—L'Onction des Malades n'est pas le sacrement de l'agonie, celui qui clôt l'action sanctificatrice de l'Église. C'est le viatique qui est le dernier réconfort du mourant et le gage de la résurrection. C'est pourquoi il serait souhaitable qu'on puisse, comme dans l'ancien Rituel, administrer l'Onction des Malades avant de donner le viatique. 4.—On souhaite que les pasteurs d'âmes fassent de ce sacrement un usage très large, conforme à la fois aux directives de l'Église et au sens des prières." There are four other conclusions that refer to the need for catechesis regarding the sacrament, education about the sacrament in seminaries, the need to conserve and venerate the oil, and the need to address the difficult pastoral problems facing families.

[41] See Aimé Georges Martimort, "Comment meurt un chrétien," *La Maison-Dieu* 44 (1955): 5–28.

[42] René Le Trocquer, "Anthropologie de l'âme et du corps devant la mort," *La Maison-Dieu* 44 (1955): 51–52. "L'âme et le corps seront réunis; l'homme, marquè par le temps, triomphera de la mort. C'est de l'homme total et concret, et non seulement de l'âme humaine, dont le christianisme définit la destinée, l'âme conférant à son corps sa perfection et son immortalité" (Translation by author.).

Because man is a unity which exists from the subsistence of the spiritual soul, communicated in the human composition, it is the whole man which aspires to immortality.[43]

In Le Trocquer's article, one detects a return to the ancient view of the human as a whole entity, not separated into body and soul. Over the next several years, theologians began to view the human person in holistic terms, which has great implications for the use of the sacrament of the sick.

Part of this shift in emphasis was due to the work of historical and liturgical theologians. One of these, the Episcopalian H. B. Porter, examined the medieval rites for the sick and dying. In his historical analysis of the Unction prayers, Porter noted that "as time went on, there was more and more stress on the spiritual and absolutory effect of Unction, and less and less expectation of accomplishing any physical cure."[44] Yet, there was concern for healing the whole person as well as the area that caused the most discomfort:

1. The simplest approach seems to have been to anoint the 'whole man' by anointing the head (or breast) as being the seat of the soul, whence the effects of the unction could radiate out into the entire body. Another approach was to encompass the whole man by anointing the extremities, whence the effects could converge, penetrating the entire body.

2. A more therapeutic conception, as we have noted, was to anoint the place of greatest ailment.[45]

Another theologian who had done a historical analysis of the sacrament of Extreme Unction arrived at the following conclusion: ". . . . unction is a sacrament of the sick, and not principally a sacrament of the dying. Viaticum is the sacrament of the dying and as such is given to all who are faced with death."[46] Who are the sick whom the Church anoints? Paul F. Palmer deduced from his study that canon 940 is not a "doctrinal demand affecting the validity of the sacrament, but a disciplinary measure controlling the liceity of Anointing in the Latin Church."[47] Therefore, he states,

---

[43] Le Trocquer, p. 57. "Parce que l'homme est une unité qui existe de la subsistance de l'âme spirituelle, communiquée au composé humain, c'est l'homme tout entier qui aspire à l'immortalité."

[44] H. B. Porter, "The Origin of the Medieval Rite for Anointing the Sick or Dying," *The Journal of Theological Studies* Volume VII, (1956): 220.

[45] Porter, "The Origin of the Medieval Rite for Anointing the Sick or Dying," p. 221.

[46] Palmer, "The Purpose of Anointing the Sick," p. 344.

[47] Palmer, "The Purpose of Anointing the Sick," p. 341.

It is understandable how the early Church could have anointed those who were apparently in no danger of death; how she could have anointed little children as well as those who were incapable of sinning; how she could have extended the term infirmity to include not only sickness in the restricted meaning of the term, but also that infirmity which results from the loss or serious impairment of such faculties as sight, speech, and hearing; how, finally, she could have anointed those who were mentally sick or possessed by devils. After all, Christ's ministry of healing extended to every category of physical infirmity. And there is enough evidence in the documents which we have seen that the early Church regarded her sacramental ministry of healing as the continuation of the healing ministry of Christ and His apostles.

Again, if danger of death from illness or old age is merely a disciplinary demand of the Latin Church today, it is understandable why the Church has never condemned the Eastern practice of anointing the sick who are in no such danger, and why in her attempts to win back the schismatic churches of the East, the Church has insisted only on serious sickness as a condition for the administration of the sacrament.

Finally, if danger of death is but a disciplinary demand, it may come about that, as the sacrament of unction is regarded more and more as a sacrament of the sick and less a sacrament of the dying and a preparation for eternal life, the Church herself will decide that serious sickness alone shall be the norm in determining whom to anoint.[48]

Paul Palmer was a pioneer in calling for a reform of the then current practice of Anointing the *moribundi* while ignoring the ecclesial roots of a pastoral care of the sick. As will be seen in the next section, some of Palmer's proposals came to fruition with the reforms of the Second Vatican Council.

At the Seventh Irish Liturgical Conference held in April 1960, the theme of "The Church and the Sick" was discussed at some length. The findings of this conference were published in *Studies in Pastoral Liturgy*.[49] In an excellent article, Placid Murray explored the liturgical history of the Anointing of the Sick. He investigated two questions: Is it true that Anointing was given to the sick who were not in danger of death? and, What were the effects attributed to and expected from the Anointing of the Sick?"[50]

---

[48] Palmer, "The Purpose of Anointing the Sick," pp. 341–42.

[49] Vincent Ryan, ed., *Studies in Pastoral Liturgy* Volume Two (Dublin: The Furrow Trust, 1963).

[50] Placid Murray, "The Liturgical History of Extreme Unction," In *Studies in Pastoral Liturgy* Volume Two, Vincent Ryan, ed. 18–38 (Dublin: The Furrow Trust, 1963), p. 36.

Using the research of Antoine Chavasse, Murray showed that prior to 800 AD, the sacrament

> was in fact administered to the sick who were not in danger of death and that of the three effects expected from the Anointing—bodily health, spiritual well-being and forgiveness of sins—the earliest sources seem to place bodily health first in order, sometimes even referring to it alone.[51]

After 800 AD it was "the association with death-bed Penance which brought about that Anointing became reserved to those in danger of death."[52]

Murray, echoing other theologians, tentatively suggests that perhaps the prescription of canon 940 was merely a disciplinary measure which the Church could modify. He bases his conclusion not only on historical analysis but also on the practical, pastoral nature of the work of the theologian whose task it is to maintain "a wise balance between the full doctrine of the Church and the actual reception and understanding of the sacraments by the faithful among whom he is living."[53]

## SUMMARY OF THE PRE–SECOND VATICAN COUNCIL PERIOD

In the official teaching of the Church before the Second Vatican Council, the subject for Anointing was one of the faithful, possessing the use of reason, and is in the danger of death because of sickness or old age. Furthermore, if the priest was in doubt about any of the above factors, he may anoint conditionally. However, repeatedly the Church reminded her pastors to administer the sacrament while the subjects were in possession of their faculties. Benedict reminded priests not to delay in administering the sacrament. Pius XI gave an opportunity for further latitude when he exhorted priests to exercise prudent judgment of the danger of death.

Theologians and canonists of the pre–Second Vatican Council period were concerned with the valid and licit administration of the sacrament of Extreme Unction. They focused on the subject as

---

[51] Ibid., p. 36.
[52] Ibid., p. 37.
[53] Ibid., p. 38.

being one who was sick and in danger of death due to *intrinsic* causes. In other words, the subject was one who was seriously ill because of an illness arising out of his or her own person. Theologians called for a restoration of the ancient practice of administering Penance-Anointing-Viaticum to those who were dying, reestablishing Viaticum as the "last sacrament." Moreover, the name *extreme unction* should be abandoned in favor of the more appropriate name *sacrament of the sick*. In addition, some canonists and theologians called for a broader interpretation of the term *danger of death* and reminded the Church of its commitment to minister to the sick who, through the "efficacy of prayer," may be healed.

Finally, in the pre–Vatican II period there is a shift to looking toward the human being as a whole entity. Healing, like sickness, affects the whole human person. When the Church through her minister anoints someone who is infirm, the whole person is commended to God's care. The sacrament of the sick is the Church's witness not only to the infirm subject and his or her family, it is a witness to the Church itself, testifying to God's healing activity in the world.

In chapter 4 we shall examine how the Fathers of the Second Vatican Council incorporated some theological and canonical reflection in reformulating the theology of the sacrament of the sick.

## QUESTIONS FOR DISCUSSION

1. Compare and contrast ministry to the sick prior to 800 AD and after 800 AD.
2. According to the Code of Canon Law (1917 Code) and the Vanves Conference, who is the proper subject for Anointing?
3. According to the Code of Canon Law (1917), may a person who is not near death be anointed? Why?

# Chapter 4

# Christian Healing: From the Second Vatican Council to the Present

## INTRODUCTION

In this chapter, we will focus on the development of the theology of the new rite of the sacrament of the sick. As in previous sections, the emphasis will be on the recipient of the sacrament. Several authors have written extensively about the proceedings of the Second Vatican Council and their impact on the development of the new rituals.[1] Our intent is not to duplicate those efforts here. Rather, the emphasis will be on the shift in focus from the sacrament as a last Anointing to the sacrament for the seriously ill.

One of the most significant areas of reflection and change during the Second Vatican Council was that of liturgy and the sacraments. While most of the changes and adaptations were accomplished after the Council finished its work, the Council Fathers issued the clarion call for further study and reform of the cultic life of the Church.[2]

In *Sacrosanctum concilium*, the Council Fathers, simply but definitively, encouraged the reform of the rites associated with the sick and the dying:

---

[1] See the work of François Bourassa, Charles W. Gusmer, Carlos G. Alvarez Gutierrez, Aimé Georges Martimort, Jerzy Stefanski, and Herbert Vorgrimler, et al., in the bibliography.

[2] See the work of Jerzy Stefanski, "Das krankensakrament in den arbeiten des II. Vatikansischen konzils," *Notitiae* 23 (1987): 88–127, and Carlos G. Alvarez Gutierrez, "El sentido teologico de la uncion de los enfermos en la teologia contemporanea (1940–1980)" (Dissertation), (Bogota 1982), especially pages 269–314. Section 3 (pp. 300–303) concerns the subject of Anointing.

> "Extreme unction," which is now called "anointing of the sick," is not a sacrament for those only who are at the point of death. Hence, as soon as any one of the faithful begins to be in danger of death from sickness or old age, the appropriate time for him to receive this sacrament has certainly already arrived.[3]

In this passage, the suggestions of many theologians was implemented; that is, to change the name of the sacrament to reflect its primary use with those who are sick rather than those who are in their last moments of life. Furthermore, the Council defined the subject for Anointing as

1. One of the faithful (that is, a baptized Christian),
2. who begins to be in danger of death,
3. due to sickness or old age.[4]

We see a convergence here of the ancient tradition with the Tridentine reform, in addition to recognition for the possibility of further adaptation. The restoration of the sacrament as being for the sick harkens back to the Jacobean text. The reference to being in danger of death recalls the theology of the scholastics canonized at Trent. The use of the verb *begins to be* allows for a broader conception of the seriousness of illness, as well as removing reception of the sacrament from the moment of death to sometime prior.

The Council also called for new rituals to be written:

> In addition to the separate rites for anointing of the sick and for Viaticum, a continuous rite shall be prepared according to which the sick man is anointed after he has made his confession and before he receives Viaticum.[5]

In this paragraph, the Council Fathers urged for a distinction to be made between the sacrament of the sick and the rites of the dying. As we saw in the history of the sacrament, this distinction blurred over time. By the time of the Council of Trent, the rites for the sick and

---

[3] *Sacrosanctum concilium*, 73. Hereafter abbreviated SC. English translation from Walter M. Abbott, Gen. Ed. *The Documents of Vatican II* (New York: Guild Press, 1966). "Extrema Unctio», quae etiam et melius «Unctio infirmorum» vocari potest, non est Sacramentum eorum tantum qui in extremo vitae discrimine versantur. Proinde tempus opportunum eam recipiendi iam certe habetur cum fidelis incipit esse in periculo mortis propter infirmitatem vel senium."

[4] These points will be further explained in the following section on the new ritual of Anointing the Sick.

[5] SC, 74. "Praeter ritus seiunctos Unctionis infirmorum et Viatici, conficiatur Ordo continuus secundum quem Unctio aegroto conferatur post confessionem et ante receptionem Viatici."

the rites for the dying were almost synonymous. Furthermore, the sick only received the sacrament when they were at the point of death. The Second Vatican Council envisioned three possibilities: a rite for the sick person, a rite for a person who was near death, and a rite for the person who was in the process of dying in which death was immanent but not immediate.

Furthermore, the Council called for a revision of the internal rites themselves:

> The number of anointings is to be adapted to the occasion, and the prayers accompanying the rite of anointing are to be revised so as to correspond with the varying conditions of the sick who receive the sacrament.[6]

While it took several years for the changes to be implemented, there was recognition that rites of the Church, while being theological, have an anthropological basis as well. Rites and rituals do not exist in a vacuum. Rather, they have an intrinsic relationship with those for whom they are designed. In other words, the prayers and actions of worship need to speak to the experience of those who engage in them. The faith of the participants must be living, active, and conscious. There is both a vertical and horizontal dimension to one's faith life. On the one hand, God interacts with humanity and humanity responds to God. On the other hand, people must also interact with one another. Worship and the sacraments contain this dual dimension by their very nature. In the Dogmatic Constitution on the Church, *Lumen gentium* (LG), the Council Fathers emphasized this dual movement when they wrote of the sacrament of the sick:

> By the sacred anointing of the sick and the prayer of her priests, the whole Church commends those who are ill to the suffering and glorified Lord, asking that He may lighten their suffering and save them (cf. James 5:14–16). She exhorts them, moreover, to contribute to the welfare of the whole People of God by associating themselves freely with the passion and death of Christ (cf. Romans 8:17, Colossians 1:24; 2 Timothy 2:11–12; 1 Peter 4:13).[7]

---

[6] SC, 75. "Unctionem numerus pro opportunitate accommodetur, et orationes ad ritum Unctionis infirmorum pertinentes ita recognoscantur, ut respondeant variis condicionibus infirmorum, qui Sacramentum suscipiunt."

[7] LG, 11. "Sacra infirmorum unctione atque oratione presbyterorum Ecclesia tota aegrotantes Domino patienti et glorificato commendat, ut eos alleviet et salvet (cfr. Iac. 5, 14–16), immo eos hortatur ut sese Christi passioni et morti libere sociantes (cfr. Romans 8:17; Colossians 1:24; 2 Timothy 2:11–12; 1 Peter 4:13), ad bonum Populi Dei conferant."

Moreover, the sick person is not alone. The whole Church (the People of God and the communion of saints) commends the sick person to God's healing mercy. Yet, the one who is ill is challenged to join his or her suffering to that of Christ; in other words, to make a response to God's invitation to healing. It is also significant in the passage that there is no mention of death in connection with the sacrament of the sick. The emphasis is on the sick person.

In the discussions that followed the promulgation of the Second Vatican Council documents, the Consilium concerned itself with the subject of Anointing. As noted several times previously, the Council saw the subject as one who was "infirmus" not "moriens."[8] Yet, as Gutierrez notes, "the language of 'danger of death' did not correspond to the language of the doctors and ran the danger of returning to Unction as a sacrament of the dying."[9] For this reason, it was necessary to clarify "danger of death" as meaning both proximate and remote.[10]

Pierre Adnès synthesizes the history of the danger of death *(periculum mortis)* clause in the following manner:

- The Council of Trent accepts the rigorous sense of the formula, but nuances its meaning being careful not to make the dying the exclusive recipients of Unction; its first words are about the sick in general.
- The Roman Ritual of Paul V, of 1614, puts without doubt Unction in strict connection with death, but does not insist on its absolute exclusivity; its last words are, to the contrary, because health may be restored to the sick person.
- Vatican II proposed explicitly the formula "danger of death," but does not control the harshness speaking of the beginning of danger as the opportune moment for Unction (SC, 73).
- The new ritual simply suppressed the formula, while conserving the proper idea of the seriousness of sickness (SC, 8). It distinguished between the ordinary rite (SC, 64) and a rite for those who are *in proximo mortis periculo* (SC, 115).[11]

---

[8] Carlos G. Alvarez Guttierrez, "El Sentido Teologico de la Uncion de los Enfermos en La Teologia Contemporanea (1940–1980)," Bogota: Typis Pontificiae Universitatis Xaveriana, 1982, p. 300.

[9] Ibid., p. 301. "el lenguaje de 'peligro de muerte' no concuerda mucho con el lenguaje de los médicos y corre el peligro de volvernos a la Unción como sacramento de moribundos."

[10] Gutierrez, "El Sentido Teologico," p. 301–302.

[11] Pierre Adnès, *L'Unzione degli infermi: Storia e teologia* (Milano: Edizioni San Paolo, 1996), pp. 70–71. "il concilio di Trento accetta il senso rigoroso della formula, ma ne sfuma la portata

While the new ritual avoids the term *danger of death*, the implication is that the illness is of such a serious nature that death could be a possibility, however remote.

In short, the Council Fathers promoted the return to the ancient tradition of the sacrament being for the sick. While not desiring to dismiss the possibility of the dying person receiving the sacrament, the emphasis was placed on the recipient as being one who was seriously ill. Following the ancient tradition, Viaticum was restored to its proper place as the sacrament of the dying.

In his monumental work, *The Reform of the Liturgy: 1948–1975*, Annibale Bugnini analyzed the work that precipitated the changes in the ritual for the sick. Two problems that contributed to the delay of the publication of the new ritual were the issue of repeatability of the sacrament and the subject who could receive Anointing. As Bugnini notes,

> The Constitution on the Liturgy had said that the sacrament is administered to "infirmis periculose aegrotantibus," thus repeating the expression used in the Ritual of Paul V. Authors writing on the subject did not make a sharp distinction between "serious" and "dangerous" illness, but medicine had made it possible to distinguish clearly between the two. Serious illnesses that of their nature can lead to death (for example, leukemia or breast cancer) may be discovered several years before they enter their acute phase. At this early point there is certainly danger of death, but it is not immediate; moreover, there can even be a cure with the right treatment.[12]

In short, because of the advances made in medicine, it was now possible to allow for the repeatability of the sacrament within the same illness when one's condition became more serious.

In terms of the subject for sacramental Anointing, the Congregation for Divine Worship reached a decision which was confirmed by Pope Paul VI on January 14, 1972:

---

preoccupandosi di non fare dei moribondi i destinari esclusivi dell'unzione; le sue prime parole sono per I maliti in generale;-il rituale romano di Paolo V, del 1614, mette senza dubbio l'unzione in stretta connessione con la morte, ma non insist sulla sua assoluta esclusività; le sue ultime parole sono, al contrario, perché la salute sia resa al malato; -il Vaticano II propone esplicitamente la formula del «pericolo di morte», ma ne tempera l'asprezza parlando di un inizio di pericolo come momento opportuno per l'unzione (SC, 73); il nuovo rituale sopprime semplicemente la formula, pur conservando l'idea molto giusta della gravità della malattia (n. 8). Distingue del resto un rito ordinario (n. 64) e un rito per chi è *in proximo mortis periculo* (n. 115).

[12] Annibale Bugnini, *The Reform of the Liturgy 1948–1975*, translated by Matthew J. O'Connell (Collegeville, MN: The Liturgical Press, 1990), p. 686.

The subject of this sacrament is any one of the faithful who is seriously ill *(graviter aegrotat)* because of sickness or old age. The sacrament can be repeated if the sick person gets better after being anointed or if the condition becomes more serious during the same illness.[13]

However, by March 4, 1972, the wording had been corrected by "replacing *graviter aegrotat* with *periculose aegrotat,* in order to avoid all ambiguity and any interpretation that may depart from the tradition."[14] Bugnini notes in the footnote to this section that the Sacred Congregation for the Doctrine of the Faith interprets the tradition as follows: "The expression 'dangerously ill' . . . applies, 'as the words themselves indicate,' to subjects whose illness is beginning to threaten their life (letter of the SCDF, June 23, 1972)."[15]

Ten years after the convocation of the Second Vatican Council, the new order for the sacrament of the sick was promulgated. In the Apostolic Constitution *Sacram Unctionem infirmorum* (SUI), Paul VI established a new sacramental form of Anointing and approved the new Rite of Anointing the Sick. SUI offers a cursory historical survey of the sacrament, giving particular attention to the theology expounded upon at Trent and at the Second Vatican Council. In addition, Paul explains the logic of change:

All these considerations had to be weighted in revising the rite of anointing in order better to adapt to present-day conditions those elements which were subject to change.

We have thought it fit to modify the sacramental form in such a way that, by reflecting the words of James, it may better express the effects of the sacrament.[16]

While Paul VI uses the term *in pericolo mortis* in the Apostolic Constitution (quoting from SC, 73), the praenotanda of the *Ordo*

---

[13] Ibid., p. 687.

[14] Ibid., p. 687.

[15] Ibid., p. 687, footnote 12.

[16] *Pastoral Care of the Sick: Rites of Anointing and Viaticum* (New York: Catholic Book Publishing Co., 1983), p. 16. Hereafter abbreviated as PCS. "Quae omnia prae oculis habenda erant in ritu Sacrae Unctionis ita recognoscendo, ut quae essent mutationibus obnoxia, ad nostrae aetatis condiciones melius accommodearentur. Formulam sacramentalem ita mutare consuimus ut, verbis Iacobi relatis, effectus sacramentales satius expreimerentur." *Ordo Unctionis infirmorum eorumque pastoralis curae. Editio typica.* (Vatican City: Typis Polyglottis Vaticanis, 1972, 1975), p. 9. Hereafter abbreviated as OUI.

*Unctionis infirmorum eorumque pastoralis curae* (OUI) prefers the term *periculose aegrotans.*[17]

This term, *periculose aegrotans,* is the key to determining the recipient of the sacrament of the sick. While the praenotanda notes that all suffering and illness "trouble the human spirit,"[18] "those who are seriously ill need the special help of God's grace in this time of anxiety, lest they be broken in spirit and, under the pressure of temptation, perhaps weakened in their faith."[19] The Church recognizes that all sickness affects not only the body, but also the soul and spirit as well. However, serious illness is particularly insidious in that it can more severely affect one's very relationship with God and the rest of humanity.

The Church made a conscious effort to use the term *serious* rather than *in danger of death* when referring to more severe illnesses. As the footnote to paragraph 8 in the American edition of the *Ordo Unctionis infirmorum* (OUI) notes:

> The word *periculose* has been carefully studied and rendered as "seriously," rather than as "gravely," "dangerously," or "perilously." Such a rendering will serve to avoid restrictions upon the celebration of the sacrament. On the one hand, the sacrament may and should be given to anyone whose health is seriously impaired; on the other hand, it may not be given indiscriminately or to any person whose health is not seriously impaired.[20]

What constitutes "serious impairment"? The second section of paragraph 8 gives a partial answer:

> A prudent or reasonably sure judgment, without scruple, is sufficient for deciding on the seriousness of an illness; if necessary a doctor may be consulted.[21]

In this case, the judgment of whether a person may receive the sacrament is reserved to the minister of Anointing. Yet what constitutes

---

[17] This is a significant shift in terminology: from "in danger of death" to "seriously ill." Compare the text of SC, 73, with that of OUI, 8.

[18] OUI, 1. "quae eorum conscientiam angerent."

[19] OUI, 5. "Homo enim, periculose aegrotans, perculiari Dei gratia indiget, ne, anxietate premente, animi demissione percellatur et, tentationibus subiectus, in sua ipse fide forsitan deficiat."

[20] PCS, p. 22.

[21] OUI, 8. "Ad gravitatem vero aegortantionis diiudicandam quod attinet, satis est ut prudens seu probabile de ea iudicium habeatur, quibusvis remotis anxietatibus et collatis consiliis si casus ferat, cum medico."

"serious illness" may vary from minister to minister. A case in point: Should a 65-year-old person be anointed? Although he or she may be in "perfect health," one priest may say that the person's age warrants reception while another priest may deny reception because the person is not "sick enough." Furthermore, there are many medical conditions that are considered by some to be illnesses, but are not so viewed by others.[22]

The OUI further delineates other recipients of the sacrament of Anointing: those who have a serious illness requiring surgery (OUI, 10), the elderly who have become "notably weakened" (OUI, 11), sick children (OUI, 12),[23] and those who are sick, yet have lost consciousness or the use of reason, may be anointed presuming that they would have requested the sacrament when they were in possession of their faculties (OUI, 14). While the sacrament is not to be administered to those who are already dead, "if the priest is doubtful whether the sick person is dead, he should confer the sacrament using the rite given in no. 269" (OUI, 15). However, those who remain in open and serious sin may not receive the sacrament.

The *editio typica* allows for adaptations to the ritual to be made by both Episcopal conferences (OUI, 38–39) and the minister himself (OUI, 40–41). In the United States edition of the rite, the American Bishops added the following emendation:

> Some types of mental illness are now classified as serious. Those who are judged to have a serious mental illness and who would be strengthened by the sacrament may be anointed (see no. 5). The anointing may be repeated in accordance with the conditions for other kinds of serious illness (see no. 9).[24]

While a seemingly innocuous statement, almost banal in tone, this amendment takes a giant leap forward in categorizing serious

---

[22] For example, alcoholism, drug addiction, sexually transmitted diseases, and mental disorders. These will be considered in greater detail in chapters 6 and 7. Regarding the case of an older person, Charles Gusmer notes the following: ". . . . old age is not so much a sickness, but rather a condition in which deteriorating health through length of years can constitute an intrinsic threat to life" (*And You Visited Me: Sacramental Ministry to the Sick and the Dying*, p. 83). As the Bishops' Committee on the Liturgy clarified, "It is not any apparent imminence of death which would determined anointing, as it is debility (weak condition)." (Gusmer, p. 83 op cit. Bishops' Committee on the Liturgy, *Newsletter* XV (March–April 1979).

[23] The ideal is that the child would have the use of reason; however, in cases of doubt, the child may be anointed.

[24] PCS, 53, p. 39.

illness. Heretofore, one of the implicit criteria for judging the seriousness of an illness was a physical manifestation or impairment. By
acknowledging that a mental disorder could also render a person
incapacitated, the Bishops broadened the concept of illness. On the
one hand, they moved closer to a holistic view of the person, illness,
and health which characterized the ancient Church's view of sickness.
On the other hand, they gave credence to using the sacrament with
a whole other class of sick persons, in effect, making the sacrament
accessible for more extensive use.

As noted above, the new ritual for sacramental Anointing
envisions several different rites of celebration. The norm is that of
Anointing one who is ill. For the person who is dying, the rite of
Viaticum is to be used (OUI, 27). Presumably, this rite would be used
with those who have been suffering for a period of time, during which
they are experiencing a slow and steady decline of health, culminating
in their death. For other cases, the continuous rite is to be used:

> For special cases, when sudden illness or some other cause has unexpectedly
> placed one of the faithful in proximate danger of death, a continuous rite
> is provided by which the sick person may be given the sacraments of
> penance, anointing, and the Eucharist as viaticum in a single celebration.
>
> If death is immanent and there is not enough time to celebrate the
> three sacraments in the manner already described, the sick person should
> be given an opportunity to make a sacramental confession, even if it has
> to be a generic confession. After this the person should be given viaticum,
> since all the faithful are bound to receive this sacrament if they are in
> danger of death. Then, if there is sufficient time, the sick person should
> be anointed.
>
> The sick person who, because of the nature of the illness, cannot receive
> communion should be anointed.[25]

There are several elements to be considered in this instruction.
First, the continuous rite is not the norm. It is to be used in "special

---

[25] OUI, 30. "Quo facilius etiam casibus peculiaribus prospiciatur, quibus aut ex morbo repen-
tino aliisve de causis fidelis in proximo mortis periculo quasi ex improviso constituatur, est in
promptu ritus continuus, quo infirmus sacramentis Paenitentiae, Unctionis et Eucharistiae ad
modum Viatici muniatur. Si vero, instante mortis periculo, tempus non suppetat omnia sacramenta
modo superius descripto ministrandi, primum detur infirmo opportunitas confessionis sacra-
mentalis, etiam pro necessitate generice peragendae, deinde ei praebeatur Viaticum, ad quod
recipiendum quivis fidelis in periculo mortis tenetur. Postea, si tempus adhuc superest, sacra
Unctio conferatur. Si vero ob infirmitatem, sacram Communionem recipere nequit sacra Unctio
illi ministranda est."

cases" when illness suddenly overtakes the person. Examples might include heart attack or stroke, accident, or a flu epidemic. Second, the person is in "proximate" danger of death. The implication is that the person most likely will not recover (although one must never despair of the mercy of God). Third, the continuous rite "telescopes" the more protracted norm of Penance-Anointing-Eucharist into a few minutes due to the proximity of death. The usual practice would be for a member of the faithful who is seriously ill to receive Anointing at the beginning of the illness and to receive sacramental Penance and Eucharist on a regular basis throughout his or her convalescence. With the continuous rite, the Church very clearly restores the ancient order and practice of the rites of Christian dying.

In the continuous rite, sacramental Anointing is not the "purpose" or the "extreme" (here meaning "last"); rather, Viaticum is. The last sacrament of the Christian life should be Viaticum, since the Eucharist is the *culmen et fons* of the Church's life.[26] In cases where there is no time to administer all three sacraments, sacramental Anointing is to be omitted. It is only in cases when the person cannot receive the Eucharist (due to unconsciousness, a medical procedure, or some other impediment which prevents swallowing of the eucharistic species) that sacramental Anointing takes precedence and replaces Viaticum.

## PASTORAL CARE OF THE SICK

The *Ordo Unctionis infirmortum* (OUI) is significant because it reflects a more open attitude toward suffering and illness. In succinct fashion, the praenotanda summarizes the tradition of the Church's concern for those who are ill. Moreover, it has an anthropological focus as it notes that sickness is not only individual and communal; it is an ecclesial concern as well. Everyone (not just the patient and medical personnel) is exhorted to "fight strenuously against all sickness . . . so that we may fulfill our role in human society and in the Church."[27] Furthermore,

---

[26] cf. SC, 10.

[27] OUI, 3. "ut homo contra quamvis infirmitatem strenue pugnet . . . ut in humana societate et in Ecclesia officio suo fungi possit."

The role of the sick in the Church is to be a reminder to others of the essential or higher things. By their witness the sick show that our mortal life must be redeemed through the mystery of Christ's death and resurrection.[28]

More importantly, Christ himself assists in both the fight against illness and in the witness of the sick person. Through the sacrament of the sick, "Christ strengthens the faithful who are afflicted by illness, providing them with the strongest means of support."[29] Through the sacrament, those who are seriously ill receive the comfort of Christ and the Church. Moreover, in Christ's own suffering, death, and Resurrection, the sick person is given the example of a model witness to overcoming evil and illness. In short, those who are ill are invited to more closely conform themselves to Christ in the Paschal Mystery. As Christ became human, in their sufferings ill persons are to become more like Christ.

This exhortation is extended to all those who suffer and are ill, but most especially to those who are in a state of serious sickness. In this particular and graced condition, the Church offers the sacrament of Anointing in order that the Lord, acting through the sacrament, may rise up and save the sick person. All those who are seriously ill, those suffering from a disease, the elderly, those about to undergo surgery, sick children, and even those who suffer from a severe mental disorder, are strongly urged to receive sacramental Anointing.

## POST CONCILIAR DOCUMENTATION: THE TEACHING OF EPISCOPAL CONFERENCES

In the years since the promulgation of the new OUI, Episcopal conferences around the world have issued their own reflections on the themes of sickness and healing. Many of these teachings highlight or further explicate what is contained in the praenotanda. However, there are some notable emendations and adaptations concerning the recipient of the sacrament of the sick. We noted some of the work

---

[28] OUI, 3. "Insuper in Ecclesia infirmorum officium est testimonio suo tum ceteros monere ne rerum essentialium vel supernarum obliviscantur, tum ostendere vitam hominum mortalem per mysterium mortis et resurrectionis Christi redimendam esse."

[29] OUI, 5. "Quare Christus fideles suos infirmitate laborantes Unctionis sacramento munit, tamquam firmissimo quodam praesidio."

of the United States Conference of Catholic Bishops in the preceding section. In the section below, we will examine the work of the Italian and Spanish Episcopal conferences, in addition to that of the American conference.[30]

## The National Conference of Catholic Bishops

The United States Catholic Conference of Bishops (USCCB), along with its Episcopal bodies, the National Conference of Catholic Bishops and the Bishops' Committee on the Liturgy, has issued several documents regarding the sacrament of the sick. Three of these documents have import for the recipient of the sacrament: the *Newsletter* of March–April 1979, the *Study Text 2: Pastoral Care of the Sick and Dying* 1984, and the *Guidelines for Celebration of the Sacraments with Persons with Disabilities* issued in 1995.[31]

In the *Newsletter*, the Bishops revisited the issue of the subject of the Anointing of the Sick.[32] They noted that the new PCS, flowing from Paul VI's Apostolic Constitution, engendered "a reexamination of the very nature of illness and what constitutes 'danger of death' [which] needed to be brought into line with the findings of modern medicine."[33] The Bishops reiterated that while the new rite does not use the phrase *in pericolo mortis*, it does note that the subject of Anointing must be "dangerously ill" *(periculose aegrotant)*.[34]

In the category of "dangerously ill," the Bishops include the following persons: persons about to undergo surgery ("routine" or cosmetic surgery are excluded), old people,[35] sick children (while noting that what applies to adults likewise applies to children, e.g.

---

[30] The work of other major Episcopal conferences, such as the French, British, and German is not included either because the conferences did not produce a text of adaptation or because such documentation was unavailable to the author.

[31] Bishops' Committee on the Liturgy, *Newsletter* Volume XV (March–April 1979), United States Catholic Conference, *Study Text 2: Pastoral Care of the Sick and Dying* (Washington, D.C., 1984), U.S. Bishops, "Guidelines for Celebration of the Sacraments with Persons with Disabilities," *Origins* 25 (June 29, 1995).

[32] The Bishops had discussed this question in a *Newsletter* dated March 1974.

[33] *Newsletter*, p. 154.

[34] The reader is invited to consult the discussion on page 75. In the PCS 1983, the question of terminology was finally settled. In the *Newsletter*, the term *dangerously* is employed; however, by 1983, the Bishops had decided that the term *serious illness* was a better translation of *periculose aegrotant*.

[35] See footnote 22 in this chapter.

weak condition, surgery, etc.), and those who have lost con⸝
or the use of reason, yet would have asked for the sacramen
were in control of their faculties. There is a fifth subject me
emotional or spiritual illness. The Bishops note the following:

> Can someone who is mentally ill or emotionally disturbed be anointed?
> Dangerous illness is not limited to physical malady. For example someone
> with definite suicidal tendencies due to mental illness or unbearable
> emotional pressures may be a candidate for anointing since the sacrament's
> benefits are spiritual.[36]

To those persons already noted in the *praenotanda*, the Bishops
broaden the notion of illness to include those with mental afflictions
as well.

In the revised edition of the *Study Text 2*, the Episcopal
conference examined the issue of serious illness:

> What does it mean to be seriously sick? To be sick means bodily pain,
> psychic depression, isolation from one's profession as well as from normal
> human society, especially as experienced in the family. To be sick means
> impatience, sulkiness, an excessive preoccupation with self. To be sick means
> discouragement or even despair, hardness of heart, spiritual dryness.[37]

While the above description could apply to almost any illness, the
Bishops felt that in a serious illness many, if not all, of the factors are
present. Furthermore, "sickness is more than a medical phenomenon.
Sickness is a crisis situation in the lives of Christians regarding their
salvation and their life with Christ in the community of the Church."[38]
In both theological and anthropological terms, the Bishops recognized
the crucial role that illness plays in the person, in society, and in the
Church.

The Bishops noted that "serious illness" could not be reduced
to a mere medical judgment; rather, the pastoral judgment of
seriousness must also take into account "the spiritual and physical
condition of the person."[39] From an anthropological perspective, the
Bishops were conscious of the unity of the person regarding both

---

[36] Bishops' Committee on the Liturgy, *Newsletter,* p. 155.
[37] United States Catholic Conference, *Study Text 2,* p. 32.
[38] United States Catholic Conference, *Study Text 2,* p. 32.
[39] United States Catholic Conference, *Study Text 2,* p. 33.

sickness and healing. They noted that the sacrament might result in a "clinical cure." However, what is more important is that through reception of the Anointing of the Sick, "the inner body-soul personal constitution of the sick Christian will be healed by the grace of Christ through a special strengthening of the entire person."[40]

In the *Guidelines for Celebration of the Sacraments with Persons with Disabilities,* the Bishops reminded pastors and parishes to make provisions for accessibility of the sacraments to persons who have disabilities of any kind: hearing, sight, and mobility as well as those with developmental and mental disabilities.[41] The *Guidelines* reiterate that "parish sacramental celebrations should be accessible to persons with disabilities and open to their full, active and conscious participation, according to their capacity."[42] In the section on particular sacraments, the Bishops note,

> Since disability does not necessarily indicate an illness, Catholics with disabilities should receive the sacrament of anointing on the same basis and under the same circumstances as any other member of the Christian faithful.[43]

In other words, the Bishops clearly indicate that a disability is not an illness. In medical terms, a disability could be termed a "condition," since it is permanent, yet not life-threatening. While it may diminish the quality of life of a person, it in no way makes them any less human or denies their basic dignity as children of God.

Because a disability is not necessarily an illness, one cannot receive the sacrament of the sick to be relieved of suffering. For example, a blind person could not receive sacramental Anointing for the purpose of healing his or her sight. However, if that person was about to undergo experimental surgery in the hopes of restoring his or her sight, he or she would certainly be a candidate for the sacrament of the sick. Likewise, a mentally disabled person[44] could not receive the sacrament to relieve him or her from the disability, but if suffering from a serious

---

[40] United States Catholic Conference, *Study Text 2,* p. 33.

[41] While the term *disability* is eschewed in some circles as being discriminatory (the preferred term being *challenged* as in *sight-challenged*), the term *disability* will be used throughout this section to remain consistent with the Bishops' document.

[42] U.S. Bishops, *Guidelines,* p. 3.

[43] U.S. Bishops, *Guidelines,* p. 28.

[44] Here we mean someone with Down syndrome or mental retardation.

illness such as pneumonia or cancer, he or she should be given the sacrament.

In these three documents, the Bishops of the United States show a broadening of the concept of serious illness. In the *Newsletter,* mental and psychological illnesses were considered as serious, which warranted Anointing. In the *Study Text 2,* the Bishops noted that serious illness cannot be merely based upon a medical diagnosis— the person's spiritual and physical condition must also be taken into account. Finally, in the *Guidelines,* a disability was not to be viewed as an illness; however, persons with disabilities could and should be anointed if the pastoral need arose.

## Conferenza Episcopale Italiana (CEI)

The Italian Bishops Conference issued the document *Evangelizzazione e sacramenti della penitenza e dell'unzione degli infermi* at the XI General Assembly in 1974. In the document, the Italian Bishops reflected on the need for evangelization regarding the sacraments of Penance and Anointing of the Sick as part of a program of spiritual renewal in Italy.[45] They noted that sickness, as well as war, hunger, dissatisfaction with work, accidents, and natural calamities are the cause of "insecurity and anxiety which permeates among the men of today."[46] The Italian Bishops are conscious of the anthropology of sickness and health when they write:

> Physical sickness, in fact, weighs down the spiritual fragility, appropriate to each Christian, and can carry it, without a special grace of the Lord, to the egotistical closing in on itself, to the rebellion against Providence and to despair.[47]

---

[45] Conferenza Episcopale Italiana, *Evangelizzazione e sacramenti della penitenza e dell'unzione degli infermi* (Torino: Elle Di Ci, 1974, 1990), 2. "Con la scelta pastorale di «Evangelizzazione e sacramenti» la Chiesa in Italia ha inteso dare l'avvio ad un programma di rinnovamento spirituale che, confermando la sua fedeltà alla missione affidatale da Cristo, la pone più concretamente nella situazione socio-culturale di oggi." Hereafter abbreviated as *Evangelizzazione.* The English translations cited in notes 45–49 are paraphrases of the original text, *Evangelizzazione e sacramenti della penitenza e dell'unzione degli infermi,* supplied by the author of this volume.

[46] Conferenza Episcopale Italiana, *Evangelizzazione,* 129. "Il problema è aggravato dalla avversità che, nonostante le conquiste dell'uomo, di continuo funestano la vita del mondo: guerre, fame, disgrazie sul lavoro, incidenti di viaggio, calamità naturali. Di qui l'insicurezza e l'angoscia che permane anche fra gli uomini di oggi."

[47] Conferenza Episcopale Italiana, *Evangelizzazione,* 140. "La malattia fisica, infatti, aggrava la fragilità spirituale, propria di ogni cristiano, e potrebbe portarlo, senza una speciale grazia del Signore, alla chiusura egoistica in se stesso, alla ribellione contro la Provvidenza e alla disperazione."

While the document does not specifically mention the recipients for Anointing, it does so in a general way that echoes both *Sacrosanctum concilium* and the 1917 *Code of Canon Law:*

> The sacrament of Anointing is therefore intended for all the gravely ill in which the state of their health is seriously compromised; its subjects are also the dying, when it is not possible to confer on them the sacrament in a most opportune time.[48]

In general, the document from the Italian Bishops was designed to provide an instruction to parishes regarding the use of the sacraments as tools of evangelization. In the section on the sacrament of the sick, the Bishops emphasized that all persons—all the baptized—play a role in ministering to the sick.[49]

## Comisión Episcopal Española De Liturgia

The Spanish Episcopal commission on the Liturgy, in accord with OUI, 38, offered some reflections on the sacrament of the sick.[50] They noted that a variety of aspects of the human person must be taken into account when ministering to one who is ill. Somatic, psychological, social, and religious aspects interact within the same illness that affect not only how that person will respond to ministry, but also how he or she will progress on the road to recovery.[51]

The sacrament of the sick is a sacrament of recovery in which the sick person is pastorally prepared for his or her reintegration into

---

[48] Conferenza Episcopale Italiana, *Evangelizzazione,* 141. "Il sacramento dell'Unzione è destinato a tutti i malatti gravi in cui stato di salute risulti seriamente compromesso; soggetti di esso sono anche i moribondi, quando non sia stato possibile conferir loro il sacramento in tempo più opportuno."

[49] Conferenza Episcopale Italiana, *Evangelizzazione,* 166. "E lo stesso invito è rivolto a tutti i battezzati, particolarmente ai religiosi e alle religiose, ai familiari dei malati stessi e a coloro che in qualsiasi modo sono addetti alla loro cura."

[50] "Orientaciones doctrinales y pastorales del episcopado español" found in the Spanish *Ritual de la unción y de la pastoral de enfermos,* 5th edition (Barcelona: Comisión Episcopal Española de Liturgia, 1992) pp. 27–43. The "Orientaciones" were written originally in 1974.

[51] Comisión Episcopal Española de Liturgia, «Orientaciones,» p. 54. "Los aspectos somáticos, psicológicos, sociales y religiosos que se entremezclan en un mismo enfermo, dan lugar a situaciones diferenciadas dentro de una misma enfermedad. Entre los aspectos somáticos y psicológicos habrá que tener en cuenta la distinta situación de un anciano, un enfermo a corto o a largo plazo, los enfermos crónicos o los que precisan una intervención quirúrgica. En unos, la esperanza de curación es grande, en otros se ha perdido totalmente; hay quien padece ansiedad, otros soledad. A ello habrá que sumar la formación cultural que, según los casos, será alivio o tortura para el enfermo. Y no faltará quien necesite ayuda material para poder sanar." (English paraphrase of the original document supplied by the author of this volume.)

ordinary life.[52] To this end, the Spanish Bishops note, pastoral care of the sick must also continue "postsacramentally" to assist in the reestablishing of relations with God, with their brothers and sisters, and with the community.[53] In this statement, the Spanish Bishops emphasize the theological and anthropological aspects of serious illness as being an alienation from God, from family and from the community, as well as from self.

On the anthropological level, the Spanish Bishops view sickness and health as encompassing the whole human person: "body and soul, heart and conscience, intelligence and will that wants to be saved and recuperated for life."[54] The Bishops specifically list the elderly, the comatose, those without reason, and the dying as the subjects for Anointing.[55] Yet, they remind us that God is always merciful, and the Church, through her minister, is God's representative of salvation in Christ.[56]

The Spanish Bishops, like their American counterparts, noted that the human person is a psychosomatic unity—that is, the body, soul, spirit, emotions, conscience—and will work together in comprising the human person. If one aspect is afflicted (such as the body with sickness), the other aspects are likewise affected. Therefore, a healing ministry must be attentive to all of the dimensions of a human being. In this sense, the sacrament of Anointing must have effects for the whole person: bodily as well as spiritually, physically as well as mentally, and intellectually as well as sensually.

---

[52] Comisión Episcopal Española de Liturgia, «Orientaciones,» p. 69. "Como sacramento del restablecimiento, la pastoral de la Unción debe preparar al enfermo para su reintegración a la vida ordinaria."

[53] Comisión Episcopal Española de Liturgia, «Orientaciones,» p. 69. "Una pastoral postsacramental le hará descubrir la urgencia de vivir más evangélicamente sus relaciones con Dios y con los hermanos y le vinculará más estrechamente con la comunidad cristiana. . . ."

[54] Comisión Episcopal Española de Liturgia, «Orientaciones,» p. 56. "cuerpo y alma, corazón y conciencia, inteligencia y voluntad, el que se quiere salvar y recuperar para la vida."

[55] Comisión Episcopal Española de Liturgia, «Orientaciones,» p. 70. "los ancianos," "los comatosos y amentes," and "los moribundos"

[56] Comisión Episcopal Española de Liturgia, «Orientaciones,» p. 70. "Dios es siempre misericordioso, y la Iglesia, a la que representa también en este momento el ministro, es portadora de la salvación en Cristo."

## Postconciliar Documentation

In the years following the promulgation of the PCS, the Church produced four texts which are very important to the recipient of the sacrament of the sick: the *Code of Canon Law (1983)*, the *Code of Canon Law for the Eastern Churches (1990)*, the *Book of Blessings (1985)*, and the *Catechism of the Catholic Church (1997)*. In order to demonstrate the broadening concept of sickness (from 1982 to 1997) we will examine and analyze below the references to the recipient of Anointing found in these four documents.

### *Code of Canon Law* (CIC) (1983)

The *Code of Canon Law*[57] was promulgated in 1983 under the authority of Pope John Paul II. It is considered the last document of the Second Vatican Council because it put the norms of the Council into juridical context.[58] The CIC is not intended to contain all of the theological concepts relating to a given topic. Rather, the law sets the parameters that govern a given topic.[59] The CIC is designed to offer guidelines to the Church as to how the norms of the Second Vatican Council are exercised in everyday life situations.

The sacrament of the Anointing of the Sick is found in Book IV, "The Office of Sanctifying in the Church" at title VI (canons 998–1007). The canons governing the recipient of the sacrament are 1004–1007. Canon 1004 lists the criteria for the candidate:

> The anointing of the sick can be administered to a member of the faithful who, after having reached the use of reason, begins to be in danger due to sickness or old age.[60]

---

[57] *Code of Canon Law Latin-English Edition,* Translation under the auspices of the Canon Law Society of America (Washington, D.C.: Canon Law Society of America, 1983). Hereafter abbreviated as CIC.

[58] For a fuller treatment of the process of promulgation see James A. Coriden, Thomas J. Green, and Donald E. Heintschel, eds., *The Code of Canon Law: A Text and Commentary* (New York/Mahwah: Paulist Press, 1985), pp. 4–8.

[59] Usually this means stating what absolutely cannot be done versus suggesting all of the possible options that may be used in a particular case. In other words, the law is restrictive rather than prescriptive.

[60] CIC, 1004. "Unctio infirmorum ministrari potest fideli qui, adepto rationis usu, ob infirmitatem vel senium in periculo incipit versari."

The criteria include membership in the Church, possession of reason, and in "danger" due to sickness or old age.

In cases where there is doubt on the part of the minister regarding the status of the sick person (such as whether the person has attained the use of reason, is dangerously ill, or whether the person is even dead), the minister is to administer the sacrament.[61] Persons who are not in possession of their faculties at the time of the Anointing are to receive the sacrament if they would have "requested it at least implicitly when they were in control of their faculties."[62] However, those "who obstinately persist in manifest serious sin" may not receive the Anointing of the Sick.[63]

The canonical commentaries refer to canons 940–943 of the 1917 CIC in formulating an interpretation of the current code. Commentators also look to other theological commentaries on the revised OUI.[64] Regarding canon 1004 of the 1983 CIC, it is significant to note that the phrase reads ". . . . begins to be in danger, . . ." while in the 1917 CIC the similar canon read ". . . . is in danger of *death.* . . ." One commentary notes that "the change from 'danger of death' of the 1917 Code to 'danger' seems to have been intended to emphasize that this sacrament is not to be exclusively connected with the dying. The danger mentioned is still, however, understood to be danger of death."[65] Another commentator explicates by noting that "the meaning is that there must be some probability, *although slight,* of death."[66] However, in keeping with the intent of the Second Vatican Council and the OUI, the 1983 CIC is deliberately unrestrictive regarding the recipient.

---

[61] CIC, 1005. "In dubio utrum infirmus rationis usum attigerit, an periculose aegrotet vel mortuus sit, hoc sacramentum ministretur."

[62] CIC, 1006. "Infirmis qui, cum suae mentis compotes essent, hoc sacramentum implicite saltem petierint conferatur."

[63] CIC, 1007. "Unctio infirmorum ne conferatur illis, qui in manifesto gravi peccato obstinate perseverent."

[64] See for example A. Marzoa, J. Miras, and R. Rodríguez-Ocaña, eds., *Comentario exegético al código de derecho canónico*, Volume III/1 (Pamplona: Ediciones Universidad de Navarra, S.A., 1996, 1997), pp. 854–92.

[65] Gerald Sheehy, et al., eds., *The Canon Law Letter & Spirit: A Practical Guide to the Code of Canon Law* (London: Geoffrey Chapman, 1995), p. 546.

[66] William H. Woestman, *Sacraments: Initiation, Penance, Anointing of the Sick. Commentary on Canons 840–1007* (Ottawa: Saint Paul University, 1992), p. 316 (emphasis added).

In brief there seems to be no solid canonical reason to restrict the wider availability of anointing, especially if one situates the canons within the broader context of the *Ordo*. One must constantly keep in mind the intent of the post-conciliar revision of the rite of anointing to make its meaning clearer and to extend the anointing within reasonable limits even beyond cases of mortal illness. There is a need for balance between the extremes of wrongfully restricting the sacrament and celebrating it for those who are not seriously ill.[67]

In the area of "use of reason," canonical commentators seem to favor this more lenient approach as well. As John M. Huels notes, "the pastoral intent of the law is to encourage the administration of the sacrament by promoting a rather flexible approach to the "use of reason" requirement.[68] Specifically, in his comment regarding OUI 12, Huels says that,

> in other words, "full" use of reason need not be attained. It suffices that the child, or mentally handicapped person, benefit in some way from the sacrament, even if it be a small measure of spiritual or emotional comfort arising from the prayerful family or caring group which assembles for the celebration of the sacrament with the young child or handicapped person.[69]

In terms of children, because of the promulgation of the new CIC in 1983, there was an emendation made to OUI, 12. In the 1972 text of the OUI, number 12 read: "Sick children *may be* anointed if they have sufficient use of reason to be strengthened by this sacrament." After 1983, the text read: "Sick children *are to be* anointed if they have sufficient use of reason to be strengthened by this sacrament. In a case of doubt whether a child has reached the use of reason, the sacrament *is to be* conferred."[70] Through linguistic nuance,[71] the Church recognized that the primary effect of the sacrament is for healing and strengthening. All those who are seriously ill (including those who might not be fully conscious of what is going on) could benefit from a celebration

---

[67] Thomas J. Green, "The Church's Sanctifying Office: Reflections on Selected Canons in the Revised Code," *The Jurist* 44 (1984): 385.

[68] John M. Huels, " 'Use of Reason' and Reception of Sacraments by the Mentally Handicapped," *The Jurist* 44 (1984): 213.

[69] Huels, " 'Use of Reason,' " p. 213.

[70] International Committee on English in the Liturgy, *Emendations in the Liturgical Books Following Upon the New Code of Canon Law* (Washington, D.C.: ICEL, 1984), p. 20 (emphasis added).

[71] That is, the shift from "may" to "are to be."

of the sacrament and therefore should not be denied reception. In any case, the sacrament should be conferred absolutely and not conditionally, as had been the practice before the 1983 CIC.[72]

In short, the 1983 CIC allows for latitude in administering the sacrament of the sick. Following the course begun at Vatican II and furthered in the new OUI, the CIC permits anyone who is seriously ill to receive sacramental Anointing. Yet two issues remain: the concept of "seriously ill" and the issue of those who "persist in manifestly grave sin."

In the *Nuovo dizionario di diritto canonico*, there is a brief explanation of *"infermo grave"* within the entry relating to the sacrament of the sick. It notes that the Second Vatican Council identified "seriously" with the beginning to be in danger of death due to sickness or old age.[73] However, "seriousness does not signify a forecast of death, also that which may happen; for example for taking no interest toward the sick person. Seriousness is perfectly compatible with the contrary forecast: that of working against sickness and the assistance of the sick person until healing."[74]

Concerning the issue of persistence in manifest grave sin, it is important to note that canon 1007 follows immediately upon canon 1006 which says, "This sacrament is to be conferred upon sick persons who requested it at least implicitly when they were in control of their faculties."[75] If a person were in a state of public (manifest) grave sin and wished to receive Anointing prior to surgery, the normal course of events would be for the person to avail himself or herself of the sacrament of Penance and then receive the Anointing of the Sick. If, however, the person were in a state of unconsciousness, he or she could not repudiate his or her sinfulness (nor ask for forgiveness) and therefore could not be a recipient of sacramental Anointing. A practicing Catholic

---

[72] E. Caparros, M. Thériault, and J. Thorn, eds., *Code of Canon Law Annotated* (Montréal: Wilson & Lafleur Limitée, 1993), p. 631.

[73] Carlos Corral Salvador, Velasio De Paolis and Gianfranco Ghirlanda, *Nuovo dizionario di diritto canonico* (Milano: Edizioni San Paolo, 1993), "Unzione degli infermi," p. 1089. "Il Vaticano II identifica detta «gravità» con l'inizio di pericolo di morte per malattia o vecchiaia (SC, 73)."

[74] Salvador, *Nuovo dizionario di diritto canonico*, p. 1089. "Gravità non significa previsione di morte, anche se questo potrebbe avvenire; per esempio per disinteresse verso l'infermo. La gravità é perfettamente compatibile con la previsione contraria: di lotta contro la malattia e di assistenza all'infermo fino alla guarigione." (Translation by author.)

[75] "Infirmus qui, cum suae mentis compotes essent, hoc sacramentum implicite saltem petierint, conferatur."

Christian may be presumed to have a desire for the sacrament. However, one may not assume the same for who is a non-practicing Catholic and in fact, persists in public actions contrary to the faith. In that person's case, he or she would first have to demonstrate the desire to return to a life of grace before being admitted to the sacraments of the Church.[76]

## The *Code of Canon Law for the Eastern Churches* (1990)

The *Code of Canon Law for the Eastern Churches* or the *Codex Canonum Ecclesiarum Orientalium* (CCEO) was promulgated in 1990 by Pope John Paul II. It is the canon law for the Eastern Churches that are in communion with Rome. The canons regarding the sacrament of the sick are found in Title XVI "Divine worship and especially the sacraments."[77] The CCEO reflects the Eastern attitude of freedom and nonrestriction. The subject for Anointing the Sick is a member of the Christian faithful who is "gravely ill and sincerely contrite."[78] Furthermore, "the Christian faithful freely receive Anointing of the Sick whenever they are gravely ill."[79] Moreover, those who are gravely ill and lack consciousness or the use of reason "are presumed to want this sacrament to be administered to them in danger of death or *even at another time,* according to the judgment of the priest."[80]

It is significant to note that that the criteria for reception are different from those of the Western *Code of Canon Law.* First, the recipient should be "gravely ill and sincerely contrite." In this phrase, the Eastern Church draws a closer connection between illness and sinfulness than does the Western Church. The use of the term *gravely* (as opposed to the use of *seriously*) implies a proximate time of death. On the other hand, canon 738 uses the terminology *freely receive* to indicate that unlike the Western Church, the Eastern Church is less concerned about the subject having achieved the use of reason, being

---

[76] See Sheehy, et al., p. 547, and Marzoa et al., pp. 890–92.

[77] *Code of Canons of the Eastern Churches Latin-English Edition,* Translation prepared under the auspices of the Canon Law Society of America (Washington, D.C.: Canon Law Society of America, 1990), pp. 364–67.

[78] CCEO, 737. "Christifideles morbo gravi affecti cordeque contriti."

[79] CCEO, 738. "Christifideles unctionem infirmorum libenter suscipiant quandocumque graviter aegrotant."

[80] CCEO, 740. "praesumuntur velle sibi hoc sacramentum ministrari in periculo mortis vel etiam ad iudicium sacerdotis alio tempore" (emphasis added).

of a certain age, or being in a state of grace. Third, all the Christian faithful who are gravely ill are presumed to want to receive the sacrament. There are no legal gymnastics denying reception to those who persist in manifest serious sin. Fourth, the "judgment of the priest" is given canonical status whereby he determines if the person is indeed a candidate for reception. In addition, the sacrament may be administered even at a time other than the danger of death (CCEO, 740).

The CCEO is written, favoring a broader interpretation of who the recipient of the sacrament of the sick may be. The priest himself is given more latitude in making this determination by the deliberate ambiguity of the canons. Finally, while making a closer connection between sickness and sinfulness, the Eastern Church seems to view both as aberrations of the human condition, which are in need of healing.

## The *Book of Blessings* (1985)

The *editio typica* of *De Benedictionibus* was promulgated in 1985. The American edition was approved for use in the United States in January 1989 under the title *Book of Blessings*.[81] In chapter two, there is an *Ordo benedictionis infirmorum,* which is a complement to the order for visiting the sick, found in the OUI.[82] There are two sections of prayers— one for adults and the other for children. In addition, there is a shorter rite that omits the responsorial psalm and intercessions. This shorter rite was designed for those occasions in which the sick person could not sustain a longer visit.

The 1989 American edition contains some additional proper blessings, which were approved for use by both the Administrative Committee of the National Conference of Catholic Bishops and the Congregation for Divine Worship.[83] Following the shorter rite, there are two additional sections for specific instances that may occasion a ministerial response. Section II is entitled "Order for the Blessing of a Person Suffering from Addiction or from Substance Abuse." Section III is entitled "Order for the Blessing of a Victim of Crime or Oppression."

---

[81] *De Benedictionibus* (Vatican City: Typis Polyglottis Vaticanis, 1985). Hereafter DB. *Book of Blessings* (New York: Catholic Book Publishing Co., 1989). Hereafter BB.

[82] DB, 290. BB, 376.

[83] BB, p. 5.

Section II is significant because it recognizes, for the first time, the particular needs of a person suffering from an addiction. As number 407 states, "this blessing is intended to strengthen the addicted person in the struggle to overcome addiction and also assist his or her family and friends." It also may be used with those who abuse alcohol or drugs, but are not yet addicted.[84] Furthermore, "ministers should be aware of the spiritual needs of a person suffering from addiction or substance abuse, and to this end the pastoral guidance on the care of the sick and the rites of *Pastoral Care of the Sick* will be helpful."[85] Here the writers of the *Book of Blessings* (BB) recognize that an addiction is classified as an illness and should be treated as such. Perhaps this is also a veiled reference to a possible use of the OUI with those who are addicted. This possibility will be explored in the next two chapters.

Section III is a wonderful addition to the repertoire of blessings and prayers. While the personal experience of crime is often traumatic, this section marks the first time that there is an official text for an ecclesial response. As number 431 notes, "this blessing is intended to assist the victim and help him or her come to a state of tranquility and peace." However, in cases of violent crimes, such as rape, the victim often has been physically assaulted, perhaps to near-death. Is there a possible use of the OUI in these situations as well? Again, this possibility will be explored in chapters 5 and 6.

In short, the BB offers a further nuance to the theme of "serious illness." Addiction to alcohol or drugs is characterized as an illness that requires the assistance of medical professionals. Victims of crimes and oppression who are physically or psychologically wounded may need medical assistance. In such situations the Church can and should be an active participant in assisting the recovery process. While the BB limits that participation to a blessing, there are indications (such as number 409) that perhaps a fuller sacramental celebration may be used.

## The *Catechism of the Catholic Church* (1992, 1997)

The *Catechismus Catholicae Ecclesiae* (CCE; or *Catechism of the Catholic Church*) was originally written in French in 1992. The Latin typical

---

[84] BB, 408.

[85] BB, 409.

edition was finally published in 1997.[86] Since 1992, the *Catechismus* has been translated into a variety of languages. The section concerning the sacrament of the sick is found in article 5 of the second section of the second part of the CCE.

In succinct fashion, the second section of article 5 responds to the question, Who receives and who administers this sacrament?[87] The subheading above number 1514 is "in case of grave illness . . . ."[88] The CCE quotes from SC, 73 and CIC, 1004, 1005, and 1007. The subjects for the Anointing include "anyone of the faithful [who] begins to be in danger of death from sickness or old age."[89] Furthermore, "it is fitting to receive the Anointing of the Sick just prior to a serious operation. The same holds for the elderly whose frailty becomes more pronounced."[90] In a curious omission, the CCE does not mention that children may also be recipients of the sacrament.

In summary, the CCE adds nothing new to our theological understanding of the sacrament of the sick. Rather, it reiterates what has been stated in the Vatican II documents, the OUI, and canon law. In fact, the CCE strictly interprets who the recipient may be and offers little latitude for creativity.

## Summary of the Postconciliar Documents

In this section, we have seen how the tension between a strict interpretation of the tradition and a more open interpretation of sacramental celebration has played itself out in the official texts of the Church. While canon law tends to be more restrictive of who the recipient of Anointing may be, there are opportunities for more broadly interpreting the canons. The American *Book of Blessings* contains an order for blessing those who are addicted or are victims of crime and oppression. It is possible that these two categories of people—the

---

[86] *Catechismus Catholicae Ecclesiae* (Città del Vaticano: Libreria Editrice Vaticana, 1997). Hereafter abbreviated as CCE.

[87] CCE, p. 405. "Quis recipit et quis hoc confert sacramentum?"

[88] "In casu gravis infirmitatis."

[89] CCE, 1514. "fidelis incipit esse in periculo mortis propter infirmitatem vel senium."

[90] CCE, 1515. "Congruum est, infirmorum recipere Unctionem ante chirurgicam cuiusdam momenti sectionem. Idem valet pro personis senescentis aetatis quarum fragilitas fit acutior."

addicted and victims of violent crime—may be candidates for the Anointing of the Sick as well. These possibilities will be explored in the following chapters in greater detail.

## Papal Documents and Discourses

In this section we will focus primarily on what John Paul II has said regarding the sacrament of the sick. Since the promulgation of the new OUI, there have been four successors of Peter: Paul VI, John Paul I, John Paul II, and Benedict XVI. Paul VI, John Paul I, and John Paul II each have made ministry to the sick important parts of their ministries. In particular, John Paul II has written extensively on the role that sick persons play in modern society. As this book went to press, the pontificate of Benedict XVI was in its infancy; however, in keeping with the work of his predecessors, Pope Benedict has also reached out to those who are sick and suffering.

Keep in mind that the focus of this section is on the recipient of the sacrament of the sick. Therefore, while the Popes have written about sickness in general or about sick persons, their focus has not been specifically on the sick person in relation to the use of the sacrament of the sick. Rather, the thrust has been to restate the Church's commitment to ministry to the sick and dying, commending the work of health care professionals and those who are ill to the crucified and risen Lord.

While there is little in the way of papal pronouncements regarding the sacrament of the sick *per se* contained in papal writing, one is able to discern an ever broadening definition of who the sick person is. This is especially true in the writings of John Paul II, in his addresses to the sick, and in his Messages for the World Day of the Sick.

### Paul VI

Paul VI promulgated the new OUI in 1972. In the remaining years of his pontificate, Paul VI did not make many significant pronouncements on the role of the sick person in society. However, two events are noteworthy. In 1975, the Holy Father held a special Jubilee Mass for the Sick during the Holy Year of 1975 during which 50 pilgrims were anointed. In his homily, the Pope noted the following:

Evidently, in this sacrament as in the others, the Church's primary concern is with the soul, the forgiveness of sins and the increase of God's grace. But she also wants, and aims to procure, as far as she can, the relief and, if possible, the cure of the sick person. Basing Ourselves on the Lord's words as transmitted by the Apostles and impelled by their sentiments of Love, We recently authorized a reform of the rite for anointing the sick, so that its complete finality might be made more evident and its administration might be facilitated and extended (within just limits) even to cases where the illness is not mortal.[91]

The Pope continued by saying that human suffering has value because it is transformed by the mystery of Christ, which enables the whole Church to profit.[92] In a particular way, the sick have a direct contact with Christ.

From this contact the Church cannot but derive an immediate spiritual profit in the form of an outpouring of new life, unity and interior growth. This means you are now helping to build up the Church![93]

In a homily delivered on World Leprosy Day, Paul VI noted that throughout the centuries, missionaries have been in solidarity with lepers in whom the missionaries saw the image of the suffering Christ.[94] Furthermore, all humans (and not just Christians) must continue to "fight against leprosy and all the forms of leprosy which are widespread throughout contemporary society—such forms as hunger, discrimination and underdevelopment."[95] In his remarks given after the liturgy, the Pope said, "leprosy is typical of the sufferings which penetrate and consume man's life in various forms." He specifically mentioned war, alcoholism, and drug addiction.[96]

While Paul VI did not specifically mention who the recipients of the sacrament of the sick could be, he did display a particular compassion for those who were on the margins of society. He was clearly

---

[91] Pope Paul VI, "The Value of Christian Suffering, Homily of Pope Paul VI at a Jubilee Mass for the Sick (October 5, 1975)," *The Pope Speaks* 20 (1975): 276 (emphasis added).

[92] Ibid., p. 278.

[93] Ibid., p. 278–79.

[94] Paul VI, "Leprosy in Our Time, Homily of Pope Paul VI during Mass for World Leprosy Day (January 29, 1978)," *The Pope Speaks* 23 (1978): 171.

[95] Ibid., p. 171.

[96] Ibid., p. 168.

interested in broadening the recipient of the sacrament of the sick to those who were not in a state of mortal danger.[97]

## John Paul I

Pope John Paul I reigned for only 33 days in 1978. While he spoke to many pilgrims and visitors to the eternal city, the brevity of his reign prevented him from expounding on any theme in detail.

## John Paul II

When Pope John Paul II died on April 2, 2005, he had been in office for almost twenty seven years. He was by far one of the most prolific Popes in terms of his writing and speaking. He had been one of the most consistent in speaking out about the rights of the sick and the elderly. While an entire volume could be written which shows the Pope's commitment in this area, the focus of this section will be to offer some "highlights" as evidence of a broadening definition of sickness in the latter part of the twentieth century.

In 1984, the Pope wrote *Salvifici Doloris* in which he noted that there is a Christian meaning to human suffering. All human beings exist in a world of suffering that has both a personal and a collective dimension. However, Christ himself entered into this world where

> he healed the sick, consoled the afflicted, fed the hungry, freed people from deafness, from blindness, from leprosy, from the devil and from various physical disabilities, three times he restored the dead to life. He was sensitive to every human suffering, whether of the body or of the soul.[98]

In the same way, the Church must be sensitive to those who suffer and work toward alleviating suffering in the world.

In the Apostolic Exhortation *Reconciliatio et penitentiae*, the Pope noted,

> The anointing of the sick, in the trial of illness and old age and especially at the Christian's final hour, is a sign of definite conversion to the Lord

---

[97] See especially Paul VI, "Value."

[98] Pope John Paul II, *Salvifici Doloris (On the Christian Meaning of Human Suffering)* (Washington, D.C.: Office of Publishing Services, USCCB, 1984), n. 16.

and of total acceptance of suffering and death as penance for sins. And in this is accomplished supreme reconciliation with the Father.[99]

In establishing the Pontifical Commission for the Apostolate of Health-Care Workers, Pope John Paul II wrote,

> In fact, illness and suffering are not experiences which concern only man's physical substance, but man in his entirety and in his somatic-spiritual unity. For that matter, it is known how often the illness which is manifested in the body has its origins and its true cause in the recesses of the human psyche.[100]

Repeatedly, Pope John Paul II stressed that all human beings have inherent dignity stemming from their relationship to God. In his pastoral visit to India, where he visited the patients at Nirmal Hriday (House of Pure Heart), the Pope again spoke of the value of each person:

> The world of a human being is not measured by usefulness or talents, by health or sickness, by age or creed or race. Our human dignity comes from God our Creator, in whose image we are all made. No amount of privation or suffering can ever remove this dignity, for we are always precious in the eyes of God.[101]

One year later, John Paul II addressed the Catholic Health Association in Phoenix, Arizona. In his speech, the Pope noted that "the immediate aim [of health care] is to provide for the well-being of the body and the mind of the human person, especially in sickness and old age."[102] Yet, health care professionals *must not* for the basic dignity be afforded to each person by virtue of their relationship to God. Repeatedly, the Holy Father defended the fundamental rights of every human person. In a telling remark, the Pope specifically mentioned the crisis of AIDS and AIDS-related complex (ARC) as an area of immediate concern.[103]

---

[99] Pope John Paul II, "Reconciliation and Penance," in *The Pope Speaks* 30 (1985): 65.

[100] Pope John Paul II, "Of Suffering Humanity," *The Pope Speaks* 30 (1985): 143.

[101] Pope John Paul II, "The Value of Each Person," *The Pope Speaks* 31 (1986): 132.

[102] Pope John Paul II, "Defending Human Dignity," *The Pope Speaks* 32 (1987): 364.

[103] Pope John Paul II, "Defending Human Dignity," p. 367. In 1990, Pope John Paul II again addressed the AIDS crisis in a speech to the Bishops of Burundi in which he called upon them to be attentive to the "*psychological and spiritual assistance* that the seriously ill or the seropositive person should not lack" [Pope John Paul II, "The Ethics of the AIDS Crisis," *The Pope Speaks* 36 (1991): 66].

In a general audience given in 1992, the Holy Father spoke directly about the sacrament of the sick. He notes that "the Sacrament of Anointing is thus an effective presence of Christ in every instance of serious illness or physical weakness due to advanced age. . . ."[104] Furthermore, he said that "experience also shows that the sacrament gives a spiritual strength which changes the way the sick person feels and gives him relief even in his physical condition.[105]

Yet, the Holy Father had not excluded the mentally ill from being considered in the image and likeness of God. As he noted, "Christ not only took pity on the sick and healed many of them, restoring health to both their bodies and their minds; his compassion also led him to identify with them."[106] In addition, "whoever suffers from mental illness 'always' bears God's image and likeness in himself, as does every human being."[107]

Finally, in the "Message for the Sixth World Day of the Sick," the Pope specifically mentioned those who are marginalized from society:

> Dioceses, parishes and all communities in the Church should devote themselves to presenting the subjects of health and illness in the light of the Gospel; encourage the advancement and defense of life and the dignity of the human person, from conception until natural death, and make the preferential option for the poor and the marginalized concrete and visible—as regards the latter, the victims of new social maladies, the disabled, the chronically ill, the dying and those who are forced by political and social disorder to leave their land and live in precarious or even inhuman conditions should be surrounded with loving attention.[108]

## SUMMARY OF PAPAL DOCUMENTS AND DISCOURSES

Through this brief examination of papal writing and discourse since 1972, we see that the definition of *sickness* has become broader. Pope

---

[104] Pope John Paul II, "Anointing of the Sick," *The Pope Speaks* 37 (1992): 366.

[105] Pope John Paul II, "Anointing," p. 366.

[106] Pope John Paul II, "The Image of God in People with Mental Illnesses," *Origins* 26 (January 16, 1997), n. 7.

[107] Pope John Paul II, "Image," n. 8.

[108] Pope John Paul II, "Christ Came to Share our Afflictions," *L'Osservatore Romano* (Weekly Edition in English), 29 (16 July 1997): n. 8.

Paul VI noted that the sacrament of the sick might be used when the illness is not mortal. He even viewed alcoholism and drug addiction as a kind of leprosy of the modern day. Pope John Paul II linked the ministry of the Church to Christ's own ministry among the sick and dying. He pointed out that in Christ's ministry he was concerned for the whole person: body, soul, and spirit. Therefore, the whole person, taken as a psychosomatic unity, is to be accorded dignity and pastoral care. In the late 1980s, the Holy Father promoted the need for pastoral ministry to those who are suffering with AIDS and AIDS-related complexes. He further noted that the sacrament of the sick gives spiritual strength and can sometimes offer physical relief to the sick person. In recent years, Pope John Paul II has reminded the Church that even those who have mental illnesses have rights and should be given dignity as well as spiritual care.

We have explored the shift that took place in the twentieth century regarding sickness and the recipient of the sacrament of Anointing. Because of changing cultural and social milieux, the Church, through the work of theologians and canonists, began to examine the need for a broader use of the sacrament of the sick.

In the theological realm, there was greater attention given to using the sacrament with those who were seriously ill rather than only with those who were in the process of dying. This shift was seen linguistically in the name change from *extreme unction* to the *sacrament of the sick*. The theological emphasis of the sacrament, while still concerned with the preparation of the sick person for eternal glory, admitted of the possibility of a physical healing. Moreover, the sick person was more strongly encouraged to join his or her sufferings to the Passion and death of Christ. The sick person was seen as a witness to the Church of the spiritual consolation offered through Anointing.

In the new *Ordo Unctionis infirmorum*, the emphasis was on the need to fight against sickness while joining one's sufferings to those of Christ on the cross. While serious illness was still a criterion for reception of the sacrament, various Episcopal Conferences recognized the need for broadening the understanding of the term *serious*. Mental disorders, the illnesses of children, and advanced age were included in the criteria. In addition, an important distinction was made between persons with illness and persons with disabilities.

In the documentation written after the OUI, the term *illness* seems to be more broadly interpreted, and ministers of Anointing are given more latitude as to whom they may anoint. In the American *Book of Blessings* there is a prayer for those who suffer from addictions to drugs or alcohol, which are classified as illnesses. In papal discourses of the past thirty years, there has been an ever-increasing push to include more types of diseases and maladies under the umbrella of illness. Moreover, in the pontificate of John Paul II, the emphasis had been on the dignity of all persons, but the Pope had paid particular attention to the dignity of those who are marginalized in society, especially the ill.

## QUESTIONS FOR DISCUSSION

1. What is the "last sacrament?" Why?
2. What are the principal aspects of the sacrament of the sick (matter, form, minister, subject, and effects), according to *Pastoral Care of the Sick?*
3. Who are the ministers to the sick? How do they function?
4. Who are the subjects for Anointing, according to papal teaching?

# Chapter 5

# Other Christian Traditions of Healing

## INTRODUCTION

In this chapter we will examine four other Christian traditions of Anointing,[1] so that we might develop some comparative insights into the sacrament of the Anointing of the Sick: the Eastern Orthodox, the Anglican Communion, the Episcopalian Communion, and the Lutheran Communion.[2] Since our subject is the Western Latin Roman Catholic tradition, a history of each of these communions will not be done in this book.[3] Rather, the discussion will center on what is

---

[1] Project Ten, an international program of the Lutheran General Medical Center in Park Ridge, Illinois, produced a series entitled *Health/Medicine and the Faith Traditions,* edited by Martin E. Marty and Kenneth L. Vaux. The books were published by the Crossroad Publishing Company of New York. The reader is invited to consult the following books for a fuller treatment of the variety of ecumenical perspectives on medicine and healing: David H. Smith, *Health and Medicine in the Anglican Tradition: Conscience, Community, and Compromise* (1986); Richard A. McCormick, *Health and Medicine in the Catholic Tradition: Tradition in Transition* (1987); Robert Peel, *Health and Medicine in the Christian Science Tradition: Principle, Practice, and Challenge* (1988); Fazlur Rahman, *Health and Medicine in the Islamic Tradition: Change and Identity* (1989); David M. Feldman, *Health and Medicine in the Jewish Tradition: L'Hayyim—To Life* (1986); Martin E. Marty, *Health and Medicine in the Lutheran Tradition: Being Well* (1986); E. Brooks Holifield, *Health and Medicine in the Methodist Tradition: Journey Toward Wholeness* (1986); and Kenneth L. Vaux, *Health and Medicine in the Reformed Tradition: Promise, Providence, and Care* (1984).

[2] Almost all the Christian denominations have some form of ministry to the sick. However, only the Roman Catholic, Eastern Orthodox, and Anglican Communion continue the practice of the laying on of hands and the Anointing with oil. Other communions may participate in this practice, but it varies from congregation to congregation and is not considered a "sacrament" in the fullest sense of the term.

[3] For a fuller treatment of the historical development of the sacrament of the sick in these traditions, the reader is invited to consult the following articles: Elie Mélia, "The Sacrament of the Anointing of the Sick: Its Historical Development and Current Practice," in Matthew J. O'Connell, translator, *Temple of the Holy Spirit: Sickness and Death of the Christian in the Liturgy* (New York: Pueblo Publishing Company, 1978); Charles W. Gusmer, "Liturgical Traditions of Christian Illness: Rites of the Sick," *Worship* 46 (November 1972); Gusmer, "Anointing of the

currently being done in those traditions in order to better understand our Roman Catholic practice. In addition, we will examine current trends in other ecclesial communions. Specifically, our interest is the subject of Anointing. What criteria do these four communities use for determining who will receive the Anointing of the Sick? Is the Anointing reserved only to certain individuals? Having answered these questions, the information will be assessed as to its relevance for the Roman Church today.

When we compare these other Christian traditions with the Roman Catholic tradition, we will see that some are more inclusive concerning the recipient of Anointing, while some have a different grasp of the connection of sickness and sin, and that still others join the healing to a full recovery for the recipient and a reintroduction to "normal" life.

## Eastern Orthodox

By the term *Eastern Orthodox*, we mean those churches of the Eastern tradition that are not in communion with Rome. These churches may trace their separation from Rome to 1054. In common parlance, the Eastern Orthodox are usually called the Russian Orthodox or Greek Orthodox. However, because these communities trace their liturgical and spiritual life to the apostles in an unbroken line of succession, they are considered "churches" and not "ecclesial communions." Moreover, their sacraments are considered both valid and licit by the Roman Catholic Church.[4] Indeed, the Second Vatican Council sees the relationship between the Eastern Churches and the Roman Church as being like that between sisters.[5]

Charles W. Gusmer notes that the rite for the Anointing of the Sick is contained in the *Euchologion*, "and is intended to be performed in public, and if possible, by seven priests with choir and congregation."[6] The earliest mention of a sacramental Anointing in

---

Sick in the Church of England," *Worship* 45 (May 1971); Gusmer, *The Ministry of Healing in the Church of England: An Ecumenical-Liturgical Study*, (London: Alcuin Club, 1974).

[4] *Unitatis Redintegratio*, 15 (hereafter UR).

[5] UR, 14.

[6] Charles W. Gusmer, "Ecumenical Perspective," *National Bulletin on Liturgy* 10 (January–February 1977), p. 30.

the Eastern tradition occurs in the *Euchologion of Serapion*.[7] The blessing over the oil "emphasizes healing of body and mind, especially spiritual healing and the forgiveness of sins."[8]

In her essay on the use of oil in the Byzantine tradition of Orthodoxy, Christine Hall notes that the present form of the Anointing of the Sick became fixed in the fifteenth century under the title the Holy Maslu, deriving from the Slavonic word for olive oil.[9] Hall notes that in Orthodoxy, the Anointing of the Sick and confession are regarded as extensions of baptismal grace. Moreover, whether the Holy Maslu is celebrated for an individual or in a communal setting, a confession is always made beforehand.[10] "The Holy Maslu normally takes place in the church, in the assembly of the faithful, but, when it is necessary for it to take place in the sick person's home, it is customary for the faithful close to the sick person to assemble there."[11]

In his useful essay on the Eastern tradition, Elie Mélia notes that in James 5 the effect of the Anointing of the Sick is both healing and repentance. It is a single action that has a twofold aim: *"prayer for the healing of the sick person and the effective remission of sins."*[12] He further illustrates that "the concern for healing makes life the focus of the euchelaion, but the life that is the dominant concern here is life in Christ and according to the Holy Spirit."[13] It is in this vein that the euchelaion is celebrated not just for the sick, but with the healthy as well. Indeed, everyone who is present at the service (including the clergy) used to be anointed. However, as Mélia notes, Orthodox bishops are trying to limit this practice.[14]

In the Orthodox Church, the solemn consecration of the oil during Holy Week is accompanied by a general Anointing of all

---

[7] See chapter 2 in this book for the text of this prayer.

[8] Gusmer, "Ecumenical Perspective," p. 30.

[9] Christine Hall, "The Use of the Holy Oils in the Orthodox Churches of the Byzantine Tradition," In Martin Dudley and Geoffrey Rowell, eds., *The Oil of Gladness: Anointing in the Christian Tradition* (London: SPCK, 1993), p. 105.

[10] Hall, "The Use of the Holy Oils in the Orthodox Churches of the Byzantine Tradition," p. 106.

[11] Hall, "The Use of the Holy Oils in the Orthodox Churches of the Byzantine Tradition," p. 106.

[12] Elie Mélia, "The Sacrament of the Anointing of the Sick: Its Historical Development and Current Practice," in Matthew J. O'Connell, translator, *Temple of the Holy Spirit: Sickness and Death of the Christian in the Liturgy* (New York: Pueblo Publishing Company, 1983), p. 157.

[13] Ibid., p. 158.

[14] Ibid., p. 158.

those present. Thus, while some sick people are brought to this service, they are in the minority. Mélia posits that the focus of this celebration highlights the penitential scope of the Anointing. Moreover,

> One kind of catechesis, however, proposes the idea of a prevention of illnesses; behind this lies the notion of a universal subjection to sickness, in the sense that we are all sick without realizing it or at least are all on the brink of falling ill.[15]

John Meyendorff explains the meaning of the Anointing of the Sick in this manner:

> Healing is requested only in a framework of repentance and spiritual salvation, and not as an end in itself. Whatever the outcome of the disease, the anointing symbolized divine pardon and liberation from the vicious cycle of sin, suffering, and death, in which fallen humanity is held captive. Compassionate to human suffering, assembled together to pray for its suffering member, the Church through its presbyters asks for relief, forgiveness, and eternal freedom. This is the meaning of holy unction.[16]

In an earlier work, Alexander Schmemann cautioned against two extreme positions regarding the sacrament of the sick. On the one hand, it cannot be seen only as a sacrament of *death*, in which the "last rites" prepare one for safe passage into eternity. On the other hand, one cannot consider the sacrament to be one of *health* or a as "complement" to secular medicine. Both views are wrong says Schmemann, "because both miss precisely the sacramental nature of this act."[17]

He notes that a sacrament is a passage or transformation of the old into the new in which God manifests "the ultimate Truth about the world and life, man and nature, the Truth which is Christ."[18] As such, the Anointing of the Sick is a sacrament because its purpose or end is not *health*, "but the *entrance* of man into the life of the kingdom, into the "joy and peace" of the Holy Spirit."[19] Finally, the defeat of a human person caused by suffering, disease, and ultimately

---

[15] Ibid., p. 159.

[16] John Meyendorff, *Byzantine Theology: Historical Trends & Doctrinal Themes* (New York: Fordham University Press, 1974, 1979), p. 199.

[17] Alexander Schmemann, *Sacraments and Orthodoxy* (New York: Herder and Herder, 1965), p. 127.

[18] Ibid., p. 128.

[19] Ibid., p. 128 (emphasis in the original).

death has been made victorious by Christ. In this sense, "the defeat *itself* becomes victory, a way, an entrance into the Kingdom, and this is the only true *healing*."[20]

In short, the *euchelaion* service clearly shows the interdependence of the physical and the spiritual aspects involved in sickness. Moreover, the relationship between sin and sickness is expressed in a clearer fashion without making a causal connection. Furthermore, the service invites all those present to reflect upon the need for not only physical and mental healing, but even more for spiritual healing, especially in the area of the remission of sins.[21] The criterion for receiving the Anointing is illness, but it is not restricted to only the seriously ill or the dying. In fact, in some cases, perfectly healthy individuals may receive the sacrament for spiritual strengthening and as a general confession and forgiveness of sins. Finally, while the healing service requests healing and strengthening from God, ultimately true healing and wholeness become reality only when one enters into God's kingdom.

## THE ANGLICAN COMMUNION

Unction in the Anglican Communion has had a long and controversial history.[22] Charles Gusmer notes that "today, under the auspices of an active healing ministry, Anointing of the Sick, together with the laying on of hands, is practiced in most of the member churches of the Anglican Communion."[23] However, Unction of the Sick has not found universal acceptance throughout the Church of England.[24]

The Anointing of the Sick must be seen in the context of a healing ministry that is addressed to the whole person. As has been noted throughout this work, sickness (and healing) encompasses the whole individual. The entire person—body, soul, mind, and spirit—is

---

[20] Ibid., p. 128 (emphasis in the original).

[21] Charles W. Gusmer, "Liturgical Traditions of Christian Illness: Rites of the Sick," *Worship* 46 (November 1972), p. 536.

[22] See Charles W. Gusmer, "Anointing of the Sick in the Church of England," *Worship* 45 (May 1971) and Gusmer, *The Ministry of Healing in the Church of England: An Ecumenical-Liturgical Study* (London: Alcuin Club, 1974).

[23] Charles W. Gusmer, "Liturgical Traditions of Christian Illness: Rites of the Sick," *Worship* 46 (November 1972), p. 536.

[24] Gusmer, "Anointing of the Sick in the Church of England," p. 268.

affected by sickness. Therefore, ministry to the sick should be directed
toward the restoration of wholeness. As Gusmer notes in his history
of the Anglican use of Unction,

> It should be made clear that the pastoral concern of the ministry of
> healing is broader than that of anointing of the sick. Holy unction,
> together with the laying on of hands, is the sacramental expression of an
> overall ministry to the sick which also comprises charismatic and psycho-
> logical approaches. Equally important within the context of the ministry
> of healing is the ministry of prayer and intercession for the sick.[25]

In the reformed rites of the Anglican Communion, a distinction is made between the Anointing and the laying on of hands.
The ordinary minister of Anointing is an ordained priest or bishop
while a layperson endowed with the charismatic gift of healing may
lay on hands.[26] "Unction is also usually considered a more potent
ministration, to be used more sparingly than the laying on of hands."[27]
Furthermore, the recipient of Anointing is restricted "to a baptized
member of the church, *understanding and using the sacramental life.*"[28]
It is interesting to note that the recipient should not be a casual
churchgoer. Nor is the Anointing considered a last-minute preparation
before one enters eternal life. Rather, in the administration of the
Anointing, the Holy Spirit is invoked for protection from the evils
that oppress the sick person and for restoration to wholeness of health.
As Gusmer notes,

> The recipient of unction is a sick person, even a child, who may be either
> physically or mentally ill. The danger of death need not at all be present,
> and the anointing may be repeated. This use of unction is thus a return
> to the primitive meaning of the sacrament as a rite of healing for sick
> Christians. The practice of sacramental healing in the Church of England
> is also marked by a genuine personal concern in the preparation, sacra-
> mental administration and subsequent pastoral care of the sick; a flexibility
> and variety manifested in the choice and manner of ministration; and the

---

[25] Gusmer, "Anointing of the Sick," p. 269.

[26] The American Episcopal Church permits, in cases of necessity, that "a deacon or a lay
person, using oil blessed by a bishop or priest, may perform the anointing." Charles W. Gusmer,
"Liturgical Traditions of Christian Illness," *Worship* 46 (November 1972), p. 536.

[27] Gusmer, "Anointing of the Sick," p. 270.

[28] Gusmer, "Anointing of the Sick," p. 270 (emphasis added).

involvement of the local church supporting the sick person by its faith and prayers of intercession.[29]

In short, the Anglican tradition views Unction has having the possibility of three results: "immediate or gradual recovery of health, a happy and peaceful death, or a non-physical healing by which the patient is invited to share more deeply in the sufferings of the cross of Christ."[30] In terms of the recipient of the sacramental expression of healing, the laying on of hands is more frequent while the Unction of the sick is reserved for one who is seriously ill, but not necessarily dying. As Gusmer points out in his classic study,

> The illness need not be solely physical, but may also have a mental or moral origin. Charles Harris advocates the use of unction for the treatment of insanity and neurosis, and even in sexual cases such as sterility, impotence and frigidity. Henry Cooper of the Guild of St. Raphael, however, wisely cautions that the sacrament should not be cheapened by indiscriminate administration and should be restricted to crisis situations in a patient's deteriorating condition or to a single application during a serious illness.[31]

## THE EPISCOPALIAN COMMUNION

The Anglican Communion has undergone a significant development in the restoration of the use of Unction as part of its sacramental system. Moreover, this rejuvenation of an ancient rite of the Church is spreading to other ecclesial communions.[32] The Episcopalian Communion has established "A Public Service of Healing," which is included in their *Book of Occasional Services*.[33] In place of a time for confession and forgiveness of sins, it contains a litany of healing that illustrates the communal nature of sickness and healing. It begins with an *audible* naming of those for whom the prayers are made.

---

[29] Gusmer, "Anointing of the Sick," p. 271.

[30] Gusmer, *The Ministry of Healing*, p. 122.

[31] Gusmer, *The Ministry of Healing*, p. 123.

[32] Gusmer, "Liturgical Traditions of Christian Illness," p. 535. This is especially true of the Lutheran and Reformed Churches.

[33] *Book of Occasional Services* (New York: The Church Hymnal Corp., 1979), p. 148f. Cited in Robert L. Browning and Roy A. Reed, *The Sacraments in Religious Education and Liturgy: An Ecumenical Model* (Birmingham, AL: Religious Education Press, 1985), pp. 283–84.

The prayer also includes a reference to the variety of persons who may be suffering:

> Grant to all who seek your guidance, and to all who are lonely, anxious, or despondent, a knowledge of your will and an awareness of your presence; *Hear us, O Lord of life.*
>     Mend broken relationships, and restore those in emotional distress to soundness of mind and serenity of spirit; Hear us, O Lord of life.

The prayer continues by mentioning those who care for the sick:

> Bless physicians, nurses, and all others who minister to the suffering, granting them wisdom and skill, sympathy and patience; *Hear us, O Lord of life.*

In an acknowledgment that sickness is related to sin, there is this petition:

> Restore to wholeness whatever is broken by human sin, in our lives, in our nation and in the world; *Hear us, O Lord of life.*

The prayer concludes with this simple, but very direct petition:

> Heal us, and make us whole.

At the conclusion of the service, those who wish may come forward to receive the laying on of hands and the Anointing of the Sick.
    It is interesting to note the variety of illnesses that are mentioned; not only physical illness, but chronic conditions, broken relationships, anxiety, and emotional distress. Both the communal dimensions of illness as well as the individual aspects of human suffering are mentioned as being in need of healing or prayer. Because this is a communal service, the language used is in the first or third person plural. Moreover, no one is considered exempt from illness or from God's healing touch. All persons are in need of being made whole again.

## THE LUTHERAN COMMUNION

In the United States, rituals for the laying on of hands and the Anointing of the Sick were included in the *Occasional Services,* a companion ritual to the *Lutheran Book of Worship.* In the public service, the minister applies the oil in the form of a cross on the sick person's forehead while saying:

O God, the giver of health and salvation: As the apostles of our Lord Jesus Christ, at his command, anointed many that were sick and healed them, send now your Holy Spirit, that _____name,_____ anointed with this oil, may

in repentance and faith be made whole; through the same Jesus Christ our Lord. (Amen)[34]

In the private service, used in the home or hospital environment, the minister says,

_____Name,_____ I anoint you with oil in the name of the Father, and of the Son, and of the Holy Spirit. (Amen.)[35]

The Lutheran Communion is still in the process of restoring the rites for the sick. Through reflection on their history as well as dialogue with other Churches and communions that have restored or rejuvenated Unction in their own sacramental ministries, the Lutheran Communion may gradually develop a fuller theology of sacramental ministry to the sick.[36]

## THE WORLD COUNCIL OF CHURCHES

In 1990, the Christian Medical Commission (CMC) of the World Council of Churches (WCC) issued a document entitled *Healing and Wholeness: The Churches' Role in Health.*[37] In commissioning the study of which this document is the result, the CMC had four objectives, to learn about

* new thinking on the Churches' involvement in healing, of both a theological and a practical nature;
* healing practices and attitudes within traditional societies in developing countries;
* ways by which local communities care for and support their sick and suffering members; and

---

[34] Charles W. Gusmer, *And You Visited Me: Sacramental Ministry to the Sick and Dying* (New York: Pueblo Publishing Company, 1984), pp. 39–40.

[35] Gusmer, *And You Visited Me*, p. 40.

[36] The reader is invited to consult Martin E. Marty, *Health and Medicine in the Lutheran Tradition: Being Well* (New York: Crossroad, 1986), pp. 82–97.

[37] The Christian Medical Commission, *Healing and Wholeness: The Churches' Role in Health* (Geneva: World Council of Churches, 1990). Hereafter abbreviated as CMC with the appropriate page number.

- theological reflection on the Christian understanding of health, healing, and wholeness; life, death, and suffering; and human values.[38]

As the document notes, health is a justice issue, a peace issue, an issue of integrity of creation, and a spiritual issue.[39] It is imperative that the Church works to empower communities to eliminate sickness and disease. Furthermore, human rights violations, war and increased militarism "have made wellness of mind, body and spirit—wholeness—an impossibility."[40] The Church needs to preserve the integrity of creation by having concern not only for the human body but also for eliminating those forces that threaten to destroy creation. Finally, the spiritual dimension of life, which is one of the components of health, is a quest for wholeness and salvation.

The role of the Church, according to the CMC document, is to be a "community-builder" in the world:

> A healing community is not a world without problems and suffering, but rather a striving together to live in God's kingdom. Jesus joined the marginalized, the downtrodden and the imperfect. Through his willingness to identify, suffer and empty himself, he gave hope, restored dignity and created community. He led the marginalized back to their own communities, and enabled them to restore their relationships.[41]

The Church as a Christian community is called to be a sign of hope and an expression of God's kingdom in the entire world. As "wounded-healers," the Church must serve the needs of all. However, particular attention must be given to those who are suffering:

> When one suffers, all suffer, when one receives honor, all rejoice together. When one part of the body/community is in pain, the whole body groans. When one part is healed, the whole body is renewed. It is not right for some parts of the body to be feeling well while other parts of the same body are suffering.[42]

In the CMC document, it is noted that the congregation is seen as a healing place, a caring community, a health teaching place,

---

[38] CMC, p. ii.
[39] CMC, pp. 1–4.
[40] CMC, p. 2.
[41] CMC, p. 15.
[42] CMC, p. 16.

and as an advocate for justice, peace, and the integrity of creation.[43] In healing rituals, the Church acts as God's instrument. The members of the congregation gathered in prayer and support for the patient and the minister, act as conduits of healing. Moreover, through its participation in a rite of healing, the congregation is itself transformed, forgiven, and healed by God's liberating presence. The context for healing and forgiving must always be within the community of faith that is gathered in prayer and worship.

At the local level, the Church brings about healing through

- praying for the sick
- confession and forgiveness
- laying on of hands
- Anointing with oil
- Holy Communion
- using creative healing liturgies
- supporting those who are committed to the healing task
- training healers
- using the charismatic gifts.[44]

However, the Church cannot be insular; it cannot only minister to its members alone. The Church needs to reach out to those who are marginalized and invite them to conversion and healing as well. The Church needs to bring about healing in illnesses that are not just of a physical or psychological nature, but those that are social: the lonely, the oppressed, the abused, the divorced, the unemployed, and those who have unplanned pregnancy.[45]

The Church can also effect healing by being a place of knowledge and teaching, not just for its particular members, but the community at large as well. Some examples include

- Bible study on health, healing, and wholeness
- facilitating self-discovery of causes for ill-health
- practical health education
- studying questions of bio-medical ethics
- learning to take personal responsibility for health.[46]

---

[43] CMC, pp. 31–33.
[44] CMC, p. 31.
[45] CMC, p. 31.
[46] CMC, p. 31–32.

Moreover, the Church, as an advocate for peace and justice, can work to alleviate oppression, racism, and injustice as they relate to health issues. Finally, the Church needs to cooperate with other healing partners such as family members, health professionals, traditional and alternative healers, other health agencies and communities, other faith groups, and the local government.[47] Health, healing, and wholeness are not just the purview of medical professionals or solely the Church's responsibility. Rather, everyone needs to take an active part in bringing about health and wholeness.

## SUMMARY OF ECUMENICAL CONSIDERATIONS

This brief survey of current trends in the ecumenical movement has shown us several insights regarding sacramental healing and ministry to the sick. By way of general commentary, please note that the Orthodox Church, the Anglican and Episcopalian Communions, and the Lutheran Communion are more inclusive concerning the recipient of Anointing. The Orthodox Church in its euchelaion of Holy Week invites all present to partake of the sacramental Anointing for strengthening and the remission of sins. There is, however, a euchelaion that is used specifically for those who are seriously ill. However, in some cases, family members and the ministers themselves may receive the Anointing as well.

The Anglican Communion considers the recipient to include those who may be suffering from mental and moral diseases to participate in a sacramental Rite of Anointing. These include various kinds of mental disorders, but also sexual disorders such as sterility, impotence, or frigidity. The Episcopalian Communion offers a Public Service of Healing, which encompasses the communal nature of sickness as well as the variety of illnesses that plague humanity today. The Lutheran and Reformed traditions are rediscovering the roots of a sacramental ministry to the sick. Perhaps they will make a further contribution to the area of ministry to the sick as the Church enters its third millennium.

Perhaps the Roman Catholic Church may learn from our Orthodox brothers and sisters the importance of seeing all persons as being in need of healing, whether physically, spiritually, or morally.

---

[47] CMC, p. 33.

The Orthodox seem to have a better grasp of the intimate connection between sickness and sin, since they emphasize that the sacrament of the sick is for healing *and* the forgiveness of sins. The Roman Church has tended to overemphasize the spiritual effects of the sacrament throughout its history. Furthermore, the Roman Church has focused on the severity of illness whereas the Orthodox seem to place *all* illness as being within the realm of needing God's healing touch via the sacrament. The Anglican Communion further broadens the concept of illness, extending it to include diseases and disorders which, although not life-threatening, can disrupt a person's normal functioning within society or family. In addition, the Anglican Communion emphasizes the need for holistic pastoral care of the sick. The Church should be concerned about sick parishioners not only during their illness, but also during the period of recovery and reentry into social life.

In the ecumenical realm, other churches and ecclesial communions have been working in the area of pastoral ministry to the sick. The Orthodox in particular have a more balanced view of sickness and sin, seeing both as conditions plaguing humanity and both being in need of healing. The Anglicans seem to take a more comprehensive approach to the recipient of sacramental Anointing, by including all those who suffer from any kind of weakened condition or dysfunction. The Episcopalians have developed a public healing service that focuses on the communal nature of illness while the Lutherans are rediscovering the value of sacramental Anointing services. Finally, the World Council of Churches challenges all ecclesial communions to work toward developing a ministry that promotes wholeness and health.

Anthropologically, the Roman Catholic Church has made great strides in viewing the human person more holistically. The body-soul dualism, prevalent in Scholastic thought, has been replaced by a body-soul unity of the human person. In other words, the human subject comprises body, soul, spirit, and mind. While there still is the tendency to give precedence to the soul, the Roman Catholic Church recognizes that one must take care of one's physical body and mind in order to appreciate God's gift of the soul.

In the area of human sickness, theologians have come to realize that when one aspect of the human person is stricken with illness, all of the other aspects are affected as well. In physical sickness, a person's mind, spirit, emotions, and even soul are touched as well.

Moreover, sickness, whether physical or mental, has the capacity to disturb one's relationship with God, with family members, and with society in general.

In recent years, there has been a greater emphasis on classifying social maladies as illnesses. For example, alcoholism or drug addiction was originally thought to be a moral disorder or a character flaw. Today, they are seen as addictions that have a medical basis and hence are classified as illnesses. Even Pope John Paul II noted that all illness has a psychological basis.[48] As we learn more about the functioning of the body and the mind, perhaps other conditions and disorders, which are now classified as "behavioral" or "conditioned," in the future may be categorized as illnesses.

In short, the Roman Catholic Church has made great strides in pastoral care of the sick and dying. However, there is still some reluctance to admit certain persons who are suffering to the sacrament of the sick. In the following chapters, we will explore the various kinds of diseases and disorders to which the medical community has given a classification. Moreover, the ways in which healing is done in various societies may shed some light on how the Church may more actively pursue a healing ministry in the years to come.

## QUESTIONS FOR DISCUSSION

1. Given the brief discussion on ecumenism, what insights can Roman Catholic ministers gain with regard to ministry to the sick and dying?
2. What rituals are used by other Christian traditions with those suffering from serious, but not life-threatening illnesses?
3. How do these rituals elucidate our understanding of Roman Catholic sacramental practice?
4. According to the Orthodox belief, what is the purpose of Anointing the Sick?

---

[48] See the discussion in chapter 4.

# Chapter 6

# A Pastoral View of Sickness

## A Definition of *Serious Illness*

In this chapter we will closely examine four characteristics of serious illness. First, serious illness comprises several components: biological, psychological, cultural, social, and the spiritual. Second, while one factor may be the dominant cause of the illness or disease, the other three components also play a role. Therefore, in treating the dominant cause, the physician must also examine and attend to the other factors as well. Third, the spiritual component, with its attentiveness to the role of guilt, is an important dimension that is often ignored, yet may be the dominant cause of disease in some cases. Fourth, for a disease or illness to be considered "serious," there should be a danger of death. That is, if the illness has the capacity to cause mortality (whether immediately or over the long-term), it should be considered serious. The severity is not diminished even in cases where the illness may be alleviated with pharmacological substances, surgery, or therapy. Karl Rahner and Herbert Vorgrimler state that serious sickness

> is one of the processes that deprive man of control over himself: a concrete but equivocal manifestation of his creatureliness (the jeopardy of his existence and his dependence on God), of his sinfulness (like concupiscence, original sin), of the approach of death (as suffering and as an act), of the inabrogable and ever mysterious declaration of man's position as both agent and patient.[1]

---

[1] Karl Raher and Herbert Vorgrimler, "Sickness," in *Concise Theological Dictionary*, 2nd Edition (London: Burns & Oates, 1965, 1983), pp. 474–75.

## Types of Serious Illness

Many factors can influence the onset of disease or illness. Certainly the most prevalent is that of biology, although social factors may also cause illnesses. However, it is important to remember from both an anthropological perspective as well as a theological position that, because the human person is multi-dimensional, all of the various factors and dimensions are affected by and affect illnesses and diseases.

A serious illness will incapacitate a person in one or more of these areas to such a degree that he or she will need to seek out medical or professional attention to alleviate the problem. An illness is considered *serious* if it is so severe or the patient is so incapacitated that death could be the result if a cure or treatment is not forthcoming. By *incapacitation* I mean the inability to function "normally" in society.[2] Moreover, an illness should be considered serious if the incapacitation is of such a severity that the person is unable to heal himself or herself and must seek out a professional healer of some type.[3]

The Church works alongside medical professionals to remind them that each person is a unique spiritual being and should not be treated for healing through physical, medical means only. Furthermore, the Church seeks to draw those who are marginalized by sickness back into society through pastoral and sacramental ministry.

The pastoral care of the sick, as was seen in the preceding chapters, has had a long history, not without its debates. The sacrament of Anointing is one component of the total pastoral care ministry that the Church offers to its suffering members. We must not discount the work of family and friends in the healing process. Moreover, health care professionals through their diligent care bring about healing of the whole person as well. As we have seen, real healing occurs when the whole person is restored to health. This not only involves the curing of the disease, but it also means that the person has a new psychological and spiritual outlook. Ordained as well as not ordained individuals

---

[2] *Normally* is an emotion-charged word. A person may rightly question, "What is normal?" The answer is simply that within a given society, a person's behavior and contribution are deemed acceptable by the other members of that society. In other words, he or she is able to fulfill the role(s) that he or she has undertaken in society or culture.

[3] These healers could be medical doctors, psychologists, ministers, homeopathic practitioners, shamans, witch doctors, medicine men—anyone who is recognized by society (or by the patient) as being able to perform a healing role.

participate in effecting this holistic restoration, especially when they work together in concert.

Those who are seriously ill should be anointed. As the liturgical and canonical legislation now stand, these are the criteria for the recipient of the sacrament of the sick:

1. The patient must be "in danger," due to sickness or old age.
2. The patient must possess the use of reason or have had the use of reason.
3. The patient should at least implicitly desire to receive the sacrament.
4. Those who obstinately persist in manifest serious sin may not be anointed.

To determine whether or not a sickness fits these criteria, one must examine the following issues:

1. Does the illness lead toward a significant weakening of the person, which could result in death?
2. Is the person aware of the implications of the sacrament?
3. Does the patient desire to receive Anointing?
4. Is the general direction of the patient's life oriented toward a relationship with God? On the other hand, is the patient openly denying God or defying Church teaching by his or her attitudes or behaviors?

Let us examine several types of serious illnesses with which the sacrament of the sick may be used. We will discuss physical illnesses and mental disorders. The illnesses, which are discussed in this chapter, are meant to be representative of the types of illness that could benefit from the use of sacramental Anointing. Certainly, other illnesses not discussed here could fit into the categories. This discussion should provide more concrete criteria for discerning the seriousness of a particular illness. If you are not sure about the seriousness of an illness, consult the patient's physician or health care professional.

## Physical Illness

*A serious physical illness is one in which a physiological ailment is of such a severity that death could result if the patient does not receive treatment of some kind.* There are three major types of physical illness:

*accidents, physical ailments,* and *general illnesses. Accidents* involving machinery of any type (cars, farm or industrial equipment, weapons, etc.) usually result in an injury that could be fatal due to blood loss or severe trauma to the person's body. It is important that the patient receive quick medical attention. If there is time, the priest may be called to administer the sacrament.

*Physical ailments* originate from within the person. They involve major organs of the body such as the brain, the heart, and the lungs. This type of illness may be rapid or prolonged. Examples include cancer, heart disease, tumors, stroke, breathing problems, and the malfunction of major organs such as the kidney, the gall bladder, or the liver.

The third type of physical illness is those of a *general type.* These illnesses, while not always fatal, can become so if they are not treated promptly and properly. They will require special attention and the same level of concern given to those in the physical ailment category. Examples of the general type of illnesses include pneumonia, allergic reactions, exposure to disease-carrying bacteria, diabetes, high blood pressure, asthma, and tuberculosis.

In determining whether a physical ailment is *serious* or not, a good rule of thumb is "can the patient heal himself or herself?" If the answer is no, the illness could qualify as serious. A word of caution is necessary: a hospital visit by the patient is not the only criteria to determine seriousness; there are many medical ailments which, while traumatic to the patient, are not critical or life threatening. These would include broken bones, cuts and scrapes, amputated limbs, minor allergic reactions, bronchitis, influenza, and even minor chronic conditions like arthritis, etc.

Because of the psychosomatic unity of the human person, one must not discount the effect that psychological factors have on physical illnesses.[4] Moreover, social and environmental factors also play a role in a person's susceptibility to and recovery from illness as well.

## The Alienation, Guilt, and Sickness

In addition to physical symptoms of serious illness, there are psychological, or spiritual dimensions of serious disease. Pierre Jacob noted

---

[4] See Timothy W. Costello and Joseph T. Costello, *Abnormal Psychology,* 2nd edition (New York: HarperCollins Publishers, Inc., 1992), pp. 135–61.

in 1973 that human health exists in three distinct, but interrelated categories: the physical, psychological, and social.[5] He notes that both social action and political action are important in the world of health. In particular, Jacob suggests that psychiatry can be of great assistance in aiding this integration of the seriously ill back into society.[6] In other words, psychiatry, psychology, and sociology have the ability to assist a person who is suffering from some mental disease to reintegrate into society if the disease is treatable and the person wishes to be reintegrated. Jacob suggests that sickness is both a biological and social phenomenon.

Whereas in the past some diseases have been considered to be the result of sins (such as leprosy, blindness, mental illness), in contemporary society, this primitive attitude is slowly being replaced by a therapeutic and educated model that is geared toward the tolerance of heretofore regarded "deviances."[7] Jacob says that anthropology shows us that sickness constitutes a sort of rupture in society because it does not operate within the normal rules of behavior of the community and that causes anxiety for the person and society in general. This anxiety gives rise to the need for non-medical or religious means to provide the answers to the questions of Why? or How come? When medicine fails to cure, the only recourse that the patient has is to magic (psychics would be an example), placebos (drugs or ointments which do not actually cure, but offer a kind of psychological relief), or religion (prayers or ceremonies that may cure the illness, or at the very least remove the feelings of alienation).

David N. Power illustrates how this theme of alienation is an essential component of what may be described as a "theological-

---

[5] Jacob, "Modèles socio-culturels sous-jacents au monde de la santé," *La Maison-Dieu* 113 (1973):10.

[6] Jacob, "Modèles socio-culturels sous-jacents au monde de la santé," p. 13. "D'autre part, en médecine mentale, le psychiatre et ses auxiliaires doivent pouvoir decouvrir les aspects culturels inconscients d'une communauté ou d'un groupe donné et les conflits qu'ils peuvent provoquer, grâce par exemple à l'analyse du secteur, fournie par le sociologue. Ainsi, ensemble, ils pourront éventuellement aider les malades à se réinsérer dans leur milieu d'origine si le développement de leur affection le permet et s'ils le désirent. En psychiatrie, en effect, c'est le mode de relation et de communication entre les différents membres de l'équipe médico-psycho-sociale dans le secteur qui détermine en partie les progrès du malade, c'est-à-dire la synthèse et la restructuration de son *moi*. Mais dans une société, les changements s'opèrent—parallèlement à une certaine conversion des mentalités—dans la structutre du système socio-politique qui affect à son tour la dynamique de la famille et, finalement, la structure psychique de la personne."

[7] See Jacob, "Modèles socio-culturels sous-jacents au monde de la santé," pp. 24–26. It is worthy to note, however, that some sicknesses are still the result of sin. Drug and alcohol abuse are stark examples.

anthropology" of the human person. Some sicknesses are not only physical but some can also be psychosomatic,[8] affecting the whole person. Furthermore, because of Christ's own suffering and Resurrection, human suffering and sickness is seen in a different light from the more medical or scientific view. In this "phenomenology of human illness," theologians attempt to see "how strengthening of faith, acceptance of suffering without loss of resolution, bodily alleviation and overcoming of sin converge in the sick person's participation in the paschal mystery."[9] Power suggests that the relationship between sickness and alleviation of sickness which, when seen within the context of the Paschal Mystery, allows the sick person to participate more fully in that mystery of Christ's own suffering and death. In a very concise manner, Power illustrates this relationship:

> In illness, the human person experiences a multiple estrangement, from one's own body, from friends and associates, from the doings of society, and from God. Sin as a global reality, rather than simply as personal offence, has a hold on the person through this alienation. The spirit is weakened by the bodily condition, and conversely weakness of spirit makes the effort to deal with the bodily condition difficult. As the evil to be overcome resides in this multiple alienation, so the grace of the sacrament, shared with the community in faith, is granted for the alleciation of this condition.[10]

While Power's principle concern is physical illness, his analysis could be equally applied to those who suffer from mental disorders.

## Sin and Sickness

In addition to feelings of alienation, some patients actually experience guilt in connection with their illness. We often hear a patient ask, "What I have I done to deserve this?" The age-old question once again is raised: "Rabbi was it his sin, or the sin of his parents that caused him to be born blind?" (John 9:2). In other words, is sickness due to biology or sinfulness or both? While guilt and sinfulness may be factors in a person's illness, it is irresponsible to assume that they are the only

---

[8] In this context, *psychosomatic* is defined as relating to or concerned with the influence of the mind on the body, especially with respect to disease.

[9] David N. Power, "The Sacrament of Anointing: Open Questions," in Mary Collins and David N. Power, eds., *The Pastoral Care of the Sick* (London: SCM Press, 1991), p.103.

[10] Ibid., p.103.

"causes." On the other hand, perhaps the Church has the responsibility to assist people in acknowledging "that they are not victims of an impersonal and amoral disease, but that their illness has a moral and theological perspective that is of vital importance to them."[11] Furthermore, "many people have not suffered from illness, per se, but they are sick (some sick unto death) of the kind of life they have lived and the interpersonal relationships they have destroyed.[12] It is important to see that illness, especially serious illness, may have a spiritual or moral component. This spiritual dimension is often overlooked by physicians and psychiatrists. However, as the Church continues to involve herself in a healing ministry, she will need to continually refer to the spirituality as well as the sacramentality of sickness as an essential dimension in the healing process. Moreover, the Church's ministers will need to work closely with health care professionals to convey this most essential need.

## ANOINTING OF THE SICK AND MENTAL DISORDERS

As Gordon W. Allport notes in his book *The Person in Psychology*, "Almost every psychological theory carries with it some presupposition regarding the body-mind relation, the function of consciousness, the issue of freedom, the nature of the self—to name a few of our riddles of the Sphinx. The more you try to solve these riddles the worse they seem to grow."[13]

Indeed, a survey of any introductory psychology book will offer a glimpse into the variety of personality theories that abound. For example, the table of contents of one work offers this sample of theories: the Gestalt school, the eclectics, the Genetic-Ganzheit psychology, and the work of Maslow, Piaget, Freud, Jung, Fromm, and Frankl.[14] It is quite clear that while psychologists know who and what a person is, defining the term *person* is much more difficult. Yet, it may be said

[11] David Belgum, "Patient or Penitent," in David Belgum, ed. *Religion and Medicine: Essays on Meaning, Values and Death* (Ames, IA: Iowa State University Press, 1967), p. 215.

[12] Ibid., p.215.

[13] Gordon Allport, *The Person in Psychology* (Boston: Beacon Press, 1968), p.19.

[14] Georges Cruchon, *A Psychology of the Person: An Introduction to Dynamic Psychology*, Translated by Grace E. Watt (London: Darton, Longman & Todd, 1965), p. 5. A detailed survey of the different kinds of personalist theories lies outside the scope of this book, however.

that "modern psychology is moving almost entirely in the direction of a conception of the totality and unity of personality."[15]

Equally difficult is defining norms of behavior for purposes of defining mental health. Perhaps it is easier to say what is not acceptable behavior than it is to say what is acceptable in terms of how one should think or act. Much has been learned about the functioning of mental illness over the past one-hundred years. We have come to understand that mental health is part of the larger schema of health. Mental health is complex, requiring years of research and observation. Moreover, answers yield only questions that are more complex. However, through the pioneering efforts of Dorthea Dix in the United States in the nineteenth century and the Mental Illness Research Association (MIRA) of the current day, the stigma of mental illness is slowly being eroded away.

While the term *mental illness* is the more popular description of psychological difficulties, the term *disorder* is preferred in clinical classifications. The *International Classification of Diseases-10* (ICD-10) notes that the term *disorder* is used "to imply the existence of a clinically recognizable set of symptoms or behavior associated in most cases with distress and with interference with personal functions. Social deviance or conflict alone, without personal dysfunction, should not be included in mental disorder as defined here."[16] Furthermore, the terms *psychogenic* and *psychosomatic* are also not used in the ICD-10 because of their "different meanings in different languages and psychiatric traditions."[17] From the above descriptions, it is clear that persons who suffer from a mental disorder are recognized as having behavior that interferes with their personal functioning. That is to say, they suffer from a dysfunction that affects not only their psyche, but their body as well. The ICD-10, while preferring to avoid the term *psychosomatic,* admits that mental disorders, to be so classified, must have a necessary relation to a bodily dysfunction as well.

---

[15] Georges Cruchon, *A Psychology of the Person,* p. 25.

[16] World Health Organization, *The International Classification of Diseases-10 Classification of Mental and Behavioural Disorders: Clinical Descriptions and Diagnostic Guidelines* (Geneva: World Health Organization, 1992), p. 5 (commonly abbreviated as ICD-10). It is interesting to note that ICD-10 is not recognized by some in the medical community as being authoritative. in all cases.

[17] World Health Organization, ICD-10, p. 5.

Contemporary medical practice has seen a return to the idea of the unity of the person. The human person is a complex psychosomatic unity that is not easily categorized or understood as a whole. More research does not always translate into expanded understanding of mental disorders. While most of the literature views the alienation caused by sickness as physical, a similar analysis could be applied to those who suffer from mental disturbances as well. When one is ill, the whole of his or her person is affected, not just the particular locale of the illness. Healing, therefore, must be holistic in nature, touching not just the physical aspects, but the psychological, emotional, and spiritual ones as well.

## What Is Severe Mental Disorder?

To answer this question, we need to examine the work of psychologists and psychiatrists because the magisterial literature is silent on the matter. While the magisterium relies on the findings of professionals in a variety of subjects to assist in creating documents and further our understanding, the primary focus of magisterial statements is to further under elucidate our theological tradition. It is worthwhile to note that the valid findings of medicine or psychology help to clarify Church teaching, yet the Church still needs to be in continual dialogue with the medical community in order to further clarify her position and promote the Gospel. In other areas, there is no contradiction between modern medicine and Church teaching, in which case the findings of medical science may be used to further the mission of the Church. Such is the case with respect to mental disease. For purposes of this book, two major scientific works are used as the gauge for measuring the gravity of mental disorders. *The Diagnostic and Statistical Manual of Mental Disorders, Fourth Edition* (DSM-IV)[18] and the ICD-10 are considered the standard psychological manuals for determining criteria of analysis and diagnosis. The DSM-IV was compiled by the American Psychiatric Association through the assistance of numerous psychologists, psychiatrists, social workers, and other mental health professionals.

---

[18] American Psychiatric Association, *Diagnostic and Statistical Manual of Mental Disorders.* Fourth Edition (DSM-IV), (Washington, D.C., American Psychciatric Association, 2000). It is also interesting to note that DSM-IV is not recognized by some in the medical community as being authoritative in all cases.

It is the standard diagnostic manual for use in the United States. The ICD-10 is a companion publication issued by the World Health Organization. While it is an international compilation, it is used primarily within the European mental health community.

Both of these volumes are designed to assist mental health professionals in making accurate diagnoses of persons who appear to have a mental disorder, which affect their normal mental and/or physical functioning. It should be noted that for an accurate diagnosis, a variety of factors is examined. Very often, it is the presence of several concomitant behaviors, which determines the overall mental health of the person. In other words, if a psychiatrist or medical professional observes that a person merely talks to himself or herself, it does not necessarily mean that he or she is mentally disordered. However, if it is observed that the person carries on conversations with inanimate objects, ignores human companionship, and seems to be in his or her own little world, it is probably safe to assume that there is a problem.

Both the DSM-IV and the ICD-10 comprise many pages of diagnostic information. It is even difficult to develop a concise definition of *serious mental disorder* because of the factors that must be taken into account. Yet, for our purposes here, it is possible to develop several descriptive criteria. In brief, when the term *serious mental disorder* is used in DSM-IV, it refers to a mental dysfunction that affects the ability of a person to function in society. It may be accompanied by a physical debilitation as well.

It should be noted that what constitutes "ability to function" or "normalcy" in society varies from culture to culture. What is considered normal and appropriate behavior in the Polynesian Islands may not be considered as such in the United States. Also, even within subcultures (i.e. the African American, Latino, Midwestern, Southern, Appalachian, Native American, etc. communities) there is variance on the concept of acceptable behavior. Richard W. Coan offers this definition of normality:

> In its most distinctive uses, the term implies that it is desirable to behave and experience in conformity with the standards that are generally accepted in our society. If a person does this, he will act and experience in much the same way as most other members of the society. Such a pattern is conducive to social adjustment. . . . In every society, of course, the conforming individual tends to be accepted, while the nonconformist is viewed with suspicion,

fear, or hostility. So normality is universally acceptable, although it means a different pattern of functioning in every society.[19]

There are two ways of distinguishing between the normal and the abnormal. Anthropologists and sociologists examine the issue as it pertains to a particular culture or society at a particular time: "abnormal is that which deviates from society's norms."[20] Psychologists and psychiatrists set "as the basic criterion the individual's well-being and the maladaptiveness of his or her behavior."[21] Observance of these two designations, deviance and maladaptive behavior, enables professionals to determine the severity of a mental disorder.

Howard Clinebell cites the following criteria as being indicative of severe mental disturbance:

a) Persons believe (without any basis in reality) that others are attempting to harm them, assault them sexually, or influence them in strange ways.
b) They have delusions of grandeur about themselves.
c) They show abrupt changes in their typical patterns of behavior.
d) They hallucinate, hearing nonexistent sounds or voices, or seeing nonexistent persons or things.
e) They have rigid, bizarre ideas and fears, which cannot be influenced by logic.
f) They engage in . . . repetitive patterns of compulsive actions or obsessive thoughts.
g) They are disoriented (unaware of time, place, or personal identity).
h) They are depressed to the point of near-stupor or are strangely elated and/or aggressive.
i) They withdraw into their inner world, losing interest in normal activities.[22]

While Clinebell's analysis is to be used by the pastoral counselor in determining if a person needs to be referred to professional mental health counseling, the points he raises are useful in defining serious mental disorders.

---

[19] Richard W. Coan, *Hero, Artist, Sage, or Saint?: A Survey of Views on What Is Variously Called Mental Health, Normality, Maturity, Self-Actualization, and Human Fulfillment* (New York: Columbia University Press, 1977), p. 72.

[20] Timothy W. Costello and Joseph T. Costello, *Abnormal Psychology*, 2nd edition (New York: HarperCollins Publishers, Inc., 1992), p. 2.

[21] Ibid., p. 2.

[22] Howard Clinebell, *Basic Types of Pastoral Care & Counseling: Resources for the Ministry of Healing and Growth* (Revised and Enlarged), (Nashville, Abingdon Press, 1984), pp. 312–13.

Psychologists point to the following criteria for judging maladaptive behavior: long periods of subjective discomfort (feelings of anxiety, depression or frenetic behavior); impaired functioning (inefficiency over a prolonged period that seems to be inexplicable); bizarre behavior (behavior that has no rational basis, is unconnected to reality, which seems to indicate that the individual is disoriented); and disruptive behavior (seemingly uncontrollable behavior that disrupts the lives of others).[23]

While there are many causes for mental disorders, psychologists group them into three major concepts: stress, coping mechanisms, and vulnerability. Everyone has to deal with stress, yet when a situation causes an overload of stress or anxiety in a person's life, an individual may experience "a breakdown of adaptive responses [which] cause the appearance of abnormal behavior."[24] When faced with a stressful situation, a person usually deals with the event directly, using task-oriented behavior. However, when the person becomes defensive in the face of a particular event, he or she may rely on a coping mechanism to deal with the situation. "A coping mechanism is defined as a process of changing the meaning or significance of an event to protect the self from psychic pain and/or psychological damage. Much maladaptive or abnormal behavior is the result of defense-oriented, rather than task-oriented, behavior."[25] Finally, all individuals have vulnerabilities or susceptibilities to the development of psychological disorders.

However, when these vulnerabilities are significant or multiple, they can cause the individual to exhibit maladaptive behavior in extremely stressful situations. "There are two principle causes of vulnerability: genetic causes, in which faulty genes create predispositions to mental disorder; and early life experiences that provide faulty parenting or other inadequate learning opportunities."[26]

The American Psychiatric Association defines a mental disorder in this way:

It is a clinically significant behavioral or psychological syndrome or pattern that occurs in a person and that is associated with present distress

---

[23] Costello, *Abnormal Psychology*, pp. 4–5.

[24] Costello, *Abnormal Psychology*, p. 7.

[25] Costello, *Abnormal Psychology*, p. 7.

[26] Costello, *Abnormal Psychology*, p. 7.

(a painful symptom) or disability (impairment in one or more important areas of functioning) or with a significantly increased risk of suffering, death, pain, disability, or an important loss of freedom.[27]

While any diagnosis must be made by a professional, some behaviors are serious, some are not. Examples of serious mental disorders include the following:

- dementia,
- Alzheimer's disease,
- delirium (reversible and irreversible) not induced by alcohol or other psychoactive substances,
- mental disorders (moderate and severe) due to brain damage and dysfunction and to any physical disease,
- schizophrenia,
- any delusional disorders, psychotic disorders, manic episodes, bipolar affective disorders,
- all depressive episodes,
- all persistent mood affective disorders, reaction to severe stress or trauma, and
- all personality disorders.

It lies beyond the scope of this book to define each of these types of disorders. However, it is sufficient for our purposes to say that if a person has been diagnosed as having a "serious mental disorder" (see the above list), he or she may be a candidate for sacramental Anointing, providing the usual criteria are met.

## Post-Traumatic Stress Disorder

The experience of the Vietnam War made therapists aware of post-traumatic stress disorder (PTSD). "Events which trigger such trauma include serious threat to life or physical integrity, destruction of property or threats of the same. . . . War, famine, earthquake, fire, flood, physical and/or sexual assault and accidents represent a selection of traumatic events."[28] Resulting from some traumatic event, the survivor

---

[27] American Psychiatric Association, *Diagnostic and Statistical Manual of Mental Disorders.* Third Edition (Washington, D.C.: American Psychiatric Association, 1987). Cited in Joseph W. Ciarrocchi, *A Minister's Handbook of Mental Disorders* (Mahwah: Paulist Press, 1993), p. 4.

[28] Ciarrocchi, *A Minister's Handbook of Mental Disorders*, p. 56.

may turn to dependence on drugs or alcohol, problems with family members or work colleagues, severe depression, and an increase rate of suicide attempts.[29]

There are three major categories of symptoms: 1) reliving the event, which may take the form of recurrent nightmare; 2) numbness to outside events or withdrawal from such events; 3) cognitive and emotional symptoms such as memory impairment, guilt, or avoidance of activities that stir up memories of the trauma.[30] These symptoms of PTSD may occur immediately after the event or have a period of delay of several months. Moreover, PTSD may be triggered years later. If the "symptoms last less than 3 months the disorder is considered acute and if more than 3 months, chronic."[31]

In short, those who are most at risk for PTSD are those who have had the following experiences: military combat, rape, being held hostage, captivity in a concentration camp, torture, or natural disasters. For example, about seventy percent of those who had prolonged combat experience in the Vietnam War experienced PTSD and ninety percent of those who survived concentration camp captivity still experienced symptoms twenty years later.[32]

PTSD is still a relatively new area of study. However, if the symptoms persist and develop into severe depression or anxiety, the survivor of the trauma may be at risk for self-inflicted damage or suicide.

## Addictions

We should briefly examine addictions to help clarify why someone who is addicted needs the Church's ministry of healing as he or she moves toward wholeness. Addictions as forms of mental disorder are sadly becoming more common in our society. Addictions are grouped as a serious mental disorder. "A large percentage of marital conflicts, spouse and child abuse, sexual dysfunctions, parent-child conflicts, and financial and legal problems are the result of addictive behavior."[33]

---

[29] Katie Evans and J. Michael Sullivan, *Treating Addicted Survivors of Trauma* (New York: The Guilford Press, 1995), p. 7.

[30] Costello, *Abnormal Psychology,* p. 116.

[31] Katie Evans and J. Michael Sullivan, *Treating Addicted Survivors of Trauma,* p. 33.

[32] Costello, *Abnormal Psychology,* p. 116.

[33] Ciarrocchi, *A Minister's Handbook of Mental Disorders,* p. 5.

Given the serious effects of addictive behavior, the Church and her ministers need to become involved in assisting the healing process of addiction both sacramentally and nonsacramentally. What exactly is an addiction?

> In traditional psychiatric usage, the term *addiction* is limited to obsessive-compulsive abuse of substances like alcohol and drugs. These are sometimes called *true addictions*. The body-mind organism of those addicted to such consciousness-changing substances has adapted to the presence of the substance. This produces five criteria that are useful in diagnosing addictions.
>
> 1. *Tissue tolerance* means that increasing amounts of the substance are required to produce the desired effects, and withdrawal symptoms (like severe hangovers) are experienced when the substance is no longer taken;
>
> 2. *Increasing dependence* on the substance, both psychological and physiological;
>
> 3. *Obsessive thinking* about and craving for the substance;
>
> 4. *Loss of control* in using the substance; and
>
> 5. *Continued usage* in spite of negative consequences.[34]

Furthermore, one may distinguish between *substance* addictions and *process* addictions. Moreover, without treatment, "although not all addictions are of equal severity, all eventually exhibit similar behavioral dynamics and processes and *lead to death*."[35] "Substance addictions— I also call these "ingestive addictions"—are addictions to substances, usually artificially refined or produced, that are deliberately taken into the body. These substances are almost always mood-altering and lead to increased physical dependence."[36] Examples of substance addiction include alcohol, drugs, nicotine, caffeine, and food. "In a process of addiction one becomes hooked on a process—a specific series of actions or interactions. Almost any process can be an addictive agent."[37] Examples include, but are not limited to, the accumulation of money, gambling, sex, work, religion, and worry.

---

[34] Howard Clinebell, *Understanding and Counseling Persons with Alcohol, Drug, and Behavioral Addictions*, (Revised and Enlarged), (Nashville: Abingdon Press, 1968, 1984, 1998), p. 24.

[35] Anne Wilson Schaef, *When Society Becomes an Addict* (San Francisco: Harper & Row, Publishers, 1987), p. 19, (emphasis added).

[36] Schaef, *When Society Becomes an Addict*, p. 20.

[37] Schaef, *When Society Becomes an Addict*, p. 22.

There have been many books written about addictions. The most common focus is on drug and alcohol addiction, but in recent years there has been increased attention given to work, gambling, sex, and food addictions.[38] Furthermore, the area of addiction counseling, whether psychological or spiritual, involves so many different areas and issues that a few pages would not do the topic justice. Therefore, in this section, we will examine those addictions that are particularly "fatal" and therefore fall within the criteria of being a serious illness.[39]

There is no single cause for addictions; rather, the process of developing addictions is complex and is said to be of multiple etiology. Howard Clinebell summarizes the causative factors of addiction:

1. *The biochemical properties of alcohol, nicotine, and other drugs or addictive substances that cause them to be inherently more or less addictive for users.*

2. *Physiological causes that seem to make some people's bodies more vulnerable to addictions than other's.* Recent studies suggest that it is increasingly likely that physiological factors in chemical addictions include *genetic vulnerability* among members of certain families with high rates of addiction.

3. *Psychological trauma or deprivation that cause deeply wounded individuals and family systems who experience high anxiety, shame, and alienation, as well as low self-other esteem and general well-being.* These factors cause them to be hypervulnerable to becoming addicted if addictive substances are used or addictive behaviors begun.

4. *Sociological and cultural causes that seem to be a major determinant of the strikingly different rates of chemical and behavioral addictions in different social contexts—meaning in different families, socioeducational classes, genders, religious or ethnic groups and cultures.*

5. *Religious, existential, or philosophical dynamics that increase vulnerability to being caught in an addictive process.* Some belief and value systems, by which

---

[38] The reader may consult any "self-help" section found in bookstores and libraries for a sampling of what is available. Some stores even have an "addiction" section as well. Noted authorities include Howard Clinebell (alcohol and drug addiction), Anne Wilson Schaef (societal addictions and co-dependence), Patrick Carnes (sexual addiction), Gerald May (addiction and grace), and Wayne E. Oates (work addictions), to name a few. Since the literature is so extensive, for more information, the readier is invited to consult the bibliographies of any of the authors cited in this section.

[39] While Schaef's thesis is correct that all addictions exhibit similar dynamics and may lead to death, some are not as severe or the movement toward death is of such a long process that one could not definitively ascribe the person's death to this particular addiction. For example, can one die from too much caffeine? Probably, but not enough studies have conclusively shown that caffeine addiction is a direct cause of death. See Schaef's discussion on page 21 of her book.

individuals and groups attempt to create meaning and purpose in their lives, are pathogenic or sickness causing.[40]

Sadly, addiction is quite common in the world today. As Anne Schaef states, "Most addicts have multiple addictions."[41]

Addiction is a process. "No matter what the addiction is, every addict engages in a relationship with an object or event in order to produce a desired mood change, state of intoxication, or trance state."[42] In short, addicts are "emotionally seduced into believing that [they] can be nurtured by objects or events."[43] Moreover, the addict confuses an intense experience with real intimacy. The object of addiction substitutes for intimacy with other human beings. For example, "an alcoholic sees his relationships with drinking buddies as deep and very personal, but they slip away when the event of drinking doesn't occur."[44] The initial attraction to an object or event produces such an intense emotional experience that the person wants to recreate it. When this process is repeated several times, with deepening emotional attachment, the addictive cycle has begun.

The process of addiction has three components:

- *movement* into addiction,
- *development of the addictive personality,* and
- personal *change.*[45]

The addict has an intense experience with an object or event that produces an emotional (or physical) "high." This experience is repeated especially when the addict seeks to relieve unpleasant feelings or situations. Gradually the addict enters a cycle of behavior in which emotional craving results in a mental preoccupation with the object or event.[46]

The cycle develops when "the addict seeks refuge from the pain of addiction by *moving* further into the addictive process."[47]

---

[40] Clinebell, *Understanding and Counseling Persons,* pp. 51–52 (emphasis in the original).

[41] Schaef, *When Society Becomes an Addict,* p. 19.

[42] Craig Nakken, *The Addictive Personality: Understanding the Addictive Process and Compulsive Behavior,* 2nd edition (Center City, MN: Hazelden, 1988, 1996), p. 2.

[43] Ibid., p. 7.

[44] Ibid., p. 16.

[45] Ibid., p. 19.

[46] Ibid., p. 24.

[47] Ibid., p. 29.

This involves the repeated abandonment of one's values and healthy relationships in favor of the addictive high. Instead of seeking out others or God to satisfy the need for emotional intimacy, an addict turns to the object of his or her addiction for support.

Finally, the addict begins to say to himself or herself that he or she does not need anyone. That person withdraws from intimate relationships with self, with others, and with God. This in turn causes the *development* of the addictive personality in which the addict loses control of the self and begins to nurture addictive logic. "Addictive logic develops as a person tries to justify the subtle changes that are starting to take place within. The first person to experience *personal change* is the person to whom it is happening. The person may be the last to *acknowledge* the change, but is the first to experience it."[48]

The addict may have thoughts of suicide because he or she cannot stop the pain of addiction. Furthermore, flawed addictive logic tells the person that suicide makes sense.[49] Even if the addict does not physically end his or her life, emotionally, mentally, and spiritually the addict is in the process of dying or is dead. As Craig Nakken points out,

> Addiction is a spiritual disease. Everybody has the ability to connect with the soul and spirit of others. Because addiction is a direct assault against the Self, it is also a direct attack on the spirit or soul of the person suffering from addiction. A person's spirit sustains life; addiction leads to spiritual death.[50]

Certainly, those who suffer from addictions are in need of prayer and pastoral support. In the *Book of Blessings*, there is a ritual that may be used with individuals who suffer from addiction to alcohol, drugs, or other controlled substances.[51] Moreover, this blessing "may also be used for individuals who, although not addicted, abuse alcohol or drugs and wish [for] the assistance of God's blessing in their struggle."[52] However, because of the serious nature of addiction, it may be suggested

---

48 Ibid., p. 33.
49 Ibid., p. 62.
50 Ibid., p. 54.
51 *Book of Blessings*, #407–429. (hereafter BB).
52 BB, #408.

that the sacrament of the sick should be used in some cases in addition to participation in a recovery program.[53]

## "Death Dealing" Addictions

In this section, we shall briefly consider some common addictions that are particularly "death-dealing." In other words, those individuals who suffer from the following addictions are more likely to experience physical death and be in need of the sacrament of Anointing if the criteria are met.[54]

### *Alcohol and Drug Addiction*[55]

Alcohol and drug addiction are the best documented and understood of the addictions. What may be said is that casual use sometimes moves into abuse of the substance, and abuse develops into addiction.[56] As a result of alcohol poisoning, the addict may eventually suffer from one of a variety of physical or psychological disorders: "polyneuropathy, pellagra, cirrhosis of the liver, Korsakoff's psychosis, delirium tremens, acute alcoholic hallucinosis, and others."[57]

The effects of using drugs are also often severe. The central nervous system depressants, such as tranquilizers, "produce diminished tension, anxiety, and pain. They may induce sleep, and if taken in sufficient quantities, stupor, coma, and even death."[58] Other effects include hallucinations, seizures, convulsions, disorientation, and temporary psychoses.[59] Central nervous system stimulants, of which amphetamines, cocaine, nicotine, speed, and inhalants[60] are the best

---

[53] See the sections on the treatment of addictions and the use of the sacrament with addictions in chapter 7.

[54] The reader is reminded that the purpose of this section is to offer some examples of persons who might be candidates for the sacrament of the Anointing of the Sick because of the acute nature of their addiction.

[55] While these two addictions are usually treated separately, for purposes of this book they are considered together as an example of chemical dependency. As Clinebell notes in his book, "the similarities between alcohol and drug addictions are greater than the differences. The differences are primarily in physical effects, diagnostic tests, and medical management of withdrawal" (Clinebell, *Understanding and Counseling Persons,* p. 109).

[56] Schaef, *When Society Becomes an Addict,* pp. 20–21.

[57] Clinebell, *Understanding and Counseling Persons,* p. 25.

[58] Clinebell, *Understanding and Counseling Persons,* p. 97.

[59] Clinebell, *Understanding and Counseling Persons,* p. 98.

[60] Such as airplane glue, nail polish remover, and gasoline.

known, cause "the release of energy, excitement, feelings of euphoria, and sleeplessness."[61] Extended use can lead to brain damage and even death. Opium, codeine, morphine, and heroin belong to a class of drugs called narcotics or opiates. "They generally have a tranquilizing and sedative effect, but physical agitation caused by withdrawal and psychological panic related to anticipation of withdrawal symptoms, may produce antisocial behavior during drug craving."[62] Moreover, these drugs are highly volatile and have resulted in numerous deaths from overdose. Psychedelic or hallucinogenic drugs, such as marijuana and LSD, "produce distortions of thoughts, sensations, and perceptions of oneself and of external reality, thereby inducing radically altered states of consciousness including visionlike states."[63] While less destructive than other drugs, hallucinogens can diminish school and work performance and may lead to psychological problems. LSD, also known as acid, "has been known to produce temporary and occasionally long-term psychoses with terrifying auditory and visual hallucinations, panic attacks, flashbacks, deep depression, and suicidal impulses."[64]

A common problem is the combining of drugs or the combining of drugs and alcohol. Various combinations of drugs are used "to counteract the side effects of one drug or synergistically increase the effect of other drugs."[65]

There are other drugs such as performance-enhancing drugs, designer drugs, and nicotine, which produce a variety of side effects. The effects of long-term smoking being cancer-causing, for example, are well known. The results of prolonged use are often fatal among the drugs mentioned above.

### Food Addictions and Eating Disorders

Overeating is more widespread in our culture; obesity is endemic. Other eating disorders are becoming more well-known: anorexia (self-starvation) and bulimia (bingeing and purging) are becoming more prevalent.[66] While overeating affects members of both sexes, anorexia and bulimia commonly affect teenage girls and young women.

---

[61] Clinebell, *Understanding and Counseling Persons,* p. 99.

[62] Clinebell, *Understanding and Counseling Persons,* p. 101.

[63] Clinebell, *Understanding and Counseling Persons,* pp. 101–102.

[64] Clinebell, *Understanding and Counseling Persons,* p. 103.

[65] Clinebell, *Understanding and Counseling Persons,* p. 104.

[66] Schaef, *When Society Becomes an Addict,* p. 21.

In the United States, especially, there is an obsession with weight. Both dieting and obesity are serious health problems. An average of 300,000 people die annually from obesity-related causes including "heart attacks, hypertension, strokes, and diabetes."[67] Moreover, most obese people, that is, those who are 20 percent over their ideal body weight, consume unhealthy foods ("junk" food) which further increases the risk of health problems. On the other hand, anorexia nervosa and bulimia are responsible for more than 150,000 deaths each year. In these conditions, the person feels "too fat" even when he or she is severely underweight. To counteract this feeling, the person goes on severe diets, use laxatives and diuretics, over-exercises, and intentionally vomits food after eating.[68]

As Anne Wilson Schaef notes,

> People with food-related addictions talk in terms of "burying" what is going on inside of them and "stuffing" their feelings. Food (or the avoidance of food) is perceived as a "cure" for anger, depression, fear, anxiety, and other unpleasant feelings—and for pleasant feelings as well. Many compulsive eaters head for the refrigerator whenever they feel too good or "alive."[69]

Like the alcoholic or drug addict, the food addict sees food as the cause (anorexics) or the solution (overeaters) to his or her problems. Food becomes the substitute for intimate relationships with others or with God.

### Sexual Addictions

Through the groundbreaking work of Patrick Carnes, more and more professionals are becoming aware of the prevalent problem of sexual addition in society.[70] Carnes notes that "sex addiction is an illness with a definite set of symptoms and it is treatable."[71] Moreover, "when a sex

---

[67] Clinebell, *Understanding and Counseling Persons,* p. 112.

[68] Clinebell, *Understanding and Counseling Persons,* pp. 112–13.

[69] Schaef, *When Society Becomes an Addict,* pp. 21–22.

[70] Patrick Carnes is recognized as a leading authority on sexual addiction. His first book, *Out of the Shadows,* broached the subject of sexual addiction for the first time. His second book, *Contrary to Love: Helping the Sexual Addict,* offers assessment, intervention, and treatment methods to help the sexual addict on the road to recovery. Another source of information on the treatment of sexual addicts is Ralph H. Earle and Marcus R. Earle, *Sex Addiction: Case Studies and Management* (New York: Brunner/Mazel, Publishers, 1995).

[71] Patrick Carnes, *Contrary to Love: Helping the Sexual Addict* (Center City, MN: Hazelden, 1989), p. 4.

addict gets a fix, it serves the same purpose as a drink or drug, and the personality dynamics that develop are essentially the same."[72]

There are many common characteristics of the sex addict. Carnes lists 14 such traits. While all are destructive of the addict's relationships and daily functioning, these are particularly deadly:

- Continue to act out despite serious consequences, including health risks, severe financial losses, injury, loss of family, and even death.
- Make futile repeated efforts to control the behavior even to the point of extreme hardship or self-mutilation.
- Feel shame and depression so severe that suicidal tendencies are one of the most common concurrent mental health issues.
- Behave in a severely abusive and exploitive way, often violating his or her own values and common sense.
- Allow family relationships and friendships to become secondary in importance to obsessional and delusional patterns that are pathological and self-destructive.[73]

In addition, the sexual addict is at higher risk for contracting a variety of sexual diseases including AIDS because of multiple sexual contacts, frequently with strangers.[74]

Moreover, sexual addiction is powerful and destructive of not only the addict, but also the addict's family and social contacts. Sexual addiction, like other addictions, exerts a powerful influence on the addict. If it is not treated, the addict continues in a downward spiral toward destruction and even death.

Sexual addiction encompasses many areas of sexual behavior. Without discussing the morality of any particular activity, Carnes notes that there are three levels of behavior.

Level One includes behavior that is perceived in our culture as acceptable. These behaviors include masturbation, heterosexual relationships, homosexual relationships, pornography, and prostitution. While some of these activities bring disapproval and may be illegal, their widespread practice indicates general public acceptance . . .[75]

---

[72] Schaef, *When Society Becomes an Addict*, p. 23.

[73] Carnes, *Contrary to Love*, pp. 5–6.

[74] Clinebell, *Understanding and Counseling Persons*, p. 135.

[75] Carnes, *Contrary to Love*, p. 79. Carnes is speaking as a psychologist, not as a moralist. While individual religions may condemn certain behaviors as sinful, Carnes's point is that society at large has come to accept certain activities as "normal" or "permissible."

Level Two specifies sexual behavior that is generally regarded as nuisance behavior. These behaviors include exhibitionism, voyeurism, transvestism, bestiality, indecent phone calls, and indecent liberties. Public reaction usually judges these behaviors as sick or pathetic or obnoxious. Often they are dismissed as innocuous, not serious, and usually not dangerous. When prosecuted, however, they may involve stiff legal penalties. . . .

Level Three includes sexual behavior that is dangerous, abusive, or life threatening. These behaviors include incest, child molestation, sexual abuse of vulnerable adults, and rape. To these acts, the public almost universally reacts with rage and the desire for revenge. The acts are seen as profound violations of cultural boundaries demanding severe consequences . . .[76]

It is important to point out that the three levels do not indicate progressive stages of addiction, but rather serve as descriptive categories of behavior whose only progression characteristics are risk—and hence excitement—as well as harm to others.[77]

It should be noted that most sexual addicts might be helped with professional treatment. However, a few persons enter the chronic phase of addiction. In classical terms, *chronic* means that the condition resists treatment. Carnes notes that the most severe chronic phase sex addicts end up in prisons or mental institutions. Their addiction is combined with severe mental problems. Moreover, the chronic sexual addict has irreparable damage to the sense of self and there is no relief from the obsession. Finally, "for chronic phase addicts, there is no life outside the obsession, and when the obsession combines with psychoses, the challenges for the therapist are legion."[78]

---

[76] "The core feature of abuse, sexual or otherwise, is that the rights and interests of an individual are ignored and/or violated to serve the purposes of another" (John C. Gonsiorek, Walter H. Bera and Donald LeTourneau, *Male Sexual Abuse: A Trilogy of Intervention Strategies,* [London: Sage Publications, 1994), p. 317]. While this volume deals specifically with the treatment of sexual offenders, there are similarities to the treatment of sexual addicts. Furthermore, many of those who perpetrate sexual abuse are themselves addicted to drugs or alcohol or were themselves victims of sexual abuse as children.

[77] Carnes, *Contrary to Love,* pp. 79–83. He notes that these levels are another paradigm for charting sexual behaviors of a *particular* addict, not for classifying addicts into subgroups. By the very nature of sexual addiction as an illness, sexual addicts elude categorization. Therefore, we cannot say that chronic masturbators are pathological and thus are a risk to themselves and others. Nor can it be said that once a person had committed rape, he is an addict. Rather, it is the repeated activity with ever-increasing intensity and ritualization that moves one from preoccupation with an activity to becoming enmeshed in an addictive pattern of behavior.

[78] Carnes, *Contrary to Love,* p. 99. However, "most sex *offenses* are extensions of antisocial behavior and cultural pathology, not addiction" (p. 98). The true chronic sex addict is someone who has sexual addiction concomitant with severe mental disorders.

## Other Addictions

There are many other kinds of addictions such as addiction to sports, work, shopping, gambling, pathogenic religion and values, television, the computer, and the Internet.[79] While these do not produce physical death as do chemical addictions, they can foster the death of relationships and personal interaction. Yet, it should be remembered,

> Each addiction is a distorted expression of a profound spiritual hunger for an integrating commitment to an object of devotion that will give lives purposeful unity. When people seek to satisfy this spiritual need by either an activity or a chemical substance, they are hypervulnerable to becoming painfully addicted to the behavior or substance.[80]

## Treatment of Addictions

While each addictive disorder has its unique form of treatment to alleviate the pain and suffering, most addictions have a similar pattern that is followed to bring about healing. Craig Nakken notes that "to recover, the addict needs loving, helpful friends, an understanding family, and a suitable Twelve-Step program. But the seed of renewal, as previously explained, resides within every suffering person, within all of us. It is a force that helps focus our attention away from our addictive impulses and toward renewal."[81] In other words, for healing and recovery, the addict needs the community, professional assistance, and his or her own desire to be healed. Moreover, he or she needs "a drive for connection" with a Higher Power or Higher Principles.

It has been found that the most successful treatment programs for addiction include a twelve-step program. Based on the Twelve Steps of Alcoholics Anonymous,[82] other programs offer a similar process for relief and recovery. The key to any recovery program is that the addict does not recover alone. He or she seeks to become whole again in community. Moreover, he or she makes an active decision to include God in the recovery process.

---

[79] See Clinebell, *Understanding and Counseling Persons,* pp. 121–45.

[80] Clinebell, *Understanding and Counseling Persons,* p. 145.

[81] Nakken, *The Addictive Personality,* p. 66.

[82] For a history of the development of Alcoholics Anonymous and how the program works, the reader is invited to consult Clinebell, *Understanding and Counseling Persons,* chapter 7, pp. 195–244.

Despite the success of the twelve-step process, only about twenty percent of addicts have any type of treatment.[83] Moreover, many addicted personalities have need for a more personal treatment conducted one-on-one with a psychiatrist or psychotherapist. Still others desire a more pastoral and spiritual approach to counseling, which could be done with a qualified minister, rabbi, or imam. However, it is important to remember that the addict needs professional help and the support of others in order to begin the road to recovery.[84]

## Summary

Persons who suffer from schizophrenia, manic depression, psychoses, neuroses, and severe depression have the possibility of having the disease controlled using drugs or therapy. Through contact with a professional, persons who suffer from these disorders can learn to live productive lives without being a danger to themselves or others. Furthermore, as has been noted previously, there are psychological factors that can affect a physical disease. Also, psychological disorders often exhibit physical manifestations such as disturbed sleep, altered appetite, or increased physical strength. Some of these disorders are given the adjective *serious* because they may cause the patient to injure himself or herself or others, even mortally. However, through biological and psychological therapy, many patients can learn to lead fairly normal lives that make a positive contribution to the society in which they live. Those who are suffering with any kind of addiction may also benefit from a variety of healing methods. They may choose to seek treatment from a counselor or, as many have done, participate in a twelve-step program or support group. As is often noted by these groups, treatment for addictions is an ongoing lifelong process of recovery. If a person is to truly be freed from his or her addictive behavior,

---

[83] Clinebell, *Understanding and Counseling Persons,* p. 245.

[84] We have not discussed the dynamics of crisis intervention, which may be necessary to obtain help for the addicted person. Some addicts need to "hit bottom" before they can be helped. "Hitting bottom" could mean ending up in a hospital or mental health center because of severe physical illness, getting arrested, or being committed to an institution by family members or the state. Others may voluntarily come to the decision that they need help and seek out treatment from a professional counselor or minister. For purposes of this discussion, the fact remains that the Church can be a vital component in the addict's road to recovery. In some cases, as will be seen in the next chapter, an element to recovery could take the form of sacramental Anointing.

it must be addressed on a daily basis and through regular contact with people who are supporting the patient in overcoming the addiction.

## QUESTIONS FOR DISCUSSION

1. What are the dynamics at work in a serious illness?
2. What are the types of illnesses with which the sacrament of the Anointing of the Sick may be used?
3. What are the characteristics of a severe mental disorder?
4. What kinds of dynamics are at work in a person with addictive personality disorder?

# Chapter 7

# An Ecclesial View of Mental Disorders, Addiction, AIDS, and Healing

## INTRODUCTION

There is a variety of illness present in society today. Illnesses range from the physical to the psychological, including addictive behaviors. It is important to keep in mind that all illness, even minor sicknesses, affects the whole person: psychologically, physically, mentally, spiritually, and relationally.

Many physical illnesses may constitute a danger to the patient. If the patient is in remote danger of death, has or has had the use of reason, desires to receive the sacrament of the sick, and is not obstinate in continuing a life of sinfulness, he or she may receive sacramental Anointing. In every illness, but especially in serious illnesses, the Church should maintain an active pastoral and sacramental presence both to the patient and to the patient's family.

Determining when to administer the sacrament of healing is probably easier when physical illness is involved. It can be relatively easy to determine when danger of death is the determining factor in deciding to contact a priest to administer the sacrament of healing. In the years since the promulgation of the revised rite, the Church has examined how it may treat and heal patients afflicted with mental disorders or addictions. In this chapter, we will examine how the Church views sicknesses and mental disorders and addictions and look at the Church's response to healing those suffering from such previously misunderstood or little-known afflictions.

## THE ROMAN CATHOLIC APPROACH
## TO MENTAL DISORDERS

How the Church assists in the healing and treatment of those with
mental disorders or addictions is an area that is gaining increased
attention. In the current edition of *Pastoral Care of the Sick* (PCS),
ministers are invited to consider administering sacramental Anointing
to someone who has a mental disorder: "Some types of mental sickness
are now classified as serious. Those who are judged to have a serious
mental illness and who would be strengthened by the sacrament may
be anointed ( see also PCS, 5). The Anointing may be repeated in
accordance with the conditions for other kinds of serious illness (see
also PCS, 9)."[1] Because this is a relatively new addition to literature
concerning sacramental Anointing, it is necessary to examine how the
Church views mental disorder. It is only recently that the Church has
taken an active role in promoting the rights and dignity of the mentally
disordered. The writings of Pope John Paul II have been characterized
by his concern for the rights of all persons. This attention has had
influence in the world and in politics. Furthermore, there have been
two major health care conferences held at the Vatican ("Disabled
Persons in Society," 1992, and "In the Image and Likeness of God:
Always? Disturbances of the Human Mind," 1996), which focused on
the rights and dignity of persons who suffer with mental and physical
disorders and handicaps.

The pontificate and writings of Pope John Paul II are distinguished by a personalist approach to the human person. From his
earliest writings to his latest, the John Paul II consistently upheld the
dignity and rights of all persons who are made in the image and likeness of God. As he noted in the encyclical *Redemptor Hominis*, 14,

> The Church cannot abandon man, for his "destiny", that is to say his
> election, calling, birth and death, salvation or perdition, is so closely and
> unbreakably linked with Christ— . . . . Man who in his reality has,
> because he is a "person," a history of his life that is his own and, most
> important, a history of his soul that his own.[2]

---

[1] *Pastoral Care of the Sick: Rites of Anointing and Viaticum* (PCS), (New York: Catholic Book
Publishing Co., 1983), no. 53.

[2] Pope John Paul II, *Redemptor Hominis* (RH), Encyclical, March 4, 1979 (Milano: Scuole
Grafiche Pavoniane, 1979), p. 30.

John Paul II further explicates this relationship to Christ in terms of the suffering that is present in the world in *Salvifici Doloris*. Although suffering is considered evil, it always in some way is connected to a good; that is, the sufferings of Christ himself. As he notes in the encyclical: "In itself human suffering constitutes as it were a specific 'world' which exists together with man, which appears in him and passes, and sometimes does not pass, but which consolidates itself and becomes deeply rooted in him."[3] As has been seen, while suffering has an alienating dimension (from self, others, and even God), it is also interpersonal and social:

> The world of suffering possesses as it were its own solidarity. People who suffer become similar to one another through the analogy of their situation, the trial of their destiny or through their need for understanding and care, and perhaps above all through the persistent question of the meaning of suffering.[4]

Yet, the late Pope reminds his readers, Christ was in the midst of the world of human suffering, healing, and consoling those who were so afflicted. Furthermore in his sufferings, Christ sanctified and redeemed the sufferings of all humanity.

In a November 30, 1996, speech to an international conference sponsored by the Pontifical Council for Pastoral Assistance to Health Care Workers, John Paul II said, "Christ took all human suffering on himself, even mental illness. Yes, even this affliction, which perhaps seems the most absurd and incomprehensible, configures the sick person to Christ and gives him a share in his redeeming passion."[5] As he had done so many times previously, the late Pope reiterated that humans are created in the image and likeness of God, which confers dignity upon their person. He notes that persons with mental illnesses often "encounter indifference and neglect" and are "exploited and abused."[6] He concludes his remarks with a very forceful definition and mandate: Whoever suffers from mental illness "always" bears God's

---

[3] Pope John Paul II, *Salvifici Doloris* (SD), Apostolic Letter, February 11, 1984 (Washington, D.C.: Office of Publishing Services, United States Catholic Conference, 1984), No. 8.

[4] Pope John Paul II, *Salvifici Doloris*, p. 6.

[5] Pope John Paul II, "The Image of God in People with Mental Illnesses," *Origins CNS Documentary Service*, Vol. 26, No. 30 (January 16, 1997): 495.

[6] Pope John Paul II, "Image of God," paragraph 6, *Origins:* 496.

image and likeness in himself, as does every human being. In addition, he "always" has the inalienable right not only to be considered as an image of God and therefore as a person, but also to be treated as such.

It is everyone's duty to make an active response. Our actions must show that mental illness does not create insurmountable distances, nor prevent relations of true Christian charity with those who are its victims. Indeed, it should inspire a particularly attentive attitude toward these people who are fully entitled to belong to the category of the poor to whom the kingdom of heaven belongs (cf. Matthew 5:3).[7]

In his message given in anticipation of the Sixth World Day of the Sick celebrated on February 11, 1998, John Paul II reiterated that all persons have the duty to assist the suffering members of the Body of Christ:

> Dioceses, parishes and all communities in the Church should devote themselves to presenting the subjects of health and illness in the light of the Gospel; encourage the advancement and defense of life and the dignity of the human person, from conception until natural death; and make the preferential option for the poor and marginalized concrete and visible—as regards the latter, the victims of the new social maladies, the disabled, the chronically ill, the dying and those who are forced by political and social disorder to leave their land and live in precarious or even inhuman conditions should be surrounded with loving attention.[8]

It is quite clear from these brief quotations that John Paul II was committed to the service of those who suffer with mental disabilities and disorders. These concerns have also been reflected in the two health care conferences held at the Vatican. As was mentioned above, these conferences offered by the Pontifical Council for the Pastoral Assistance to Health Care Workers were designed to explore the issues surrounding health care in the world today.

In the first conference, Disabled Persons in Society, the term *disabled* was used to describe any person who suffered from any kind of debilitating disease—physical or mental. In a significant article, Julius Axelrod noted that many mental diseases could be controlled

---

[7] Pope John Paul II, "Image of God," paragraph 8, *Origins:* 497.

[8] Pope John Paul II, "Christ Came to Share Our Afflictions," paragraph 6, *L'Osservatore Romano Weekly Edition in English*, N. 29 (1500), 16 July 1997: 4.

and even cured using medication. He says that the principle mental illnesses are schizophrenia, depression, mania, amnesia, and toxic-codependency.[9] He further notes that medications such as valium and librium can often alleviate serious mental disorders and psychiatric conditions, especially those that have a biological cause.[10]

As noted above, at the health conference held in 1996, In the Image and Likeness of God: Always? Disturbances of the Human Mind, John Paul II focused on mentally ill persons always being in the image and likeness of God. In Dolentium Hominum, 34 (1997), the writings and reflections of the participants continually highlight the need to welcome those afflicted with mental disorders. Consistently, the conference participants reminded their audience of the dignity that the mentally disordered possess because of their relationship with God. Furthermore, many of the participants noted that often there is a bio-logical cause for the mental disorder.[11] Furthermore, several partici-pants called for the Church to develop a pastoral attitude as well as programs to assist the mentally disordered in our society.[12] They noted that because the mentally disordered are a part of the Body of Christ (and thus possess dignity), the Church has an obligation to serve them both pastorally and spiritually.

Pope Benedict XVI, continues this tradition of concern for those who are suffering. The annual World Day of the Sick held in Adelaide, Australia, on February 11, 2006, focused on those who suffer from mental disorders. In his message inaugurating the 14th World Day of the Sick, Pope Benedict noted, "On this occasion, the Church intends to bow down over those who suffer, with special concern, call-ing the attention of public opinion to the problems connected with mental disturbance that now afflicts one-fifth of humanity and is a real

---

[9] Julius Axelrod, "Mental Illness, Drugs, and Neurotransmitters," Dolentium Hominum 22 (1993): 76.

[10] Axelrod, "Mental Illness, Drugs, and Neurotransmitters," see pp. 77 and 80.

[11] See especially the articles by Carlo Lorenzo Cazzullo, "The Acceptance of Mental Illness," (pp. 81–84), Julio Licinio, "The Biology and Psychology of Depression," (pp. 116–20), Malcom Lader, "Abnormalities of the Mind in Schizophrenia" (pp. 121–24), Ignacio, Carrasco de Paula, "The Dignity of Madness" (pp. 126–28), Dina Nerozzi Frajese, "A Measureless Mind: Manic-Depressive Illness" (pp. 132–36), and Wanda Poltawska, "Nonhuman Man" (pp. 137–39) in Dolentium Hominum 34 (1997).

[12] See Janos Füredi, "Integrated Therapies for Schizophrenic Patients and Their Families," (pp. 183–85), Franco Imoda, "Psychotherapy" (pp. 186–92), Pierluigi Marchesi, "The Role of the Church in the Treatment of the Mentally Ill" (pp. 205–207), and Hervé Itoua, "Pastoral Care and the Spirituality of the Mentally Ill" (pp. 208–16) in Dolentium Hominum 34 (1997).

social-health care emergency."[13] The late Pope further notes that those who suffer from mental disorders should be "given access to necessary forms of care and treatment."[14] To this end, Benedict suggests that more integration needs to take place between "appropriate therapy and new sensitivity towards disturbance, so as to enable workers in the sector to deal more effectively with these sick people and their families, who would be unable on their own to care adequately for their relatives in difficulty."[15] Furthermore, the Pope urges that professionals need to be trained and updated to better care for those who are suffering, and he notes that every Christian "is called to make his contribution so that the dignity of these brothers and sisters may be recognized, respected and promoted."[16]

In summary, the work of John Paul II and the recent health care conferences on the mentally disordered indicate that the Church is concerned about the dignity and rights of those who suffer from mental afflictions of any kind. More importantly, the Church is encouraging direct involvement of health care professionals and ministers in developing cures, therapies, and pastoral approaches for the elimination or control of these afflictions. While the articles point to the need for a new pastoral practice concerning the mentally disordered, they stop short of encouraging direct sacramental contact under the form of the Anointing of the Sick.[17] However, in recent years the Church has taken positive steps toward the alleviation of the suffering of the mentally disordered. Perhaps under the pontificate of Pope Benedict XVI there will be more attention given and research done regarding the use of the sacrament of the sick with all sick persons, but especially with those who are afflicted with mental disorders.

---

[13] Benedict XVI, *Message of His Holiness Benedict XVI for the 14th World Day of the Sick,* Vatican, 8 December 2005. http://www.vatican.va.

[14] Ibid.

[15] Ibid.

[16] Ibid.

[17] Hervé Itoua hints (but does not explicitly say) that Anointing may be an option for pastoral practice. "It may be observed that up to the present time our pastoral assistance to the mentally ill has involved the development, above all, of the dual dimension of charitable assistance (material help and visits) and sacramental help *at the moment of death*" (emphasis added) (p. 212). See Hervé Itoua, "Pastoral Care and the Spirituality of the Mentally Ill," pp. 211–16.

# The Use of the Sacrament of the Sick with Mental Disorders

In applying the criteria for administration of the sacrament, it is important to emphasize that a mentally disordered person should be under the care of a physician or psychologist, etc. Furthermore, the medical professional, knowing the patient's psychological history, should be consulted: Would reception of Anointing help or hinder the patient's recovery? For example, if the patient is dealing with deep-seated aversions to religious persons, having a priest anoint him or her might cause a severe reaction. Because the sacrament has an impact not only physically and spiritually, but also emotionally and psychologically as well, it is necessary that the patient be able to sustain an encounter with the prayers and gestures of the ritual.

In a book written in 1963, Norman Autton offered several practical suggestions for priests who will use the sacrament of the sick with those who are mentally disordered. He says,

> *The Sacrament of Holy Unction*, a recognized apostolic practice, giving grace to withstand the assault of the evil one, and inner liberation from the power of sin and disharmony of soul, can mean much to the mentally ill. The definite feel of the holy oil as the sign of the Cross is made on the forehead inspires courage and confidence. It should never be administered without very careful instruction and preparation, which should include an act of penitence.[18]

However, each patient should be considered on an individual basis. It is imperative that the priest have insight into the mental, moral, and spiritual state of the patient if spiritual healing is to be effective.

Autton suggests that "to avoid all danger of misinterpretation and 'person-centeredness' it is often good to make it a corporate act whenever practicable, with a few of the faithful present upholding in prayer both priest and patient."[19] Autton also suggests that mentally disordered patients be given prayers and meditations or short scriptural passages, which may assist in alleviating their isolation, loneliness, and

---

[18] Norman Autton, *The Pastoral Care of the Mentally Ill* (London: SPCK, 1963), p. 135 (emphasis in the original).

[19] Ibid., p. 136.

despair. In speaking to the mentally disordered, a priest should avoid "phrases couched in psychological terminology" or dwell continually on the themes of sickness, suffering, hell, or punishment. Instead, he should focus on the word of God, faith, and love.[20]

Finally, Autton says that "religion can only be salutary to mental health when it offers enduring values that foster personal growth and integration. . . . Piety is not all-sufficient or a panacea against a psychic disorder, neither will religion eliminate the need for psychiatry."[21] In addition, in the ministry of healing, the spiritual life of the priest is of prime importance. "He must, therefore, be conscious of a deep sense of vocation and mission, for the value of his example is immeasurable. His patients should see him as a recognizable minister of God, testifying at all times to the fact of God's overruling power and love towards the rehabilitation of the patient."[22] The priest, as sacramental minister, cannot allow himself to imitate the other disciplines of health care. His ministry is distinct from that of the physician, the nurse, the psychiatrist, or the orderly. Each one has a crucial role to play in the rehabilitation and restoration of the mentally disordered person.

When dealing with a mentally disordered individual, it is important that one consider all the criteria for reception of the sacrament of the sick. Certainly, the criterion of "danger of death" is crucial. Will the patient's psychological condition or illness seriously impair his or her functioning in society or put the patient (or others) in danger of death? In some illnesses, self-mutilation and suicide can be very real possibilities.

The "use of reason" is more problematic because it touches the heart of a psychological illness. Is the patient aware enough of what is going on in order to make an informed decision whether he or she wishes to receive the sacrament or not? Moreover, has he or she at any time before the onset of the illness enjoyed the use of reason? This criterion is important because the Church does not wish to administer the sacraments indiscriminately. Not only does the person need to

---

[20] Ibid., p. 138.

[21] Autton, *The Pastoral Care of the Mentally Ill,* p. 139.

[22] Autton, *The Pastoral Care of the Mentally Ill,* pp. 140–41. This quality of priestly ministry extends to all priests in every ministerial situation, not just in the mental health sphere.

desire reception (or in the case of children, the parents or caregivers), the Church needs to ensure that the person is ready to receive the sacraments. The priest should do a discrete inquiry as to the nature of a *mentally disordered* person's illness in this area.

Finally, is the patient aware of his or her relationship with God? Is he or she currently or had he or she been moving toward God in social and religious life? Was the patient a good person who is now suffering from a psychological disorder? Alternatively, was this person engaging in sinful activities that then brought about the psychic disorder?[23]

In short, a person should be anointed for a psychological disorder if it truly is a disease that can lead to death of the patient. Moreover, the person should be under the care of a mental health professional who should be consulted by the priest to ascertain whether the patient is capable of receiving the sacrament. At no time should the priest interfere with the patient's therapy, even if he himself is trained in psychology. The role of the priest is to bring the healing presence of Christ through the sacrament. The priest is not the healer, Christ is. The patient has the right to refuse the sacrament even if his or her family (or the priest) thinks it would do some good. However, the priest and the parish should make a concerted effort to offer pastoral care to the patient and his family both during the illness and after. At no time should the Church's ministers deny pastoral or sacramental assistance if all the criteria for reception of the sacrament are met.

## Addiction and Sin

As noted previously in chapter 6, addictive behaviors have been classified as mental disorders. While some may be minor, other kinds of addictions such as alcoholism, drug addiction, or sexual addiction are quite serious and can often lead to death. But as we have noted, there is a connection between sickness and sin. Is there a similar connection between addictive behavior and sin?

In his 1989 study, Patrick McCormick examines the issue of sin in society. [24] He examines six models of sin that have been used

---

[23] For example, someone who suffers a nervous breakdown because he or she has been stealing money from an employer, or a professional "hit man" who has been torturing or killing others for money.

[24] Patrick McCormick, *Sin as Addiction* (Mahwah, NJ: Paulist Press, 1989).

throughout history, pointing out their strengths and limitations. He notes that sin may be viewed as stain (the defilement model), as crime (a cry for punishment), as personal, as a spiral that encompasses not just the person but the community as well, as a sickness, and finally, as an addiction. McCormick points out that while each of these models has value, viewing sin as an addiction seems to encompass all of the models and invites the sinner to see his or her whole life as one of "recovery from sin." The characteristics of sin and addiction are quite similar. In both, there is an aversion to God and an attempt to be god. "A core element of both sin and addiction is the refusal to accept our own limitations, our own imperfections, our own creatureliness."[25] Furthermore, in both processes, we become idolatrous. We replace God with a created thing.

"Sin, like addiction, seems to involve a progressive enslavement to our compulsions. . . . With the growth of sin's power the sinner becomes less able to change, grow, or repent. Instead there is a sort of hardening of the heart, a deadening of one's soul."[26] Both sin and addiction lead to disintegration of one's emotional, psychological, physical, and spiritual integrity. Consequently, a person becomes alienated from himself or herself, from others, and from God. Both the addict and the sinner distort all the relationships in which they are engaged.

"Furthermore, sin, like all addictions, is based on and fed by lies."[27] These deceptions hide the truth and lead one closer to death. In short,

> The sinner is like an addict—denying his creatureliness, refusing to let God be God, creating a delusional world through deception, denial and projection, becoming alienated from all others and destroying the self in a spiral of disintegration ending in death.[28]

Sin is like an addiction in that while it may begin as a "private" or "personal" activity, it soon encompasses and destroys everything around it. Moreover, sin, like addiction, usually begets other sins, creating cycles of behavior that "flourish on personal, interpersonal and societal levels."[29]

---

[25] Ibid., p. 161.
[26] Ibid., pp. 161–62.
[27] Ibid., p. 162.
[28] Ibid., p. 163.

Although sin can be an addiction, is the reverse true?
Is addiction sinful? Howard Clinebell summarizes some common
statements that compare the two:

1. Addictions are the result of personal sin. At no point are they
   sicknesses.
2. Addictions begin as personal sin that result in an obsessive-
   compulsive disease process called addiction.
3. Addictions are sicknesses that are caused by the sin of voluntary
   excessive drinking or drug use.
4. Alcoholism and other substance addictions are sicknesses caused by
   the convergence of a variety of factors involving both sin and
   sickness, responsibility and compulsivity.
5. Alcoholism and drug dependence involve sin in the sense that they
   have destructive consequences. These include preventing people
   from developing their God-given capacities for living fully and
   productively.
6. Addictions are illnesses resulting from social sins.[30]
7. Alcoholism and other addictions involve original sin.[31]

Clinebell notes that, at one time or another, each of these statements
were believed to be true. He is critical of statement 1. because it
blames the addiction on a misuse of free will. As we have seen, the
addict's personal freedom of choice can be constrained by genetic,
familial, or social factors. The second statement begins from the view
that all drinking and drug use is sinful. However, once voluntary control is lost, it becomes an addictive illness. "Victims are no longer fully
responsible, since their drinking and using are now done compulsively
to some degree, beyond the control of their wills. However, they are
responsible for having caught the compulsion or disease. In this sense
addictions are sin sicknesses."[32]

The third statement is also weak in that it focuses on the
abuse or misuse of alcohol or drugs, rather than on their use. "The sin

---

[29] Ibid., p. 172.

[30] Examples of social sins include racism, sexism, greed, or genocide. For example, if a man
has grown up in a society that devalues women and views them as objects, he may develop an
addiction to visiting prostitutes or using pornography.

[31] Howard Clinebell, *Basic Types of Pastoral Care & Counseling: Resources for the Ministry of
Healing and Growth* (Revised and Enlarged), (Nashville, Abingdon Press, 1984), pp. 287–91.

[32] Ibid., p. 288.

is the sin of excess involved in becoming addicted."[33] The problem is in establishing the line of demarcation between what is acceptable use and excessive use. Statement 4. "emphasizes that alcoholics have a psychological compulsion joined with a physical addiction to alcohol. It goes on, however, to express the belief that one is driven to drink by selfishness and its symptoms."[34]

It is Clinebell's view that an acceptable position on the relationship between sin and addiction would include "the responsibility factors in the definitions of sin described in [statements] 5, 6, and 7. The concept expressed in statement 4 will undoubtedly prove meaningful to some clergy, although the difficulties involved should be faced."[35] Stated simply, sin is involved in addictive behaviors. However, instead of placing blame, twelve-step programs are aimed at helping addicts to "grow in their capacity for self-determination and responsibility."[36] The fact is, alcoholism and other addictions arise from a person's inability to control his or her behavior. The addiction is oftentimes used as a substitute for accepting responsibility for one's actions that may become sinful. For example, a man is having difficulty at work because his performance is not up to par. He begins to drink to forget about his problems. The drinking becomes excessive, which leads to destructive behaviors such as viewing pornography on the Internet and being abusive to his wife and children. He finds that the alcohol makes him feel better and so he continues to use it more and more frequently to the extent that he becomes addicted to its use. While the addiction is not sinful, the behavior that results from the addiction can be sinful. The man is culpable for the sin, even though he may not be aware of it at the time. However, while he is undergoing treatment it may be pointed out to him that he was abusive. At that time, he should apologize and seek forgiveness because although he may no longer be committing the sin of abuse, the effects of the sin remain, for which he is responsible. The difficulty in dealing with persons who suffer from addictive behaviors is ascertaining the degree to which they are culpable or responsible. Some people would like to

---

[33] Ibid., p. 288.
[34] Ibid., p. 289.
[35] Ibid., p. 291.
[36] Ibid., p. 293.

excuse the behavior as "being under the influence" and thereby dismiss culpability. However, the courts recognize that driving while intoxicated does not absolve a person from responsibility for any accident. I would concur that the same is true in the realm of sin. If an addict commits an action that is sinful while he or she is addicted, he or she is morally obligated to atone for that sin once he or she becomes aware of it.

A goal of therapy, like that of confession, is to enable persons to see their shortcoming and failures to "hit the mark," to learn from them, and to move toward growth and conversion. The beginning point of conversion is acceptance of the self. Addicts carry the burden of guilt and shame. If this is not transformed into a liberating experience, the addict will continue in a downward spiral of depression and self-rejection.

Twelve-step programs work toward transforming this guilt and shame into personal responsibility, which then moves the addict toward personal growth. On the one hand, the addict is told, "You are not responsible for the fact that you have an allergy to _____" (fill in the appropriate addiction). On the other hand, the program utilizes the addict's growing capacity for self-acceptance and responsibility by saying, "but you do have a responsibility to face your loss of control over _____ and to use the program to re-educate your attitudes toward _____ so that you won't be driven to take the first step and engage in this behavior."[37]

In summary, the goal of addiction counseling and participation in a twelve-step program is health and wholeness of the entire human person. Those who are addicted and make the choice to become whole again recognize that it is a lifelong process. It involves attentiveness to the physical, psychological, social, and spiritual dimensions of the person. When one of these aspects is out of balance with the others, sickness develops.

## The Church and Addictions

In 1992, the Pontifical Council for the Family issued the document *From Despair to Hope: Family and Drug Addiction.*[38] In it the authors point out that drugs are a problem for the person, the family, and

---

[37] See Clinebell, *Basic Types of Pastoral Care & Counseling,* pp. 294–95.

society. They note that "basically, the drug user is one who is sick because of a lack of love: he did not know love; he does not know how to love correctly because he was never loved correctly."[39] Because of this lack of love and the ultimate search for love, the drug addict turns to a substance to satisfy his cravings. Moreover, the family "is the key element in the formation of a person's character and attitudes towards society."[40] The document cites many causes for the family crises, which may result in drug addiction, including stress, divorce, lack of communication, and selfishness; "in a word, the inability to raise children in an open and wholesome way."[41] Finally, today we have "a society without ideals, permissive, secularized, where the search for escape expresses itself in so many ways, one of which is the flight to drug addiction."[42]

In an effort to combat drug addiction, the Church needs to adopt an evangelizing presence in which she proclaims the inherent dignity of all persons. This evangelization should include

1. The proclamation of God's paternal love directed to the salvation of every person, a love that is above every sense of blame;
2. The condemnation of personal and social evils that should include the proclamation of God's love for all people, the condemnation of personal and social evils which lead to drug abuse, and the personal witness of those who work with drug users to assist them in getting the help they need.
3. The witness of those believers who dedicate themselves to the treatment of drug users according to the example of Christ Jesus, who did not come to be served but to serve and give his life.

Citing Pope John Paul II, the document notes that "the possibility of recovery and redemption from the terrible slavery has been concretely proven."[43] Therefore, the Church must actively support efforts that combat drug use and promote recovery and healing at all societal levels: the family, the parish, in the communities that treat drug users, and in culture.[44]

---

[38] Pontifical Council for the Family, *From Despair to Hope: Family and Drug Addiction*, (Vatican City, 1992). Hereafter cited as *From Despair* with the appropriate page number.

[39] Ibid., p. 2.

[40] Ibid., p. 2.

[41] Ibid., p. 2.

[42] Ibid., p. 2.

In a 1990 document released by the United States Catholic Conference, the Bishops attested to the fact that "ultimately, we are all casualties of substance abuse and chemical dependency. Besides the millions of individuals and families personally ruined by abuse of alcohol and other drugs, the economic and social costs are immense."[45] They noted that "chemical dependency then can lead to disorders of the nervous system, physical deterioration, and even death due to drug-related physical problems, accidents while intoxicated, or by suicide—tragically prevalent among drug using adolescents."[46]

Because of their addiction, chemically dependent persons will progress more deeply in the downward spiral of "addictive illness and self-destruction." "Their condition cries out for others to recognize the problem and intervene to confront and support them. Responding effectively is the challenging task of family, co-workers, friends, and faith community."[47] Specifically, the Church needs to get more actively involved in pastoral ministry to those who are addicted. In addition to prayer for the addict, those in recovery, treatment, prevention, enforcement, and their families, the Church can initiate the following responses in parishes around the country:

1. Our parishes can offer individuals and families struggling with substance abuse the abundant resources of personal and communal prayer, the power of God's word in the scriptures, and the rich treasure of our sacramental life. They can experience healing and strengthening for life without addiction in the sacrament of Reconciliation and know the loving presence of Christ Jesus in the celebration of the Eucharist in the midst of a supportive faith community.

2. An alcohol and drug awareness effort should develop educational, informational, preventive, and advocacy programs of service to the entire community. Wherever possible, our parishes should offer

---

[43] Ibid., p. 5.

[44] Ibid., see pp. 5–8.

[45] United States Catholic Conference, *New Slavery, New Freedom: A Pastoral Message on Substance Abuse* (Washington, D.C.: United States Catholic Conference, Inc., 1990), p. 6. Hereafter cited as *New Slavery* with the appropriate page number.

[46] USCC, *New Slavery*, p. 7.

[47] USCC, *New Slavery*, p. 8.

adult education programs on a regular basis to make this knowledge available to as many families as possible.

3. Parish facilities could also be made available to self-help groups such as Alcoholics Anonymous (AA). The Twelve-Step Program, the centerpiece of these powerful groups, has a profoundly spiritual foundation based on trust in God.

4. Parish schools and religious education programs should include an appropriate substance-abuse curriculum, with maximum appropriate parental involvement and collaboration with other schools and community educational efforts.

5. Pastors and all parish and school professionals should learn to recognize early signs of abuse of alcohol and other drugs and respond by making appropriate referrals.

6. Parishes can help people in the process of recovery, including those who return to the community after treatment.

7. Where possible, parish efforts should be joined to those of other churches, ecclesial communities, and other religiously sponsored programs for prevention, treatment, rehabilitation, and advocacy.[48]

The Church has a crucial role to play in the prevention, education, and treatment of those who are addicted to alcohol and drugs.

On November 21–23, 1991, the Pontifical Council for Pastoral Assistance to Health Care Workers sponsored a conference entitled "Drugs and Alcoholism against Life." The proceedings were published in *Dolentium Hominum* in 1992.[49] At this conference, experts in science, medicine, psychology, ethics, and pastoral theology from around the world discussed the issues of drug and alcohol addiction in the world. At his welcoming address, Pope John Paul II noted,

> The phenomenon of drugs and alcoholism cannot be combated nor can effective action be taken for the healing and recovery of their victims unless the human values of love and life are first restored—the only ones capable, especially if illuminated by religious faith, of giving full meaning to our existence. . . .
>
> As it is up to the Church, then, to work on a moral and pedagogical level, intervening with great sensitivity in this specific area, so it is up to public institutions to adopt a serious policy aimed at healing situations

---

[48] USCC, *New Slavery,* pp. 11–12 (emphasis in the original).

[49] "Drugs and Alcoholism against Life," *Dolentium Hominum,* 19 (1992).

of personal and social unease . . . . In this campaign for prevention, treatment, and recovery the interdisciplinary research to which this Conference has made such a significant contribution has a decisive role to play.[50]

The Church is not only to be a moral force in the fight against addictions, it is also to be an active participant in assisting addicts to reach their full potential.

In a noticeable lacuna, the Church has not really spoken out about other kinds of addictions, restricting itself to alcoholism and drug addiction. Perhaps in the future the Church will recognize other forms of addiction and lend support to their treatment and alleviation in a more systematic manner.

## The Use of the Sacrament of the Anointing of the Sick with Addictions

In an article written in 1989, Mary Grace Benedict suggests that the sacrament of the sick should be made available to struggling alcoholics.[51] She believes that the biggest obstacle to using the sacrament stems from society's (and the Church's) attitude toward alcoholism.[52] She notes that "Anointing is not intended to—and will not—do away with the need for medical and psychological help. We are not attempting to accomplish in a "magical" act a recovery that leapfrogs over the daily program of A.A., even though the same Spirit is active in both."[53] Benedict correctly states,

> The Church says that this sacrament may and should be celebrated with anyone whose health is seriously impaired. Recovering alcoholics know in stark terms how seriously impaired they are physically, mentally, emotionally and spiritually. The Sacrament of Anointing is certainly suitable for them.[54]

Moreover, the decision to participate in sacramental Anointing rests with both the alcoholic and the faith community (in the person of the priest). Since the Rite of Anointing emphasizes healing, libera-

---

[50] Pope John Paul II, "Drug Addiction and Alcoholism Frustrate the Person's Very Capacity for Communion and Self-Giving," *Dolentium Hominum,* 19: 8–9.

[51] Mary Grace Benedict, "Open the Sacrament of the Sick to Struggling Alcoholics," *St. Anthony Messenger* 96 (March 1989): 37–39.

[52] Ibid., p. 38.

[53] Ibid., p. 38.

[54] Ibid., p. 38.

tion, and reconciliation, the alcoholic who is in recovery could benefit from a further strengthening of those activities in a spiritual manner. Furthermore, if the alcoholic has a relapse and begins to drink again, yet returns to recovery, he or she would certainly be able to celebrate the sacrament again.

Thomas Weston notes that liturgical healing services can be a powerful moment in the life of someone who is recovering from an addiction.[55] In his retreat work with recovering alcoholics and drug addicts, Weston often uses sacramental Anointing to bring about healing. He says,

> Healing happens in a couple of ways. One, people start to have greater emotional freedom. A lot of folks drink and use drugs in order not to feel. A lot of it is self-medication. So a lot of people come into recovery with huge amounts of rage, huge amounts of grief, and huge amounts of loss. They're disconnected from their emotions. So they'll come to Eucharist or they'll come to Anointing, and they'll cry for the first time in 15 years. That's a healing. Their world starts getting bigger. They start getting a lot more tolerant. Thoughts start coming up of reconnecting with a praying community.[56]

Weston sees his work as building community by inviting those who are isolated by addictions to get to know other people on a basic level. Gradually, they will develop a curiosity and a hunger for prayer. For some, this will lead them back to a church. "Building community, building a sense of together, and building a sense of welcome, and also the notion that we're people on the way. This is a pilgrim church."[57]

Using both Benedict's and Weston's reflections as a starting point, it may be said that the sacrament of the sick may be used with all those who are suffering from serious addictions.[58] Again, the criteria involved are similar to that which was used with those who are mentally disordered. The addiction must be one that imposes a danger to the patient or to others, e.g. pedophilia. In other words, the addiction

---

[55] Thomas Weston, "Open the Sacrament of the Sick to Struggling Alcoholics," *Modern Liturgy* 19 (October 1992): 6–10.

[56] Ibid., pp. 6–7.

[57] Ibid., p. 10.

[58] Charles Gusmer notes, "Some rehabilitation centers for alcoholics under Catholic auspices regularly conduct communal Anointings, for alcoholism is considered a disease, as drug addiction might also be" (*And You Visited Me*, p. 85). Unfortunately, there has not been much written about

must so impair a person's functionality that he or she could die. Moreover, the addict must be under the care of a medical professional or be participating in a recovery program. He or she should be on the road to health and wholeness. Of course, those who have "hit bottom" are also candidates for Anointing because they are in many times very close to physical death. Because of the process of recovery, when an addict relapses and returns to his or her former addictive behavior, he or she could also receive the sacrament again (in accord with canon 1004 §2). As with mental disorders, the sacrament must not be administered to those who do not desire it. Finally, while some addictions (such as sexual addiction) may appear to be a defiance of God's law (and therefore sinful), it must be remembered that all addictions are illnesses and should be treated as such.

## Summary

In many ways, the road to recovery from addiction is like the road to recovery from sin. As redeemed sinners, our lives are a continual process of conversion away from sin and recommitment toward God. Despite our daily transgressions, we still seek out God's forgiveness and mercy. When we "miss the mark" of being a complete human being in our personal, communal, or religious lives, we do not stop in our relationality; rather, we continue to try to build deeper and more intimate relationships with ourselves, our neighbors, and our God.[59]

Just as "recovery" in the addictive healing process refers to an ongoing and vital part of the addict's life, so in addition we are considered "recovering sinners" who are in continual need of God's grace. "Recovery is an experience of getting better, getting freer, getting

---

the use of the sacrament of the sick with those who suffer from addictions. Major theologians and liturgists seem to ignore the issue. Perhaps this current discussion may encourage other theologians and liturgists to explore the issue in greater detail.

[59] In an excellent article, Kenneth F. Dougherty notes that "the priest can play a central role in motivating the sick alcoholic—and all who are sick—to regain physical and spiritual health . . . . The priest who is informed of the AA steps of recovery and understands the alcoholic as a person in need, can be of genuine service, especially in the second and third steps of AA, in which the alcoholic comes to an active belief and surrender of will and life to God. In this divine-human encounter the priest can mediate between the divine Physician and the penitent seeking help" [Kenneth F. Dougherty, "Battle of the Bottle," *The Priest* 28 (July–August 1972): 25]. While his comments are directed toward the alcoholic, they are applicable to all the different kinds of addictions. As he notes in his conclusion, "Truly it is a man-made mystery why the alcoholic drinks: and it is a God-given mystery why he or she stops. Priests should be prophetic witnesses to this mystery" (p. 27).

healthier, getting reconciled."[60] In short, recovering from sin or from an addiction is a lifelong process that involves integration of all the different dynamics of a person's life. Furthermore, it is not done in isolation. The recovering sinner or the recovering addict learns to become whole again in the context of a loving community of faith. The addict and the sinner need to learn that they are not God. Instead, they need to come to self-acceptance, forgiveness, and peace in the knowledge that God is present and active in their lives and in the lives of those around them. Moreover, all people in the community are "in recovery." No one has accomplished total integration. All are "on the road" to wholeness and holiness.

## Anointing People with AIDS

There have been many articles written about the AIDS virus. "The underlying cause of the acquired immunodeficiency syndrome (AIDS) is the human immunodeficiency virus (HIV), discovered by Professors Robert C. Gallo and Luc Montagnieur."[61] The origins of the HIV virus still elude us; however, evidence of the emergence of AIDS began in the mid- to late 1970s.[62] Because it emerged first in the homosexual communities, it was first thought to be particular to homosexuals. However, throughout the 1980s it spread to other parts of the general population through direct or indirect contact with homosexuals.

"The HIV virus is unusual because of the time between infection and subsequent development of disease."[63] In other words, while someone may be infected with the HIV virus, it may lie dormant for years before it evolves into full-blown AIDS. There are three stages to the process of infection. The first stage is the asymptomatic carrier stage. In other words, after infection, there are no detectable signs of AIDS. Once infected, a person is infectious for the remainder of his or her life. Moreover, the incubation period of the HIV virus can be protracted over a long period of time.[64] The second stage in

---

[60] McCormick, *Sin as Addiction*, p. 181.

[61] William Blattner, "Epidemiologic Considerations on AIDS," *Dolentium Hominum*, 13 (1990): 61.

[62] Blattner, "Epidemiologic Considerations on AIDS," p. 61.

[63] Blattner, "Epidemiologic Considerations on AIDS," p. 62.

[64] John F. Harvey, *The Truth about Homosexuality: The Cry of the Faithful* (San Francisco: Ignatius Press, 1996), p. 202.

development is the appearance of several symptoms including sudden unexplained weight loss, persistent diarrhea, the swelling of the lymph nodes, and chronic fatigue. This is often called AIDS-related complex (ARC). Persons who develop ARC are critically infected with the HIV virus. "The virus itself can directly attack the brain and central nervous system and bring about severe psychiatric and neurological disturbances."[65] The third stage is full-blown AIDS and involves the breakdown of the immune system of the body. "It leaves the body vulnerable to a series of opportunistic infections, including the development of various cancers and the occurrence of deadly infections from normally nonlethal organisms."[66] To date, this stage is always terminal. There are several ways to contract the virus:

I. Route
    A. Sexual
        1) male-to-female
        2) female-to-male (rare)
        3) male-to-male
    B. Parenteral
        1) Transfusion
        2) IV Drug Abuse
        3) Needle stick
    C. Mother-to-child
    D. Mucous Membrane/Cutaneous (rare)
II. Cofactors
    A. Lifestyle
        1) Large number of sexual partners
        2) Sexually promiscuous partner
        3) Drug abuse with needle sharing
        4) Crack cocaine abuse
    B. Traumatic sexual practice
    C. Coincident sexually transmitted diseases
    D. Host factors
III. Infectivity
    A. Virus strain
    B. Virus replication—antigenemia

---

[65] Ibid., pp. 202–203.
[66] Ibid., p. 203.

C. Immune status
    1) CD4 count
    2) Immune response to virus.[67]

The most common method of contracting HIV is through risky behavior; that is, transmission of bodily fluids through sexual activity and intravenous drug use. "Ultimately, the major goal of HIV prevention strategies is to bring about fundamental changes in behavior that eliminate risk of infection."[68]

At the present time, research is still being conducted to find a cure for AIDS. There have been some remarkable advances in the years since the virus was first discovered.[69] Moreover, there are many psychological aspects to consider in persons who suffer from AIDS. Some of these include risk of ostracism, discrimination, social isolation, pre-existing psychopathological and behavioral disturbances, and AIDS-Dementia Complex.[70] However, despite these advances in our understanding of how the HIV virus works, there still is no cure for AIDS. In fact, some have called the disease an epidemic because it has spread from the homosexual population to the heterosexual population. Moreover, there has been a marked increase of the transmission of AIDS from mothers to newborns.[71]

## Treatment of AIDS

AIDS is a terminal disease. There is no cure. The only steps that can be done to stop the virus are prevention and education. Because AIDS has risen to epidemic proportions, there are those who advocate strong, decisive measure for preventing its spread. These measures include the allocation of more funding for research and sexual education in schools, "including information on homosexual and heterosexual

---

[67] Blattner, "Epidemiologic Considerations on AIDS," p. 62. Low CD4+ T lymphocyte counts (CD4 counts) are associated with a variety of conditions including infections. In addition to the diagnosis of AIDS, CD4 counts are regularly used to make treatment decisions in people diagnosed HIV-positive, such as when to start antiretroviral medications and when to begin preventative antibiotics. (AIDSPanelReport.com, 15 May 2001, *Low CD4+ T lymphocyte counts,* p. 1).

[68] Blattner, "Epidemiologic Considerations on AIDS," p. 64.

[69] For example, the discovery of AZT as a selective anti-HIV agent. See Erik De Clercq, "Prospects for the Chemotherapy of AIDS," *Dolentium Hominum,* 13 (1990): 99–109.

[70] Carlo Lorenzo Cazzullo and Costanza Gala, "Psychological and Neuropsychiatric Aspects of AIDS," *Dolentium Hominum,* 13 (1990): 142–47.

[71] Harvey, pp. 205–11.

relationships."[72] Other methods include the promotion of condom use for both heterosexuals and homosexuals. Some have proposed self-control and sexual abstinence as well. In addition, more stringent requirements and precautions are now in place for those who donate blood and work with blood transfusions and needles.[73]

In terms of actual care of those infected with HIV and the AIDS virus, much work has been done. Hospices and hospital units have been specifically erected for the care of AIDS patients. Dioceses and civil governments have developed plans for educating the public about the virus. Moreover, there have been concerted efforts to urge compassion for those who are suffering with this terrible disease.[74]

Despite the education, two phenomena still occur. On the one hand, the virus is still being spread. In spite of calls for abstinence or "safe sex practices," more people are infected each day. On the other hand, as John F. Harvey points out, "many women and children are the innocent victims of the disease."[75]

## Church Teaching on Persons with AIDS

Since the outbreak of the AIDS virus, the Church has been in the forefront of promoting compassion and education to the world. From the efforts of Mother Theresa of Calcutta in establishing hospices to a host of documentation from Rome and local dioceses, the Church has pointed out the need to find a cure for the virus, but more importantly, has invited the world to be in solidarity with those who suffer.

In 1989, the Pontifical Council for Pastoral Assistance to Health Care Workers organized an international congress whose topic was "To Live: Why? AIDS."[76] At this congress, experts from the fields of medicine, psychiatry, the social sciences, and health care gathered to discuss a variety of topics pertaining to the spread of HIV and the AIDS virus. The titles of the various speeches illustrate the scope of this illness. Like other sicknesses, AIDS has ramifications in the historical, theological, medical, and anthropological spheres. Moreover, it

---

[72] Harvey, p. 208.

[73] Harvey, pp. 207–11. These measures are mentioned without prejudice to moral or ethical considerations. Those issues will be discussed in the section on Church teaching.

[74] Harvey, p. 211.

[75] Harvey, p. 212.

[76] The acts of the congress are found in *Dolentium Hominum*, 13 (1990).

not only attacks individuals, but families, communities, the Church
and the world are all affected. In subsequent congresses, the subject of
AIDS is always mentioned because it has become such an integral
health problem over the past twenty years.

At the local level, the United States Bishops have issued three
documents that discuss the issue of AIDS. *The Many Faces of AIDS:
A Gospel Response* was written in 1987.[77] Two years later, the National
Conference of Catholic Bishops issued *Called to Compassion and
Responsibility: A Response to the HIV/AIDS Crisis.*[78] The third document was *Always Our Children*, issued in 1997. In these documents,
the Bishops offer a brief historical sketch of the development and
progress of the AIDS virus. They also present some data about AIDS
and the persons whom it affects.

In *The Many Faces of AIDS*, the Bishops summarize their reflections: 1) AIDS is a human illness; 2) The Church has the responsibility
to stand in solidarity with those who suffer by providing spiritual
and pastoral care; 3) The Church also must offer a clear presentation
of Catholic moral teaching with respect to human sexuality; 4) Discrimination and violence against persons with AIDS is immoral;
5) Society must develop educational programs to prevent the spread
of the disease; and 6) Those who are infected must live in a way in
which others will not be endangered.[79]

In terms of morality, the document reaffirms the Church's
stance against "safe sex" practices. The Bishops note, "So-called 'safe
sex' practices are at best only partially effective. They do not take into
account either the real values that are at stake or the fundamental good
of the human person."[80] Moreover, the Bishops promote the need for
medical care of those who suffer with AIDS.

On the pastoral level, the Church offers "solidarity, comfort
and support" to persons with AIDS, their friends, and families.
"Offering or ensuring this human companionship is especially impor-

---

[77] United States Catholic Conference Administrative Board, "The Many Faces of AIDS:
A Gospel Response," *Origins* 17 (December 24, 1987): 481, 483–89. Hereafter *Faces* with the
appropriate page number from *Origins*.

[78] National Conference of Catholic Bishops, *Called to Compassion and Responsibility: A
Response to the HIV/AIDS Crisis* (Washington, D.C.: National Conference of Catholic Bishops,
1989). Hereafter *Called to Compassion* with the appropriate page number.

[79] *Faces*, p. 483.

[80] *Faces*, p. 486.

tant lest those who would diminish respect for life by encouraging euthanasia or suicide determine how to 'care' for persons with AIDS."[81] In an unfortunate lacuna, the document does not mention the use of the sacrament of the sick with those who suffer from AIDS, although it does encourage training programs for hospital eucharistic ministers, visitors to the sick, and confessors.[82]

In *Called to Compassion*, this lacuna is eliminated. Under the subtitle of "Ministry to Persons with HIV/AIDS," we read this:

> The Church offers all its members the rich treasury of grace through its sacramental life. For those who are ill, the Church offers the Sacrament of the Anointing of the Sick, together with the Sacrament of Penance and the Eucharist. These encounters with Christ in forgiveness, healing, and the restoration of the life of grace are profound moments of conversion and renewal.[83]

Moreover, the document also urges daily prayer for those who are suffering from HIV and AIDS. Furthermore, "Catholic health facilities should continue to provide local professional leadership in responding to the needs."[84]

In *Always Our Children*, the Bishops strongly assert: "Without condoning self-destructive behavior or denying personal responsibility, we reject the idea that HIV/AIDS is a direct punishment from God. . . . Nothing in the Bible or in Catholic teaching can be used to justify prejudicial or discriminatory attitudes and behaviors."[85]

Church ministers are encouraged to educate themselves about homosexuality and Church teaching as well as about HIV/AIDS so that they can be resources for the community. Moreover, ministers should

> include prayers in the liturgy for those living with HIV/AIDS, their caregivers, those who have died, and their families, companions and friends. A special Mass for healing and anointing of the sick might be connected with World AIDS Awareness Day (Dec. 1) or with a local AIDS awareness program.[86]

---

[81] *Faces*, p. 487.

[82] *Faces*, p. 487.

[83] NCCB, *Called to Compassion*, p. 27.

[84] NCCB, *Called to Compassion* p. 28.

[85] *Origins*, p. 101.

[86] *Origins*, p. 102.

In these three documents there is a progression of understanding about the AIDS virus. Furthermore, the Bishops more explicitly call for the use of the sacraments, especially the Anointing of the Sick, with those who suffer from HIV/AIDS. The Church has effectively taken a stand on supporting all of those who are afflicted with this disease. The Church further encourages all of its members to stand in solidarity with those who suffer.

### Summary

Infection of the HIV virus can lead to the development of AIDS. At the present time, the disease is always fatal, although new treatments are being developed to arrest the progression of the virus. While the majority of persons who have AIDS received it resulting from their own behavioral activity, increasingly, many are contracting the disease through no fault of their own.

The Church has consistently preached God's love for all creation. It also has highlighted the need for both compassion and responsibility in dealing with the AIDS crisis. As a Church, we are called to be compassionate and caring with those who suffer. Moreover, we have the duty to work toward alleviating that suffering and preventing the further spread of the HIV virus through education and research. However, the education must always be done in reference to the moral teaching of the Church. Finally, the Church commends to God's care not only those who suffer, but those who care for them as well.

### The Use of the Sacrament of the Sick with Persons with AIDS

While initially the Church did not propose sacramental Anointing for AIDS, in recent documentation, not only is sacramental Anointing encouraged, so is the public celebration of healing Masses and prayer services. Because AIDS is a terminal disease (like cancer or leukemia), those who suffer from this affliction are certainly candidates for receiving the sacrament. However, the AIDS patient must desire to receive the Anointing of the Sick. Because the illness is progressively degenerative, the sacrament may be repeated several times during the patient's sickness. In the case of those who are unconscious, they must have implicitly desired to receive the sacraments of the Church while they were still in control of their faculties.

Because of the origin of the disease (namely, sexual transmission and drug use), some priests may be tempted to deny reception of the sacrament or insist on sacramental confession and absolution prior to receiving Anointing based on canon 1007. This is a misinterpretation of the intent of the law. A person who requests a sacrament is presumed to do so in good faith, unless he or she publicly announces that he or she is flaunting God's law or Church teaching. The fact that the person is suffering with AIDS is sufficient for reception of the sacrament. If he or she is able to participate in sacramental confession prior to receiving the Anointing, this should be done. However, if he or she has requested sacramental Anointing, the priest should presume that the AIDS patient has contrition for his or her sins. Furthermore, in some cases, by the time the priest has been called, the disease is so far advanced that the patient is incapable of participating in a sacramental confession. It has been my experience that sometimes when I anoint a person with AIDS, the celebration of the sacrament causes a conversion in the person and he or she will call me back at a later date to discuss his or her life in an extended review of life followed by sacramental confession. In other words, God's grace is active even though the person may not be as contrite as the minister may like at that time. It is only by the presence of the priest and the celebration of Anointing that the person realizes that he or she needs to be more fully reconciled to God.

The Church offers to those who are afflicted with HIV and the AIDS virus pastoral and sacramental ministry in order to draw the patient out of isolation from himself or herself, from the community, and from God. In its ministry, the Church invites all people (not just the healthy) to community and solidarity with Christ as a result of repentance and a restoration of their relationships.

## CONCLUSION

This chapter has examined the ecclesial view of mental disorders, addiction, and sin. Because all illness encompasses the physiological, biological, cultural, social, psychological, historical, and spiritual dimensions of the human person, the Church has responded by adapting its ministry to the ill and suffering.

For the Church, illness is always seen in relation to the mission and ministry of Jesus Christ. Through the Paschal Mystery, Jesus became one with creation in order to redeem it. Through his Passion, death, and Resurrection, Christ transformed the created order and gave it a new purpose and meaning. Moreover, through his suffering and death, sickness and death have a new significance. Sickness and death no longer are seen as a punishment sent by God for disobedience and sin, but they are still a consequence of both original and personal sin. Rather, sickness and death become opportunities for an intimate, transformative encounter with the Trinity.

In serious illness, this encounter takes on an added meaning because the patient is confronted in a very real way with his or her own mortality. However, because of this experience, the patient may come to glimpse what awaits in paradise. A serious illness may be the occasion for conversion and reassessment in one's own life. Moreover, in serious illness, the patient has the opportunity to witness to the faith community as priest, prophet, and king. As priest, the patient may offer his or her sufferings as atonement for sin. One's sufferings are joined to Christ's and thus become salvific. As prophet, the patient is called to give testimony to what God has been doing in his or her life. The patient may share what he or she has learned from the illness and encourage others to bear their sufferings with humility and grace. Finally, as a king or leader of God's people, the seriously ill person may teach the Church how to suffer and die with dignity. He or she can be a person who builds community and becomes a leader of prayer within his or her own family. Furthermore, the patient is capable of leading others toward Christ by an example of faith and love.

The community gathered around the sick person may also bring about comfort and healing. It is a reminder to the patient that he or she is not alone. The community gathers to support the sick person physically, morally, and socially. Through its presence, the community reaches out to the patient and removes him or her from isolation. The Christian community, the Church, offers an additional dimension: that of faith. Through the presence of the faith community, the patient is reminded of God's healing presence. The Church draws the patient out of his or her isolation and alienation to manifest the vision of eternal life. In other words, the Church can assist the patient in transforming his or her perspective of illness from one of despair to one of hope.

It is clear that the Church is involved pastorally and sacramentally with those who are seriously ill, along with their families and caregivers. However, more needs to be done. In the pastoral realm, the Church must take a role of leadership in education, research, compassion, and ministry to all who suffer. Finally, the Church needs to continually examine her role as a healer in society, working toward building community, and bridging the gap between those who are alienated from society by illness and those who are healthy.

In the next chapter we will examine the role of healing in the world today. Various healing ministries will be studied to ascertain how men and women can more fully be healed in all dimensions of their personalities. We will also look at and evaluate a new vision of the Church as healer.

## Questions for Discussion

1. What is serious illness?
2. How can ministers (sacramental and pastoral) assist in healing the sick?
3. Besides Anointing persons with addictions, what other forms or rituals of leading to wholeness may be employed?
4. How can the Church more effectively minister to persons with sexual addictions?
5. Given that HIV and AIDS are still a major health threat, how can the Church more effectively minister to those who have these diseases, along with their families and their caregivers?

# Chapter 8

# The Church as Sacramental Healer

## INTRODUCTION

What does it mean to say that the Church is a healer? In this chapter we will discuss two areas: the role of the Church in healing, and the method of healing that the Church uses.

It is clear that the Church has a ministry of healing. This role was instituted by Christ's earthly ministry and promulgated in the letter of James. Furthermore, over the centuries the Church has taken an active interest in the welfare of those who were sick, suffering, or marginalized from society. It is safe to say that this role will continue into the future.

As members of the Church, we are called "to be signs of encouragement and models for all Christians and other persons of goodwill to be engaged in the struggle for health, healing and wholeness at the personal, community, national and global level."[1] In a small pamphlet written in 1982 for the Center for Applied Research in the Apostolate, Bernard Häring notes that the Church's role in healing in health care needs to shift. As members of the Body of Christ, the Christian community needs to be a sign of the loving and healing presence of Christ. "It is a presence that protects the sick from a feeling of alienation in the large hospitals, a presence that humanizes to the extent possible a success-oriented 'health industry' by focusing coherently on personal relationships and promoting a spirit of community."[2]

---

[1] Christian Medical Commission, Healing and Wholeness: *The Church's Role in Health* (Geneva: World Community Curches, 1990), p. 29.

[2] Bernard Häring, *The Healing Mission of the Church in the Coming Decades.* Washington, D.C.: Center for Applied Research in the Apostolate. 1982.

Moreover, the Church should take an active part in preventive medicine and searching for new models of health care[3] in the world. Some areas of development, which Häring sees as important, are home health care, educational programs, assistance to the handicapped, and health care in the prison system. "In all these services, great attention should be given to an integrated approach; in visits to the home of the sick, the elderly and the lonely, there should be spiritual assistance offered as well as physical and psychological care."[4]

Finally, Häring suggests that the Church should be a leader in promoting new types of preventive care. He notes,

> There are other great threats to health which cannot be overcome by the traditional approach or by preventive medicine. I am referring specifically to the devastating illnesses attributable to our style of life and our lopsided scale of values. This, in my opinion, is the major field where the Church should come in strongly, for within this area is the tangible connection between salvation, wholeness and health.
>
> In concert with the state and all social forces extant, but specifically through her own initiative, the Church should undertake and provide a program of holistic health education. From childhood through the twilight years, people should be thoroughly and systematically instructed on the all-encompassing meaning of ideal health, on the relationship between wholeness and health, on the personal and social responsibility to be assumed for one's own health and that of our neighbor. People should learn to appreciate, to discover and to mobilize their own inner resources and be of mutual assistance in this basic process of maintaining well-being: physically, psychologically, morally and spiritually.[5]

He continues to say that "the primary goal of a health education effort should be on healthy relationships with God, with fellowman, with oneself and with our environment."[6]

One role of the Church is to foster essential Catholic values in the world. These values include redemption and the worldwide mission and vision of faith, hope, and love. Häring notes that people are rediscovering age-old wisdom that involves a wholeness of mind,

---

[3] By *health care*, I mean methods of healing and restoring to health as opposed to insurance plans or governmental agencies.

[4] Häring, *The Healing Mission of the Church*, pp. 4–5.

[5] Ibid., p. 5.

[6] Ibid., p. 6.

body, and spirit interacting with others in a social context. "Any truly Christian health design has to be particularly attentive to these values and seek to diffuse them systematically as part of the healing-redeeming ministry of the Church."[7] Finally, Häring notes that the Church must be, in the words of Carl Jung, a "wounded-healer" so that in the process of healing, both the patient and the healer "will suffer together and grow together."[8]

Finally, the role of the Church in pastoral care is to say by her presence, attitude, nonverbal symbols, and even more importantly, the exhortatory word, "that God is present to sick persons in their fear or suffering, that God as loving, caring Father, as co-suffering Lord Jesus, as healing Spirit is present and acting, but this presence is in *mystery,*"[9] In other words, the task of the Church is to make present the mystery that is God. This mystery may be even more veiled in a person's sickness. The Church, through its ministers, helps to make present the *Deus absconditus* in order to allow the *Deus revelatus* to effect healing in the patient. In short, the Church reveals God and in turn is revealed by God as God's instrument of healing.

Since Häring made these suggestions, the Church has made remarkable strides in the area of pastoral care. Through the ministry of Pope John Paul II and the work of pastoral caregivers and theologians, the Church addressed many of Häring's concerns. As this book has shown, the Church has reiterated the need to heal the whole person—body, soul, spirit, and mind. Furthermore, the Church recognizes the role that the whole community plays in assisting in pastoral care and healing. The role of the Church in the health care setting is to be a community builder between the patients, their caregivers, and the community of faith. The Church serves as a wounded healer that is sign, symbol, and sacrament of both suffering and healing. More importantly, the Church reveals God as mystery and invites those who are ill to enter into this mystery with faith and trust. Finally, the Church has taken a leading role in addressing health care concerns (both medical and financial) within the global context.

---

[7] Ibid., p. 10.

[8] Ibid., p. 19.

[9] Benedict M. Ashley and Kevin D. O'Rourke, *Health Care Ethics: A Theological Analysis,* Fourth Edition (Washington, D.C.: Georgetown University Press, 1997), p. 446.

# The Methodology of the Church's Healing Mission

The question before us is one of methodology. How does the Church function as God's instrument of healing in the world? The short answer is "by celebrating the healing process in word and sacrament."[10] Pastoral care must deepen into experiencing the presence of God in prayer, worship, celebration, and communion.[11] The celebration of word and sacrament is not merely confined to a pastoral counseling situation or in a visit to the sick. We encounter word and sacrament on a daily basis in a variety of situations.

The Church, and especially the local community, faces many challenges. The Church is an instrument of both word and sacrament. The word is preached and lived through the Church's ministers and the congregation. While the minister may have the charism of being an "alter Christus" by virtue of ordination, all men and women are called to be like Christ by their Baptism. In some senses, we are all invited to become sacraments for one another by revealing, through our words and actions, *the* sacrament, Jesus Christ.

However, the Church, especially the Roman Catholic Church, has given her ministers the task of preaching the word and dispensing the sacraments. The challenge for all ministers is that they preach the word that is lived out in their lives. When they speak, it is Christ who speaks; when they act, it is Christ who acts. Moreover, in a sacramental rite, the minister stands in the person of Christ and in the person of the Church *(in persona Christi, in persona ecclesiae)*. In short, their task is to make present the primordial sacrament through human words and events.

From the previous chapters we have seen that the subject for Anointing is anyone who has fallen into serious illness. This includes those who are elderly, children, persons who suffer from a variety of addictions, those who are afflicted with mental disorders, and especially those who are in a state of actively dying.[12]

---

[10] Ashley and O'Rourke, *Health Care Ethics,* ibid, 1997, p. 447.

[11] Ibid., p. 447.

[12] See the *Catechism of the Catholic Church,* 1514 and 1515 (hereafter CCC).

Paragraphs 8 through 15 as well as 52 and 53 from *Pastoral Care of the Sick* outline the proper subjects for reception of sacramental Anointing. However, there are many others who are ill, yet are not in a state that requires sacramental action. These persons may include those who suffer from chronic illnesses that are kept in check by medicine (diabetes or asthma), those who are recovering from surgery, and those who are incapacitated by a broken limb or disease.

The Church has a responsibility to minister to anyone who has fallen into a state of illness or impairment. These include members of the Roman Catholic Church as well as individuals who do not share our beliefs yet are connected in some way to the ecclesial communion by blood, marriage, or fraternal association.

We have a responsibility to minister with compassion to those who request of us the presence of Christ the healer. In my experience this often occurs when a priest visits a nursing care facility or hospital. After he has anointed a parishioner, on occasion the person in the next bed also wishes to receive some sort of blessing as well. (This can often happen when an Extraordinary Minister of Holy Communion distributes the Eucharist in a public setting. The priest or minister is often asked by a non-Catholic person if he or she can "have some too." While the Extraordinary Minister must deny Communion to one who is not in union with the Roman Catholic Church, the situation is slightly different for the priest who is administering Anointing as well as the one who is visiting the sick.)

According to the *Ecumenical Directory*, sacramental Anointing may be given to someone who is not Roman Catholic provided that the subject ask for Anointing of his or her own accord and that a minister of that person's own ecclesial communion is not available. Also, he or she should manifest a belief in the Church's ministry to the sick. Given these parameters, the priest may make a pastoral judgment to anoint the person. At the very least, however, he should pray with the patient and his or her family if they are present. He may also offer a blessing and promise to remember them in his Masses or prayers.

For the minister who is not a priest, he or she may also minister to the patient and the patient's family even if they are not Roman Catholic. This is a noble task on two fronts. First, the minister is acting *in the person of Christ*, which flows from his or her Baptism as a Christian. Each of us is called to do corporal works of mercy for the building up of God's kingdom, and no distinction is made whether the recipient of our ministry is Roman Catholic or not. Second, when we minister, we participate in the New Evangelization about which Pope John Paul II had often written and spoken. As the decree which promulgated the ritual states: "When the Church cares for the sick, it serves Christ himself in the suffering members of his Mystical Body. When it follows the example of the Lord Jesus, who 'went about doing good and healing all' (Acts 10:38), the Church obeys his command to care for the sick (see Mark 16:18)."[13]

## THE MINISTERS OF PASTORAL CARE TO THE SICK

Who are the ministers of pastoral care? We all are. Every person has the duty to fight against illness: the one who is ill, his or her doctors, nurses, and caregivers, the patient's family and friends, the pastor, the deacon, the other ministers of healing, the parish community, and the Church at large. When one member of the mystical body suffers, all suffer. Yet because of this communion, each and every individual participates in the ministry of healing.

*Pastoral Care of the Sick* illustrates this so beautifully with this reminder:

> Part of the plan laid out by God's providence is that we should fight strenuously against all sickness and carefully seek the blessings of good health, so that we may fulfill our role in human society and in the Church. Yet we should always be prepared to fill up what is lacking in Christ's suffering for the salvation of the world as we look forward to creation's being set free in the glory of the children of God (see Colossians 1:24; Romans 8:19–21).[14]

Each of those individuals mentioned has a particular role to play in the restoration of the patient. The one who is ill must cooperate fully in achieving his or her recovery. The patient must follow the doctor's orders in terms of taking medication, participating in therapy, and pursuing a proper diet and exercise regimen. Medical professionals should be honest with the patient and his or her family regarding

---

[13] PCS, p. 13. See also CCC, 1509.
[14] PCS, 3.

the diagnosis, prognosis for recovery, as well as alerting them to any potential problems in the healing process. Moreover, they must treat the patient with dignity and respect. They are to remember that the individual who has come to them for treatment is a human being, who needs to be treated physically as well as spiritually, and certainly never as an object for scientific research or a statistic. Since the patient is a child of God with free will and intellect, his or her wishes should be respected by family members and caregivers. A bond of intimacy exists between the patient and the caregivers, but this intimacy can be broken or distorted when the caregiver forgets that the patient is ultimately responsible for his or her own recovery.

While medical professionals play an important role in the healing process, it is the Church that reminds us of the mystery of human sickness. All who minister to the sick, whether sacramentally or not, must be aware of the link between suffering and salvation. As debilitating as sickness and disease are, there is always a ray of hope. The minister must help to keep that hope alive in the patient. This is not to give a false sense of recovery; rather, the hope that is given is that all suffering has value if viewed as a passage to a deeper relationship with God. For example, the minister should not tell the patient that God will heal the afflicting cancer if only he or she gives up smoking. Nor should the minister contradict anything that the medical professionals are saying. On the contrary, the ministers of healing should cooperate with the doctors and nurses and encourage the patient to do the same. This can be particularly helpful if the patient is resistant to medical procedures.

The parish community supports the patient, the family, and the medical professionals through their prayers both at the Eucharistic liturgy as well as in private. In their prayer, the members of the local Church keep the patient connected to the wider community of faith. The power of prayer has many wide-reaching effects, not the least of which is reminding all those who pray of the essential and higher things.

The wider Church community also assists the patient in recovery by including him or her in the universal prayer of the Church at each Eucharistic celebration. In its universal prayer, the Church calls to mind that no one is isolated. All those who feel estranged from the wider community are not forgotten. In the Prayers of the Faithful, each parish community commends its sick and suffering to the intercession of the whole Church. In this way no one is anonymous. Although we may not know an individual's name, we know that there are individuals who are suffering and in need of our prayerful support, and we can—and should—offer up prayers for them.

## Preparing the Patient to Meet God

The *Catechism of the Catholic Church* notes that there are four primary effects of the sacrament of the sick. "The first grace of this sacrament is one of strengthening, peace and courage to overcome the difficulties that go with the condition of serious illness or the frailty of old age."[15] The second effect of the sacrament is to unite the patient with the Passion of Christ. In other words, the suffering that one endures becomes a participation in the saving work of Jesus.[16] Moreover, through this sacrament, the patient contributes to the sanctification of the Church.[17] Finally, participation in the sacrament of the sick prepares the patient for the final journey.[18] We know that not every illness will be healed. Some are too far along to be cured. Furthermore, it may not be in God's plan that this particular individual should be restored to full health. In these situations, the role of the Church is to prepare the patient to meet God face to face. This is done in a variety of ways. First, honesty is the best policy. It only exacerbates the situation when a patient is kept in the dark about his or her prognosis. If the patient is lied to and later comes to realize the truth, he or she will feel betrayed and this may lead to further depression. Second, in proclaiming hope, the minister should recognize that the patient may not be there yet, but may still be at one of the earlier stages on the Kubler-Ross continuum.[19] The minister should take into account that a person may not move quickly to the acceptance stage. It is not the minister's role to force patients to move toward a particular stage, but to minister to them where they are currently. The minister may encourage the patient to move toward acceptance of the inevitable; however, if the patient

---

[15] CCC, 1520.

[16] CCC, 1521.

[17] CCC, 1522.

[18] CCC, 1523.

[19] Elisabeth Kubler-Ross identified the stages of grieving in this way: denial and isolation, anger, bargaining, depression, and acceptance.

is currently in the denial phase, the minister will need to assist the patient in working through the disbelief at his or her situation.

Once the patient has moved into the stage of acceptance, the minister can assist him or her in preparing for death. This means helping the patient to tie up loose ends spiritually as well as relationally.

## The Minister of the Sacrament and the Community

As the *Ordo Unctionis infirmorum* (OUI) states, the minister for the sacrament of the sick is a priest. "This office is ordinarily exercised by bishops, pastors and their assistants, chaplains of health-care facilities, and superiors of clerical religious institutes."[20] There has been an effort, especially in the United States, to allow permanent deacons and non-ordained lay and religious chaplains of health care facilities to administer the sacrament of Anointing the Sick. The argument given is that since they deal with the sick and their families on a daily basis, "it is pastorally awkward to have a priest who may be a total stranger or who has had little contact with a patient to celebrate that sacrament that epitomizes the Church's total pastoral concern for the sick person."[21] While some address this issue from a historical perspective,[22] it seems to me that the problem solves itself if the patient or the patient's family were to call their parish priest at the first signs of serious illness. Moreover, as the length of a hospital stay has become shorter, there really is not ample time for the lay chaplain of a large hospital to get to know his or her patients.

From a theological perspective, the priest, by virtue of his ordination, functions *in persona Christi capitis, in persona ecclesiae*. He stands in the person of Christ the head and in the person of the Church. He represents the community of the faithful. Deacons cannot do this, nor can any other member of the community. The priest is the officially recognized representative not only of his local parish community, but the Church universal as well. In the sacrament of the sick, the Church (not just the local community) comes to the patient in the person of the priest. The Church offers comfort and healing in the person

---

[20] PCS, 16.

[21] John J. Ziegler, "Who Can Anoint the Sick?" *Worship* 61 (January 1987): 26.

[22] Ziegler's article is an excellent historical survey of the issue. However, he concludes that the Church should address this issue and open the administration of the sacrament to deacons and lay ministers "so that the church can more effectively give witness to that special concern that the Lord Jesus always had for those burdened by the cross of illness" (p. 44).

of the priest. The Church reconciles, heals, and reintegrates the patient back into the community through the ministry of her priests.[23]

However, given all that has been said in this chapter about the role of the community as instruments of healing, it is imperative to remember that the priest represents the community, but he is not *the* community. His ministry as sacramental healer needs to be supported and sustained by a praying, worshipping community of faith. He *should not exercise* his ministry in isolation. It is true that God works through the person of the priest and the sacrament, but the members of the Church who are gathered around the sickbed are also conduits of healing energy and power. Through their service of the sick person, parishioners (as well as medical professionals) can also bring about healing, through prayer, through presence, through conversation, and through performing household tasks such as cooking, cleaning, and changing bed linens.

In short, only priests may anoint those who are ill. However, all persons are to "assist the sick by being with them in difficult moments, encouraging them to receive the sacraments of Penance and the Anointing of the Sick, by helping them to have the disposition to make a good individual confession, as well as to prepare them to receive the Anointing of the Sick."[24] Moreover,

> Kindness shown toward the sick and works of charity and mutual help for the relief of every kind of human want are held in special honor. Every scientific effort to prolong life and every act of care for the sick, on the part of any person, may be considered a preparation for the Gospel and a sharing in Christ's healing ministry.
>
> It is thus especially fitting that all baptized Christians share in this ministry of mutual charity within the Body of Christ by doing all that they can to help the sick return to health, by showing love for the sick, and by celebrating the sacraments with them. Like the other sacraments, these too have a community aspect, which should be brought out as much as possible when they are celebrated.[25]

In the process of celebration, all the members present, not just the sick person, are given hope and are strengthened in their faith in Christ.

---

[23] CCC, 1516.

[24] *Instruction on Certain Questions Regarding the Collaboration of the Non-Ordained Faithful in the Sacred Ministry of Priest* (Vatican City: Libreria Editrice Vaticana, 1997). Art. 9, § 1.

[25] PCS, 32–33.

Furthermore, because the ritual is efficacious, *all* who participate are renewed, restored, and touched by the healing presence of Christ.

In a fairly recent article, Todd E. Johnson examined the issue of ritual healing.[26] He noted that when one participates in a ritual event, one cannot help but to be affected by the ritual action:

> Therefore, one's physical participation in ritual affects one's mind; and because one's mind is the result of somatic activity in the brain, there is an ontological link between metaphoric or ritual action and somatic states. In other words, one does not have a body, one is a body. A mental state is a physical state; physical states affect mental conditions, and mental conditions alter physical states.[27]

In terms of healing, those who participate in the healing ritual are affected by it in some way. Some people may be physically cured while others will experience a calming effect of their anxiety.

Johnson refers to the work of Emile Durkheim, Bronislaw Malinowski, Mary Douglas, Daniel Moerman, T. J. Scheff, Abraham Maslow, and Meredith McGuire in examining the issue of efficacy in ritual healing. While it is beyond the scope of this book to thoroughly analyze Johnson's work, he does raise some interesting points regarding the role of the community in sacramental Anointing.

In citing Mary Douglas's work, Johnston notes that ritual healing creates a hermeneutic frame for experience. The ritual helps to create a new reality or perspective:

> Ritual healing for Douglas need not have a miraculous outcome to be efficacious. Instead the locus of efficacy in ritual healing can be found in the realm of individual consciousness, as it embodies that which transcends one's own existential reality. Hence, ritual healing is the process of symbolic role and world definition for those who participate, creating new alternatives for as long as the rituals and their symbols are valued.[28]

In other words, participation in the ritual becomes transformative. The ritual of Anointing of the Sick is a vehicle for communication between the human and the divine which conveys meaning and power.

---

[26] Todd E. Johnson, "Ritual Healing: A Model of Ritual Efficacy?" *Questions Liturgiques: Studies in Liturgy* 78 (1997): 148–63.

[27] Ibid., p. 150.

[28] Ibid., pp. 151–52.

Johnson further notes (based on the work of Abraham Maslow) that "a ritual of healing, because of its corporate nature, creates a shelter under which the community may stand protected from the fear of death and is reinforced by their mutual support."[29] Johnson posits that

> healing rituals must be understood to operate on three levels: 1) on the physical level they attempt to thwart illness and ward off the impending death which it foreshadows; 2) they negate the social implication of death, that being isolation; and 3) they provide an existential context in which to live in spite of death. Therefore an efficacious ritual of healing is a central and dominant myth which subordinates all other mythic systems under its world view and offers mediation on the physical, social, and existential levels.[30]

Sacramental Anointing, as an efficacious ritual of healing, transforms the meaning of illness and death by offering the hope of eternal life for both the patient and the community of faith. Moreover, the sacramental ritual removes the patient from isolation by reintegrating him or her into ecclesial communion. Finally, through the sacramental Anointing, a person is freed from sin, saved, and raised up; in other words, he or she is given a new existential context for living. The community, for its part, is invited to see the patient, not as a sick person, but as one who is living in the love and mercy of the Lord, graced by the Holy Spirit.

## QUESTIONS FOR DISCUSSION

1. What is the role of the Church in healing ministry?
2. How does the Church effect healing?
3. What is the role of the non-ordained in the ministry of healing?
4. Who are the ministers to the sick? How do they function? How do they cooperate with one another in the ministry of healing?
5. What is the relationship between the medical practitioner and the sacramental minister?

---

[29] Ibid., p. 154.
[30] Ibid., p. 156.

Chapter 9

# The Liturgical Praxis of the Roman Catholic Church

## INTRODUCTION

What is distinctive about the Roman Catholic Church is the emphasis on sacraments as actions of encounter with Christ, the primordial sacrament.[1] In her practice the Church not only preaches about health care and healing, the Church also heals sacramentally. The Church must certainly function as a "wounded healer" and give witness to the healing power of God. Moreover, the Church should be a leader in health care education and in providing health services. However, the primary role of the Church is not to be a "quasi-religious social service agency," nor solely a teacher about health. The Church as sacrament is called to heal through the sacrament of Anointing the Sick. The minister of Anointing stands in the person of Christ and heals the patient through the forgiveness of sins, the strengthening of the will and spirit, and through a sacramental encounter with Christ.

As was discussed earlier, the ultimate goal for many alternative and mystical medical practices was not so much health, but wholeness. In those contexts, wholeness came to mean spiritual wholeness. In a sacramental encounter, the person becomes whole again. While the person may not be physically restored to health, in the performance of the rite, he or she touches the holy and becomes restored to life itself.

The shamans and witch doctors of some pagan religions speak about a transformation and a restoration of balance within a person's

---

[1] The Orthodox Church and other ecclesial communions have sacramental practice as well; however, the primary focus of this section is how the sacrament of the sick is used in the Roman Catholic Church.

life. Alternative medical practices often refer to a growth of self-awareness within the patient and the need to harness the healing energy that each person has within himself or herself. In the sacramental encounter of the Roman Catholic rites of the sick, the patient is transformed and restored to balance. The force that energizes and heals is life and love, which we call God. The sacrament of the Anointing of the Sick heals by allowing people to encounter the mystery of God. In that encounter, many things happen: the forgiveness of sins, the healing of broken relationships, the restoration to the community of faith, and the transmission of peace and wholeness that can only come from Christ. More importantly, in the sacramental encounter, the patient and his or her family and friends are given a glimpse of the eschatological reality of the resurrection.

This chapter's focus is on the sacramental praxis as it currently stands. Some theologians, permanent deacons, and health care professionals have called for at least a clearer explication of the healing effect of the sacrament of the sick. However, given the history of the sacrament (see chapters 2, 3, and 4) and the definition of *serious illness* in our world today (see chapter 6), the sacramental rite offers many opportunities to express the Church's healing ministry. What is needed is a focus on the healing effect of Anointing, which may be accomplished through catechesis and the homily. Moreover, ministers (especially priests, pastoral ministers, and hospital chaplains) should be aware of the various illnesses and diseases with which the sacrament may be used. We will consider some practical considerations and suggestions for using the sacrament of the sick in various parish situations:

1. Private celebrations of the sacrament
2. Public celebrations of the sacrament
3. Nonsacramental celebrations for those who are ill

## PRIVATE CELEBRATIONS OF THE SACRAMENT

The presumption of this section is that the patient is in a non-emergency setting. That is, he or she is seriously ill, but is not in immanent danger of death but merely in proximate danger. Because the sacrament is a communal act of the Church, it is important that the community be gathered even when the rite is celebrated in a private setting.

If the purpose of the sacrament is to help patients escape their sense of isolation, it is best if family and friends can be present, which would include when possible the nurse and physician. Furthermore, if the sacrament is not to mark the end of life, but to help in the healing process, both physical and spiritual, it is certainly not separated from or in competition with the medical work of the hospital. Rather, it is part of the healing process. In fact, it is a celebration of God's healing work, which God performs not only through the ritual, but also through the *ministry* of the physicians, nurses, and administrators. Priests are not the only ministers of health; they are part of a psychosomatic healing *team,* every member of which is called by God to a healing work and empowered by him through their natural gifts and education. The priest's special role on this team is to make explicit and eucharistic (thankful) the work of all.[2]

In short, in the private celebration (especially when done in a hospital or nursing home setting), the patient, the patient's family, and care-givers should be present throughout the rite, participating in it by reading scripture and saying some of the prayers. An opportunity should be given for offering gratitude to the medical staff, both by the priest and by the patient.

For some of the illnesses mentioned in chapters 6 and 7, the patient may feel embarrassed or self-conscious about having family members or medical staff present. In these cases, the priest and the patient could celebrate the sacrament in private. Such illnesses might include mental disorders, addictions (especially in the case where the family is unaware of the addiction), and AIDS (especially when the patient has just been diagnosed and no one else is aware of his or her condition). However, in any case, because the priest acts *in persona ecclesiae,* the community is always present, not just the earthly community but the communion of saints as well.

In the private celebration of the rite, it is important that the minister and patient "connect" socially and sacramentally. In sickness, as we have noted, a patient often feels alienated and fearful. The personal, humane presence of the priest may put the patient at ease and relax him or her. Moreover, when the priest touches the patient with a handshake, by an imposition of hands or in the Anointing itself,

---

[2] Benedict M. Ashley and Kevin D. O'Rourke, *Health Care Ethics: A Theological Analysis,* 4th edition (Washington, D.C.: Georgetown University Press, 1997), pp. 449–51.

it conveys the sense of "acceptance." A physical touch lets the patient know that he or she is accepted by God, by the Church, and by *this* particular minister. A touch is especially important in cases where the patient has been scarred or has a disease that is abhorrent to many people.[3]

On the sacramental level, the priest should use generous amounts of oil and a soothing touch to convey "the sense of soothing pain and infusing life and movement."[4] Finally, in any sacramental ritual whether private or public, but especially in the sacrament of the sick, at no time should the priest give the impression that "this Anointing is one of seven I have to do today" or that "I've got to get back to the parish because I've got more important work to do." Body language, attitude, and touch, probably more important than the words spoken, convey much about the minister and his approach to sacramental healing. If the priest gives the impression that Anointing is superstition or really should be reserved for those who are dying, patients will react accordingly. However, if the priest tries to convey a sense of efficacy—that this sacrament really does heal—patients will begin to respond in a more positive manner.

The sacrament of the Anointing of the Sick is a powerful catechetical tool as well as an instrument of God's healing. It can teach the patient, his or her family, and caregivers about the power of God's love and concern for all of his children, but especially for the sick. The minister, by his attitude and presidential style, conveys the richness of the sacrament and teaches the theology of the sacrament in both word and action.

## PUBLIC CELEBRATIONS OF ANOINTING

The public Anointing service, usually celebrated within the context of the Eucharistic liturgy, is also a tool for catechesis on a much wider scale. In the preparation for a public communal celebration, there are many opportunities to offer catechesis on the theology of the sacrament,

---

[3] Examples would be someone who has survived a vicious physical attack or who has leprosy or AIDS. Of course, precautions should be taken if the illness is highly contagious or if the priest could infect the patient. In those cases, even if the priest is wearing protective clothing or gloves, he should still make the effort to touch the patient or shake the patient's hand.

[4] Ashley and O'Rourke, *Health Care Ethics*, p. 449.

the praxis, and the recipient of Anointing. In a parish celebration, for example, in the weeks preceding the liturgy it is necessary to publicize the date, but also to invite those who are ill, either privately or through bulletin announcements. However, the recipients should be known to the pastor and priests who are conducting the liturgy, before the moment of reception. In other words, when advertising a public communal Anointing liturgy, those who intend to receive the sacrament should contact the parish office to make their intention known. Furthermore, they should indicate the nature of their illness and how long they have been suffering with it. If possible, the priest himself should compile the list of recipients in order to ascertain the seriousness of their illnesses and to persuade those who are not seriously ill to refrain from receiving the sacrament.

At the liturgy itself, the recipients for Anointing should be identified by a nametag. They should be seated with their caregivers or family members in such a way that the priest may perform the laying on of hands and Anointing with ease. The medical staffs from local hospitals, nursing homes, and hospices should be invited to attend as well. The environment should be festive and welcoming—like an infant Baptism. The parish should also be invited to participate in roles of service and hospitality as well as attend the liturgy. An announcement reminding the congregation that only those who are identified as recipients will be allowed to receive the sacrament should be given at the beginning of the liturgy.

During the homily, the priest should open up the riches contained in the scripture readings and do a short catechetical reflection on the theology of the Anointing of the Sick. As the sick are receiving the sacrament, songs could be sung or music played softly in the background. Moreover, the liturgy should never feel rushed or thrown together. Those who are seriously ill may already feel alienated from the community. A poorly planned liturgy will convey the message that "you're really not wanted here, but we have to do this." At the end of the liturgy, there should be an opportunity for hospitality and fellowship in the parish center or other suitable place.

As I mentioned before, because of the nature of their illnesses, people with mental disorders, addictions, and AIDS may not wish to take part in a general Anointing service. Ministers may consider the possibility (and feasibility) of offering "specialized" communal Anointing liturgies. For example, those who are part of the local Alcoholics Anonymous group may wish to celebrate the sacrament in their group. Anointing services could be planned for those who are confined to a mental hospital for treatment. On December 1, AIDS Awareness Day, consider planning a communal Anointing liturgy for the vicariate or diocese. HIV and AIDS patients along with their families, friends, and caregivers could plan and participate in the liturgy. There may be other "special interest" groups that could also benefit from a communal Anointing liturgy, which is geared to their particular illness. In all of these cases, it is imperative that there be planning and coordination so that the liturgy truly can be a more uplifting, Spirit-filled, and effective sacramental experience.

## Communal Anointing Abuses

It should be remembered that the Anointing of the Sick is a *sacrament,* not a sacramental. Anointing is not for everyone; it is not even for everyone who is sick or "doesn't feel well." The sacrament of the sick is only for those who are seriously ill. Unfortunately, there have been many abuses in the area of communal Anointing. Three are mentioned below as examples.

A very common abuse (perhaps done out of ignorance) is to invite everyone present at the communal Anointing liturgy to come forward to receive the sacrament. While everyone present may be sick or suffering in mind, body, or spirit, not everyone is seriously ill. When this invitation is made, people who are in a state of perfect health might come forward. This action has the potential to "cheapen" the sacrament. The Anointing of the Sick is not to be compared to Ash Wednesday, Palm Sunday, or Saint Blase Day, recalling the words of James, "if anyone is sick among you, let him send for the presbyters of the Church." The Church comes to the sick person, not vice-versa. Therefore, as I noted above, it is important that the priest knows who is coming to receive the sacrament. By making an appointment to be present at the communal Anointing liturgy, the sick person has "summoned the presbyter." Moreover, if the person is not already on the parish sick list, he or she may be included for prayers and additional pastoral follow-up after the Anointing service. If the suggestions mentioned above are taken, many potential problems in this area will be eliminated.

A second abuse, related to the first, is to create a "quasi-sacramental" Anointing service. At a recent parish mission in a large Midwestern American diocese,[5] the theme was "What would you like God to heal?" After the opening rites, scripture readings, and homily, the congregation was invited to reflect on these questions: What needs healing in my life? Do I really *want* to be healed? What makes me afraid to "be like clay" in God's hands? Following this reflection was the "ritual action," which I quote here:

> You will be invited to come forward and be "anointed." There are three oils: an Oil of Healing, an Oil of Renewal and an Oil of Endurance. Donna _____ will have the Oil of *Healing* in the *center* (in front of the altar), Sister _____ will have the Oil of *Renewal* on the *right* and Sheila _____ with the Oil of *Endurance* on the *left*. You may choose to be anointed with any oil(s) for which you feel the most need. You may choose to be anointed with more than one of the oils.

I offer a few brief comments. Theologically, a service of this type further confuses the issue of the sacrament of the sick. Moreover, the oil of the sick which is blessed by the Bishop has the capacity to heal, renew, and strengthen those who are seriously ill. We do not distinguish between the different types of healing. All those who are seriously ill are in need of healing, restoring, and strengthening. Also, in this example the ministers of "Anointing" are all women. Perhaps to avoid confusion between this Anointing service and sacramental Anointing, the priest who presided at this service did not anoint. Finally, this service was conducted two years after the promulgation of August 15, 1997, on the *Instruction on Certain Questions Regarding the Collaboration of the Non-Ordained Faithful in the Sacred Ministry of Priest*.[6] The *Instruction* offers this clarification: "Since they are not priests, in no instance may the non-ordained perform anointings either with the Oil of the Sick or *any other oil*."[7] Perhaps this parish was unaware of the *Instruction* or they deliberately chose to ignore it.

---

[5] The diocese and parish shall remain nameless, to protect the parties involved.

[6] *Instruction on Certain Questions Regarding the Collaboration of the Non-Ordained Faithful in the Sacred Ministry of Priests* (Vatican City: Libreria Editrice Vaticana, 1997). Hereafter abbreviated as *Instruction* with the appropriate citation.

[7] *Instruction*, Art. 9,§ 1, (emphasis added).

A third abuse is rooted in the history of the sacrament. Father Joseph Champlin in his book *Healing in the Catholic Church* writes,

> A growing number of people today have begun to employ a blessed oil similar to the sacramental oil applied to the body during the ritual for anointing of the sick when they pray for those who are in any way ill or hurting.
>
> The older Roman Ritual contains a blessing for such oil immediately after the blessing of lard and immediately before the blessing of oats. This prayer of blessing (limited to a bishop or priest) as well as the rubrical directions do not restrict its use to the clergy. In fact the text almost presumes lay persons will be the main people employing this oil: "Grant, we pray, that those who will use this oil, which we are blessing in your name, may be delivered from all suffering, all infirmity, and all the wiles of the enemy. . . ."
>
> Parish leaders need to explain the oil's value, indicate its difference from the oil in the sacrament of anointing, and show how in practice the oil can be applied during prayer for healing.[8]

While Champlin is correct in citing the prayer from an ancient source,[9] the fact is that the new ritual does not provide for an Anointing of oil for use by the non-ordained. Moreover, the ancient prayers over the oil were used at a time when there was much fluidity between what was considered a "sacrament" and a "sacramental."[10] Although it is an ancient source, the liturgy and theology evolve. What may have been a practice in the ninth or tenth century no longer exists or has been abrogated for a variety of reasons. Lay Anointing is one such example.

In short, public communal Anointing liturgies need to be well planned in order not to add to the confusion that already exists and to provide for an enriching, healing experience. Many options may be used and adapted to the recipients involved. While there may be some confusion or ambiguity about the sacrament being for the sick or for the dying, the role of the priest and parish staff members is to clarify

---

[8] Joseph Champlin, *Healing in the Catholic Church: Mending Wounded Hearts and Bodies*, (Huntington, IN: Our Sunday Visitor, Inc., 1985), pp. 115–16.

[9] Unfortunately, he cites a secondary source instead of the primary one. Many of the early prayers mentioned oil, so it is difficult to ascertain to which he is specifically referring. The source cited is Francis MacNutt, *The Power to Heal* (Notre Dame, IN: Ave Maria Press, 1977), pp. 247–49. It was unavailable to the author for verification.

[10] Also is the issue of whether "lay Anointing" was considered a sacrament. By the twelfth century, it was fairly clear that the sacrament of the sick was performed by a priest.

and catechize. In organizing a celebration of communal Anointing, there are many opportunities for education before, during, and after the liturgy. Finally, pastoral care of the sick does not begin with, nor end with, the Anointing liturgy. The care of the sick and dying is the responsibility of the whole faith community.

## NONSACRAMENTAL CELEBRATIONS WITH THE SICK (NOT SERIOUSLY ILL)

As noted throughout this book, the sacrament of the sick is for those who are seriously ill. However, some people are not seriously ill, yet could benefit from some liturgical celebration. What options are available? First, sacramental Anointing is not an option. Nor is a quasi-sacramental service (such as was described in the previous section) an option. However, the Church does provide for ministry to the sick in a sacramental or liturgical setting. Some of these services are found in the *Book of Blessings*. The scripture passages and prayers from *Pastoral Care of the Sick* (PCS) also offer some elements that may be included in a rite of prayer.

While there is a temptation to simulate the Rite of Anointing, priests and other liturgical ministers should avoid confusion. Prayers for healing are always appreciated by those who are ill. However, the use of oil is always to be avoided. The *Book of Blessings* provides some rituals for use with parents who have miscarried or with those who were victims of a crime or oppression. Moreover, there is a section of prayers for those who are sick.[11]

For those who have died, the PCS provides prayers to be used with the family. Although the new rite has been in existence for many years, people still want their dying relatives to receive the "last rites." In the previous ritual, a person could be anointed conditionally if there was some doubt that life still remained (however minimal) after "death." "Perhaps a better procedure is to assure the family that the patient

---

[11] *Book of Blessings* (American Edition), #279–301 concern the Order for the Blessing of Parents after a Miscarriage; chapter 2, #376–450 contains the Orders for the Blessing of the Sick, including those suffering from addiction or substance abuse (#407–429) and those who are victims of crime or oppression (#430–450). However, based on the research of chapter 3, some people who are addicted or who have been victimized may also be candidates for reception of the sacrament of the sick.

received the proper rites of the Church, meaning by this that the priest has prayed for the departed and blessed the body, since in such circumstances these are the proper rites according to the present discipline."[12]

## Rite of Exorcism

In 1999, the Church published the new ritual for exorcism.[13] Discussion of exorcism lies outside the scope of this book; however, it is important to note that exorcism as a rite is a sacramental, not a sacrament. Moreover, it is only to be used in the most extreme of cases. Because someone with a mental disorder could manifest similar symptoms to demonic possession, the exorcist must be sure that the person truly is possessed. Furthermore, the exorcist must distinguish between superstition and real possession. Finally, the exorcist should consult with Church-approved physicians and psychiatrists before deciding to perform an exorcism.[14]

In the next chapter we will discuss the various options available for sacramental and nonsacramental healing rituals that may be used with those who are ill to varying degrees.

## VIATICUM AND "LAST RITES"

Chapter five in *Pastoral Care of the Sick* concerns the celebration of Viaticum. Simply put, Viaticum is the Eucharistic "food for the passage through death to eternal life."[15] When the dying Christian receives Eucharist for the last time, he or she is reminded of the Lord's promise of the resurrection. It is recommended that those who participate in the rites of Viaticum receive Communion under both kinds if they are able. Furthermore, if the dying person lingers after receiving Viaticum, he or she may continue to receive it on successive days leading up to his or her death. The Church envisions two ceremonies: *Viaticum Within Mass* and *Viaticum Outside Mass*. In the event that it is possible for the patient to participate in the Eucharistic sacrifice,

---

[12] Ashley and O'Rourke, *Health Care Ethics*, p. 451.

[13] *De Exorcismis et supplicationibus quibusdam* (Città del Vaticano: Typis Vaticanis, 1999).

[14] Crista Kramer von Reisswitz, "Exorcism Rite Reformed," *Inside the Vatican* (March 1999): 30–33.

[15] PCS, 175.

the Mass may be celebrated at the person's bedside or in the home. In this case, the priest celebrant should ensure that all of the requisite materials (vestments, ritual books, bread, wine, vessels, etc.) are made available. Clearly, the celebration of Viaticum Within Mass is the preferable. More often than not, however, the dying person will receive Viaticum Outside Mass.

As we discussed in the historical chapters of this book, the usual pre–Vatican II order for the sacraments of those who were sick followed the pattern of Penance, Anointing, and Viaticum. The ritual celebration of Viaticum was seen as the "last rite" prior to death. As the sacramental praxis evolved, however, Anointing became the "last rite," especially if the dying person was unable to receive Eucharist. In the revision of the rites following the Second Vatican Council, the original order was restored.

This is of great significance. In recent years, there has been discussion about the possibility of deacons or lay ministers being allowed to become ministers of sacramental Anointing. However, as was seen earlier, this is not possible because of the close connection between Anointing and sacramental Absolution. However, with the restoration of Viaticum as the "last rite" of a dying Christian, any baptized Roman Catholic (both ordained and non-ordained) may give the last rite to the dying person. In fact, all Christians are encouraged to minister to those who are dying as being a corporal work of mercy.

The distinctive aspect of the ritual of Viaticum is that the minister leads the dying person in renewing his or her baptismal promises. In this way, all who are present are reminded of the intimate connection between our Baptism and our participation in the Passion, death, and Resurrection of the Lord. Following reception of the Eucharist, the minister prays over the recipient these words: "May the Lord Jesus Christ protect you and lead you to eternal life."

In the event that the patient is in the process of actively dying (and thus not able to receive the Eucharist), the "last rite" becomes the Commendation of the Dying. The ritual and prayers are found in chapter six of *Pastoral Care of the Sick*. It is becoming more and more the case that a priest or deacon is not able to be present during the active dying process, so it is important that hospital and nursing home staffs as well as the family of the patient should have access to these prayers.

In short, the ritual is a simple Liturgy of the Word. There are short scriptural texts that may be prayed with the dying person in an antiphonal or ostinato style. These are followed by reading from the word of God and a litany of the saints. When death seems near, the minister or leader of prayer recites one or more of the prayers of commendation. These are taken from ancient sources and remind the dying person of God's love and mercy. One of the most ancient is the *Profiscere:*

> Go forth, Christian soul, from this world in the name of God the almighty Father, who created you, in the name of Jesus Christ, Son of the living God, who suffered for you, in the name of the Holy Spirit, who was poured out upon you, go forth, faithful Christian.
>
> May you live in peace this day, may your home be with God in Zion, with Mary, the virgin Mother of God, with Joseph, and all the angels and saints.

When death has occurred, the minister leads those present in commending the soul of the deceased to God. Finally, mindful that this is a painful time for those who remain, the minister prays for the family and friends that God will offer them his peace and consolation.

## Conclusions and a Look at the Future

There are two broad areas for future research and consideration. The first concerns illness and the subject for Anointing. The second relates to liturgical praxis.

As the Church moves into the third millennium of its existence and as medical science uncovers more cures and treatments for serious illness, it may be necessary to rethink the issue of "seriousness." As was pointed out earlier in this chapter and in chapters 1 and 6, all illness is alienating, all illness can be a traumatic experience. Even when the illness is not life threatening, it does affect one's relationships with family and friends. All illness can cause a person to ponder his or her existence. It may even lead to thoughts of mortality. For some, even a minor illness or accident (such as being hit in the eye with a baseball, or suffering with severe influenza) may result in a conversion experience whereby a person changes his or her life's direction. For others, an illness or accident may cause such intense feelings of anger or hostility that they are unable to function properly. In some ways, all illness causes "death"—perhaps not in the physical sense, but it may result in the death of a person's psyche.

In this spirit, and based on the research found in the previous chapters, perhaps the Church may wish to look again at the sacrament of the sick and more clearly articulate a theology of sickness. This theology could still refer to the eschatological tension; however, perhaps the Church could put more emphasis on the "already" found in sickness and less emphasis on the "not yet." Furthermore, in examining the miracle stories of Jesus, some of those healed were not in danger of death (the woman with the hemorrhage for thirty-eight years, the man born blind, the man with the withered hand, and so on). Yet, they still received Christ's presence and healing touch. Could not people in similar situations also benefit from the Church's presence and healing touch?

A second issue is that of liturgical praxis. While there is a rite of visitation to the sick in the PCS, there is no complementary communal rite. In response to people who feel "sick" in our society today, perhaps the Church could consider establishing a nonsacramental liturgy for those who feel burdened by sin, sicknesses, and life problems such as those found in school, the workplace, or home life. There are sacramental rituals for those who are burdened with sin (Reconciliation) or who are seriously ill (Anointing), but there are no official rituals, individual or communal, which specifically ask for God's healing of everyday malaise, depression, and heartache.

Obviously, such a rite would need to be clearly identified as nonsacramental. Moreover, oil could not be used as part of the ceremony to avoid confusion with the sacrament of the sick. However, the liturgical gesture of the laying on of hands or the inscription of the cross on one's forehead should be retained. There could be two versions of the rite: one within the context of a Eucharistic liturgy for the sick (using the collects and readings suggested in the Sacramentary) and one in the context of a prayer service or Liturgy of the Word. If such a ritual were to be developed, it could respond to the needs of those who otherwise might seek out more esoteric alternative medicines or become involved with groups that perhaps are health-giving, yet are non-Catholic or even non-Christian.

The Church needs to continue to respond to people's need for God in their lives. We have a rich liturgical, scriptural, and pastoral tradition of caring for the sick in our midst. However, we need to re-appropriate the tradition of caring for *all* the sick, not just those who are seriously ill or near death.

## Questions for Discussion

1. What resources may be used in developing rituals for the sick?
2. How may other ministers of healing (medical professionals, family, friends, etc.) also minister to the sick and the dying?
3. How does your parish minister to the sick? Is it effective? What could be improved?

# Chapter 10:

# A Closer Look at the Ritual of Healing

In this chapter we will focus on the practical considerations that must be undertaken when preparing rituals of healing, whether sacramental or nonsacramental. I don't want to duplicate what is contained in *Pastoral Care of the Sick*; rather, the rubrics and rituals will be nuanced for the North American Church. We will examine several examples of both sacramental and nonsacramental healing services. Finally, we will briefly examine the notion of "last rites" as it pertains to Viaticum.

## PRACTICAL CONSIDERATIONS

When arranging any kind of healing service, several preliminary determinations need to be made.

- What are the needs of the patient?
- What are the needs of his or her family?
- Will this service be done in the home, at the institution (hospice, nursing home), in the hospital, or in the church?
- Who will be present as participants?
- Will this service be private, semiprivate, or public?
- What is the purpose for this service?
- Is this healing ritual being conducted as an emergency?
- Is this healing ritual being done prior to surgery?
- Is this healing ritual for general healing?

These questions need to be asked prior to actually performing the healing ritual. The answers to these initial questions will help to determine if the ritual should be sacramental or nonsacramental.

Once the type of ritual has been established, the ministers need to be contacted. Obviously, if this is an emergency Anointing, only the priest and possibly a pastoral minister need attend. However, if this is to be an Anointing in a hospital or institution, consideration might be given to include family members and health care professionals as additional ministers of healing. If the healing service is to take place in the church building, ministers of hospitality, ministers of music, Christian service volunteers, and worship volunteers will need to be a part of the preparation. It cannot be stressed enough that careful, diligent preparation is necessary for any kind of worship experience. The best ritual, without proper preparation, can turn into a disaster. What follows in the next section are some checklists and sample liturgical celebrations to assist in putting together semipublic and public rituals of healing. For ease of use, I have divided them into sacramental and nonsacramental celebrations.

## SACRAMENTAL CELEBRATIONS

For sacramental celebrations it is assumed that *Pastoral Care of the Sick* is the ritual to be followed and that the patient or patients will receive sacramental Anointing by a priest or priests. This is not to exclude the ministry of deacons, health care professionals, or other parishioners. In fact, these persons will provide much needed assistance to the priest and presider in that they are probably better known to the patient than the priest is. There are three distinct situations in which the sacramental ministry of the priest may be needed: by an individual, for a group, and in specialized ministerial settings.

Prior to engaging in the sacramental ministry, the priest (or the one gathering information for the priest such as a parish secretary or other minister) should ascertain the answers to these questions:

- What is the nature of the illness that occasions the participation of a priest?
- Is the request for this ministry coming from the patient or the patient's family?
- What kind of medical care is the patient receiving to aid in his or her healing?

In short, the sacramental minister should see his or her ministry as an extension of the ministry of medical professionals. He or she cooperates with the work of dedicated doctors, nurses, and other health care personnel to ensure that the patient is receiving the best care. In some rare cases, the priest may have to act as a patient advocate to assist the patient and his or her family in making well-informed and moral medical decisions.

When ministering to an individual patient, the priest may perform his sacramental role in the home, in the hospital or institution, or at the local parish. He may be called upon in an emergency situation or in a more relaxed manner. In either case, the priest minister must be attentive to the needs of the patient, his or her caregivers, and the various needs of the particular locale.

For a non-emergency situation, the priest should refer to chapter four in *Pastoral Care of the Sick*. The ritual to be followed is that entitled "Anointing Outside Mass." The basic structure is as follows:

*Introductory Rites*
>Greeting
>Sprinkling with Holy Water
>Instruction on the letter from James
>Penitential Rite

*Liturgy of the Word*
>Reading
>Response

*Liturgy of Anointing*
>Litany
>Laying on of Hands
>Prayer over the Oil (or the blessing of oil)
>Anointing of the patient's forehead and palms
>Prayer after Anointing adapted to the patient's circumstances
>The Lord's Prayer

*[Liturgy of Holy Communion]*
>Communion
>Silent Prayer
>Prayer after Communion

*Concluding Rite*
>Blessing

Within each of these areas is an opportunity for various options as well as the inclusion of any other participants such as family members or medical personnel.

Prior to offering the greeting, the priest should engage in appropriate bedside conversation. This puts the patient at ease and helps to lessen any anxieties. It is also an opportunity for the priest to get to know the patient and the patient's family. As stated before, when beginning the ritual, the priest should never appear hurried or pre-occupied. This sends a wrong message to the patient. Eye contact, body language, and body movement convey the priest's inner disposition. "In this situation, he is acting in the person of Christ the healer. After the greeting and sprinkling with holy water, the priest offers the brief instruction from the apostle James.

If the patient so desires, he may go to confession in which case the others withdraw from the room. If the patient elects not to go to confession, the ritual continues with the Penitential Rite in which all participate.

Following the act of Penance, all present will listen to the word of God, which should be proclaimed by a capable reader other than the priest. This could be a family member or caregiver or even the patient. Following the reading (which may be chosen from a variety of passages), the priest may offer a brief exhortation or homily.

The liturgy of Anointing comprises several parts. The litany is a reminder of God's healing grace. The laying on of hands is an ancient tradition, signifying the presence of God come down to be among his people. This epicletic gesture, analogous to the epiclesis found in the Eucharistic liturgy, visually reminds all present of the descent of the Holy Spirit upon the patient. Therefore, this gesture should never be rushed or omitted. In fact, the hands of the priest should be on the head of the patient for a significant length of time. During this time, all are silent. The priest and people should be praying in their minds and hearts for the health and well-being of the patient.

Then the oil is prayed over. If the oil has been blessed by the Bishop at the Chrism Mass, the priest offers a prayer of thanksgiving, which is done in the form of a litany. The people's response "Blessed be God who heals us in Christ" is an important aspect to this litany since it calls to mind the healing ministry of Christ. If for some reason the priest does not have the oil of the sick with him, he may bless ordinary olive oil according to the formula provided.

Having heard the word of God and prepared himself or herself in prayer, the patient is now ready to be anointed. The patient is anointed on the forehead and on the hands, accompanied by the verbal formulary. He or she may also be anointed on other parts of the body, especially the areas of ailment. This is done in silence, however.

In the ancient ritual of Anointing, all the senses were anointed to heal the patient of any sins that may have been committed. In the current ritual only two locations are anointed. The forehead represents the mind, which is often the origin of our sinfulness. In addition, the patient is healed of any sins he or she may have committed with the eyes, ears, or mouth. The priest prays: "Through this holy anointing may the Lord in his love and mercy help you with the grace of the Holy Spirit." The Anointing of the hands symbolizes those sins that were committed through physical action. In the prayer that accompanies the Anointing, the priest says: "May the Lord who frees you from sin save you and raise you up." This is an acknowledgment that if the patient is in a state of sin, the prayer of faith is salvific.

After the patient receives Anointing, the priest offers a prayer that may be adapted to the situation of the patient (elderly, before surgery, incurable illness, etc.). All of the prayers are gathered together into the prayer of Jesus, which precedes the reception of Communion. If the patient is able to receive Communion, he or she should partake. In some cases, it may be easier for the patient to receive the Precious Blood rather than the host. Also, a small particle of the host may be given to the patient with a glass of water prior to and following the consuming of the host if this will help him or her to swallow. Following the Prayer after Communion, the priest imparts the blessing upon those gathered.

The priest should never be afraid to invite others to assist him with the various ritual actions. Non-ordained persons may proclaim the readings and litanies, act as servers, and assist as caregivers to the patient. Obviously, to avoid confusion, only the priest should impose hands and anoint the sick person; however, during the recitation of the Our Father, friends and family members may wish to join hands as an act of prayerful solidarity.

The presider and/or preparer of the ritual of Anointing should pay special attention to the various options that are available. These include choices of readings, the variety of orations, as well as the litanies and formularies. Part III of the PCS gives a variety of selections from Sacred Scripture. It is easy to fall into a pattern of using the same prayers and readings time after time. The priest must especially guard against becoming rote in the way he celebrates any kind of ritual.

In an emergency situation, the priest may be the only one present (such as at the deathbed of an elderly person) or he may be working alongside medical personnel (as in the case of a victim of an automobile accident or a heart attack victim being attended to in the emergency room). In either case, the priest should avoid two extremes: either being perfunctory or getting in the way. His role is to assist the person spiritually while allowing other trained professionals to do their job.

If it becomes apparent that the person is near death, the priest should offer the ritual prescribed in chapter eight of the PCS. In these cases, the Apostolic Pardon should be given. The ritual envisions that the person *in extremis* receives the sacraments in this order: Penance (if able), Apostolic Pardon, Viaticum, and Anointing. In practice, however, the patient usually receives the Apostolic Pardon and Anointing since he or she is either unable to offer a confession or consume the Eucharist. Even if the ritual is celebrated in an emergency setting, the priest should ensure that real pastoral care is being given. Even if the patient appears unconscious, the priest should still speak the words aloud, because in many cases hearing is the last sense to stop functioning. Even though the patient is unable to respond to the prayers audibly, he or she may respond in the heart and mind.

In the event that the dying person has not yet been fully initiated into the Church, the priest may follow the ritual prescribed as Christian Initiation for the Dying. In practice, this ritual is rarely used. There are two situations in which a priest may be called upon to utilize it: when a catechumen is in danger of dying or when a person who was known to be desirous of conversion to the Catholic faith is *in extremis*. Obviously, in the latter example, the priest would have to have known this in some fashion, either because he was evangelizing the patient or because the patient's family or friend informed the priest of the patient's desire. In either case, the priest must be relatively certain that full initiation is the true desire of the patient.

It is to be noted that in this case, the "last rite" is Viaticum; Anointing is *not* celebrated. The patient (either adult or child) receives Baptism, Confirmation, and Eucharist as Viaticum. If the minister is a deacon, he may baptize and give Viaticum; he does not celebrate Confirmation, but instead anoints the newly baptized with chrism while saying the prescribed prayer.

## Sacramental Celebrations with Groups of Patients

Because illness is alienating, some parishes have the practice of gathering the homebound and those who are seriously ill at least once a year to celebrate Mass and receive sacramental Anointing. In other parishes, the priest visits the local nursing home or convalescent center to offer Anointing to the patients who live there. In either situation, there is the possibility of celebrating ritual Anointing for a group. These kinds of celebrations require planning and the assistance of several volunteers to ensure that it is a good ritual experience for all involved.

In terms of preparation, those to be anointed should be identified prior to the celebration. One suggestion is to have the patients register for the service. This does several things:

- It provides an accurate count of the number of persons (patients and their caregivers) who will be anointed.
- It allows for the parish to establish a connection with those who are ill, which will be valuable for follow-up care and a continued pastoral ministry.
- Depending on what kind of information is taken, the priest and pastoral minister have some idea of the needs of the patients who will be attending.

A second aspect to the preparation is engaging the services of people in a variety of ministries. While the parish priest is key, he may wish to have other priests assist him with the Anointing of the Sick. The deacon and pastoral associates should be invited to participate as well. The deacon could proclaim the Gospel, offer the homily, and lead the litanies. The pastoral associate could serve as lector or as overall coordinator of the project. Music ministers, ministers of hospitality, ministers of Holy Communion, servers, and family members of the patients should be invited to exercise various roles within the liturgy itself.

On the day of the celebration, every effort must be made to help the patients feel welcome and important. They and their families or friends should be greeted warmly and escorted to their seats. For patients seated in a wheelchair, a special place should have been prepared. The patients could receive a flower and/or nametag to identify them as a recipients of Anointing. Hospitality ministers should be readily available to answer questions, give directions, and assist with any potential problems. Following the liturgy, patients and their caregivers should be offered some nourishment in a relaxed environment. Finally, in the weeks and months after the liturgy, the parish should keep in contact with the patient and his or her family as part of a program of ongoing pastoral care. This may be done with notes or letters, periodic phone calls, or even continued or regular visitation with the patient.

## Sacramental Celebrations in Special Situations

As part of the healing process, the priest may be invited to assist a patient in overcoming certain difficulties. These include addiction, mental illness, persons who have procured an abortion, and children who have a serious illness. In all cases, but especially in the aforementioned, the priest should be especially attentive to determining what the exact needs are and how sacramental Anointing can be of benefit. In other words, in these cases, a priest must often make pastoral judgments as to the suitability of Anointing.

It is my opinion that the sacrament of the sick should be used whenever the illness has the potential of leading the person to death—either physical or spiritual death. In some cases, it may be necessary to consult with the patient's physician or counselor to ascertain if Anointing would help the patient's progress toward recovery. In other cases, the priest upon consultation with the patient may determine that Anointing would be of benefit. Again, the priest is urged to avoid two extremes: a too restrictive use of sacramental Anointing or reducing the sacrament to a sacramental by Anointing anyone who appears to have some kind of illness. The sacrament of the sick is for the living to help them with God's grace to come to eternal life.

There are several kinds of illnesses that could benefit from sacramental Anointing. Very often, a non-ordained person will be the point of first contact with someone who is in need of spiritual healing. This person could be a counselor, a nurse, a family member, or friend. When this person discerns that the patient is in need of medical or psychological help, he or she should also try to determine if the person needs spiritual guidance as well. As noted earlier in this book, physical illness also affects a person's psychological or spiritual well-being. It may be prudent for the caregiver or friend to suggest to the patient that he or she could benefit from spiritual healing.

Some specialized situations in which this may take place include addictions counseling, those undergoing psychological or psychiatric care, those recovering from post-abortion trauma, and children with serious illnesses. Because these situations are sometimes a source of embarrassment or shame, those who are involved in them may keep them private. However, a good friend or perhaps even the caregiver may gently suggest that the patient invite his or her spiritual guide to participate in the healing process.

At the outset, a non-ordained minister may simply hear the person's story and engage in ordinary conversation. As the patient becomes more comfortable, the minister may offer to pray with him or her. At some point during the encounter (or in the course of several encounters), the minister may suggest to the patient that he or she be anointed. If the patient agrees, the minister should be present while the priest offers sacramental Anointing. This serves two purposes. First, the minister acts as a bridge between the patient and priest; second, the minister serves as a reminder and symbol of the whole Church community that offers its prayers in support of the patient's recovery.

For those participating in addiction counseling, the Anointing service may take place within the group that the fellow patients have participated in to some degree. Or, to protect anonymity of the other counselees, the patient may elect to have a more private service. The psychiatric or psychological patient may desire to have his or her close friends and family participate in prayer. For example, a woman who had procured an abortion and comes to the realization that she needs healing and forgiveness, may approach a priest to participate in the sacrament of Reconciliation. The priest may suggest to her that she also receive sacramental Anointing, especially if she is also undergoing psychiatric care or harbors deep feelings of depression, guilt, or suicide.

The Anointing of children is a pastoral judgment that should not be made lightly. If the child has not been fully initiated, the usual course of action is to fully initiate by administering Baptism, Confirmation, and Eucharist. Because these sacraments are forgiving and healing in and of themselves, there is no need for also celebrating sacramental Anointing. However, if the child is already initiated, the priest may feel that it is pastorally prudent to offer the child the sacrament of the sick. In this case, extra catechesis may be needed to help the child (as well as the parents or guardians) understand more fully what is going on.

## Nonsacramental Healing Services

Having examined sacramental services and rites in the previous section, we now turn our attention to nonsacramental forms of worship and celebration. "Nonsacramental services" refer to those rituals of healing that do not contain either the sacrament of Penance or Anointing of the Sick. They may, however, include the reception of the Eucharist or Viaticum. These services may be used when a sacramental ritual cannot (or should not) be used. One such example is when a person is suffering from a serious albeit non life-threatening illness such as minor depression over the death of a loved one or pet. Another example is a person who suffers from a chronic condition like asthma or diabetes, which is kept in check by medication. However, because of the effects of the illness, a person feels a general malaise. A third type of situation is when a person is involved in an accident or is a victim of a crime. The immediate life-threatening danger has passed, yet he or she is still in need of healing and comfort. Another example occurs when a person suffers from general malaise, depression, or ill-feeling occasioned by an upcoming stressful situation such as the loss of a job, an impending divorce, pre-wedding jitters, worries about taking the bar exam, etc. A final example occurs when the priest is not able to attend to the dying patient because he is impeded. A deacon, religious, family member, or member of the parish or hospital pastoral staff could lead the rites of Viaticum and the prayers for the dying. In all of these situations, the baptized Catholic Christian exercises his or her role as a healing minister and stands *in persona ecclesia* for the patient and his or her family.

The situations mentioned above point out two realities. First, human beings can become impaired in their daily functioning that involves a psychosomatic reaction leading to illness of some type. Second, while this suffering is not life-threatening, it could be serious enough to warrant the attention of the Church's healing ministry.

In these cases, who is the minister? Certainly, the patient's caregivers (doctors, nurses, family members) act as ministers of healing. However, other members of the Church community, priests, deacons, religious, and trained laypersons may also assist as officially recognized ministers of healing. In this day and age, because of the priest shortage, it is necessary to empower and train deacons and the non-ordained to function as healing ministers. This power flows from one's Baptism by which a person is incorporated into Christ who anoints him or her as priest, prophet, and king. It is this partici-pation in the priesthood of the baptized that allows a layperson or deacon the capacity to act as a minister of healing.

In nonsacramental services, any trained person may function as a representative of the local parish community and come to the aid of one who suffers. While some patients may prefer to have a priest or deacon minister to them in their need, the reality is that all baptized Christians share in the ministry of healing. In a hospital setting, the chaplain may not always be a priest. In some cases the chaplain may not even be Roman Catholic. When an individual requests spiritual guidance or prayer and a priest is not available, someone from the local parish community could offer his or her services.

In terms of training these individuals, workshops may be offered at the local Catholic college or seminary. Priests, hospital chaplains, and professional ministers should make it their duty to offer professional assistance in helping the local parish community to develop a ministry of healing. These workshops should include the following components:

1. The mystery of illness and healing
2. A brief history of the Church's healing ministry
3. A discussion of the kinds of illnesses that are prevalent today
4. A clear delineation of the roles of priest, deacon, and lay minister in the ministry of healing
5. A discussion of the resources available to the minister of healing

6. Copies of the kinds of healing services that a non-ordained person may lead
7. A listing of professional ministers of healing who may serve as resource persons to assist the lay minister

As the Church continues to develop her ministry to the sick and the dying, all ministers—both ordained and non-ordained—will need to be empowered to use their healing gifts. It is imperative that all ministers be given training to do their tasks. Moreover, as our population ages and people live longer and healthier lives, it will become necessary to educate all Catholic Christians as to the necessity of visiting the sick, praying with the sick, caring for the dying, and ministering to the families and caregivers of those who are ill. While sickness is often alienating, ministry to the sick should be empowering and rejuvenating.

## Questions for Discussion

1. In rituals for the sick and dying, how many participants other than the presider should be included in the ritual action?
2. Should a person who has received an abortion (or procured one for someone else) receive sacramental Anointing? Why or why not?
3. Is there any case when the rites of the dying would not be given to a dying person? When and why?

# Epilogue: Some Concluding Reflections

## UNDERSTANDING SACRAMENTAL HEALING

We have examined the historical antecedents of sacramental Anointing from the perspectives of theology and anthropology. The definition of *sickness* changed over time. In the ancient world, illness was often attributed to the capriciousness of the gods, demonic forces, the weather, personal sin, or even simply to poor diet. Whatever the cause, illness was alienating. The sick person was separated from family, friends, and society as the result of his or her malaise. Healing was accomplished by a variety of persons who acted as mediators between the sick person and society or between the sick person and the god or demon who caused the illness.

Over the centuries, there was a tendency to compartmentalize the wholeness of the human person. Because of Aristotelian and Platonic philosophy, and its canonization by theologians, the human person was divided into body and soul. Moreover, the soul took preeminence while the body was seen as the container. Hence, sickness was viewed as a temporary discomfort soon to be replaced by divine glory.

Theologically and liturgically, there was a shift in the nature of the sacrament of the sick. In the early Church, Anointing was both self-administered and administered "sacramentally" in the person of the priest. Gradually, as the Church coalesced the various rites and rituals, Anointing was given the status of sacrament—to be administered only by a priest and only to those who were seriously ill. Moreover, some theologians like Peter Lombard believed that the sacrament could only be given to those who were on the brink of death as a way of preparing them for their final journey. The sacrament came to be

called "extreme unction" or the "last rites." While the Church continued
to offer a *via media* between offering the sacrament to the *moribundi*
and to the *infirmi*, it was clear that, in practice, Scholastic theology
prevailed and the sacrament was reserved to the dying.

A shift took place in the twentieth century. Resulting from the
changing cultural and social milieu and the experience of two world
wars, some theologians, canonists, and liturgists began to examine the
history and use of the sacrament of Extreme Unction. They concluded
that the sacrament should more properly be called "the sacrament
of the sick" or "the anointing of the sick." While the emphasis was still
on the sacrament being used with those who were dying, some theologians felt that Anointing could be used in a broader context.

At the Second Vatican Council, the Council Fathers agreed
with some of the theologians and recommended that the ritual for
Extreme Unction be revised. The revision was completed in 1972
when the *Ordo Unctionis infirmorum* (called *Pastoral Care of the Sick* in
English) was promulgated by Pope Paul VI. The sacrament was no
longer seen as primarily for the dying, but for anyone who was in
danger due to old age or sickness. In both language and ritual, the
shift was made from *articulum mortis* to *magna infirmitas*.[1] No longer
did the patient need to be "at the point of death" to receive the sacrament; he or she could participate in the healing ritual whenever he
or she was seriously ill. Moreover, the sick person could receive sacramental Anointing more than once during the same illness.

Despite the change in terminology, the practice of Anointing
the dying still remained in the popular mind. Several Episcopal
Conferences, papal allocutions, and theological treatises encouraged
the use of the sacrament with those who were seriously ill. The definition of *serious illness* was the primary focus of this book. We examined
the theological, ecumenical, and canonical literature to ascertain the
elements necessary for an illness to be classified as serious.

---

[1] In the ritual, the term *periculose aegrotans* is utilized. However, in this concluding chapter I
would like to suggest that given the cultural, anthropological, and religious milieu in which the
sacrament of the sick is used, the term *magna infirmitas* provides an opening for more pastoral
ministry to those who are ill to such a degree that they could benefit from the presence of the
Church. The word *infirmitas* (much more than the word *aegrotant/aegrotans*) indicates a weakness,
feebleness, infirmity, inconstancy, or sickness which debilitates a person's functioning within
society. Perhaps the Church should examine its pastoral presence with those who are ill, but not
yet at the point of death or even in a state of serious illness to warrant the use of the sacrament
of the sick.

We explored the theological, anthropological, and medical aspects of serious illness and healing. We saw how any illness, but serious illnesses in particular, affects the physiological, psychological, biological, cultural, social, historical, and spiritual dimensions of the human person. Anthropologically, illness has an alienating effect on the person who is ill, but the illness also has an effect on the community. Both patient and community have the opportunity to educate and be educated about the experience of illness. The one who suffers can give witness to what graces God has given to him or her as a result of his or her sickness. The community for its part may be instruments of healing through its presence and pastoral care toward the sick individual.

To this end, different types of physical, mental, and addictive illnesses and disorders were examined and evaluated. In addition, AIDS was explored to illustrate the confusion that still exists regarding the nature of illness and healing in the world today. Finally, we evaluated the different types of illnesses as to their using the sacrament of the sick.

We concluded with the assertion that the Church is a healer both sacramentally and ministerially. The ministry of various members of the Church complements that of other medical practitioners, but moves the patient and the community to a deeper understanding about faith, healing, and life.

Finally, more work needs to be done in the area of the healing practices of the Church. All persons, both ordained and non-ordained, need to participate actively in helping those who are ill to be restored in health, mind, body, and spirit.

# Appendix 1

# Sample Liturgies, Liturgy Preparation Worksheets

## INTRODUCTION

In this book we examined the theology of pastoral care to the sick and dying. In this appendix are materials that offer a practical application of the theology within a liturgical context. These materials are not intended to be normative of the way in which liturgies must be celebrated; rather, they are samples of how one may design liturgies for the sick and the dying. The worksheets are contextualized and presented with commentary to assist the reader in developing liturgical resources for use in the parish or diocese.

These materials are grouped under three major headings: Appendix 1: Sample Liturgies, Liturgy Preparation Worksheets; Appendix 2: Resources for Education and Celebration; and Appendix 3: Musical Resources. It is my hope that the practitioner (whether ordained or non-ordained) may find these resources to be of benefit for his or her ministry. They are designed to be samples; the reader is invited to develop his or her own based upon the particular parish situation.

## SAMPLE LITURGIES

In this section, I provide resources for a variety of ministerial situations. These sample liturgies may be adapted for use by the presider, pastoral associate, or medical practitioner. In situations where there is only one person who is in need of pastoral attention, the presider should consult *Pastoral Care of the Sick* or the *Book of Blessings* for the proper formulas, prayers, and scriptural passages.

## Some Preliminary Issues to Consider

Prior to having any kind of Anointing service, the parish should be educated as to what Anointing means. This may be done by a series of bulletin articles or pulpit announcements. The invitation to be a part of this healing Mass or service should be given at least a month in advance. Patients, as well as their caregivers and families, should be encouraged to attend by asking them to RSVP. If there are specific problems, like transportation or particular medical needs, the patient should be invited to make those needs known in order that the parish could provide the necessary accommodation. The parish should arrange for members of a hospitality team as well as nurses or trained care-givers to be present during the liturgy as well as to have some kind of reception for fellowship following the service. When the patient arrives for the liturgy, he or she should be given a name tag so that the priests who will be anointing them may use a proper name. This also ensures that only those who have legitimate medical issues will be anointed.

In terms of set-up, the ones who are to be anointed should have a special area for seating. Accommodation should be made for those who may attend in a wheelchair. When seating patients in a pew, leave one pew empty between each pew. This will allow easier access to the patients for the priests who anoint. A special order of worship may be provided for those who are attending this liturgy to assist in their participation and as a memento of the event. When putting this pamphlet together, it is important to use a larger font size (16 or even 18 point) for those who may have trouble seeing. Finally, the parish should continue to keep in contact with the patient and his or her family after the service is over. This may be done with postcards or notes. If the patient is amenable, members of the parish could visit periodically, in addition to the parish priest.

## ANOINTING WITHIN MASS FOR A GROUP

Ideally, this Mass should be one of the regularly scheduled parish litur-gies during Ordinary Time. The reason is twofold: First, those who are to be anointed are witnesses of joining their sufferings to those of Christ. They become a reminder of the wider ecclesial community. Second, the congregation at large welcomes those who are sick back into their midst, reminding them that they are not abandoned or forgotten. However, if it is not feasible to do the Anointing during a regularly scheduled Mass because of the number of patients to be anointed, another Mass may be scheduled to accommodate. In this instance, the parish community should be invited to participate at this special Anointing Mass as well. The various prayers and rubrics for this liturgy are found in *Pastoral Care of the Sick* (PCS) chapter four.

## Order of Mass

- Introductory Rites as usual with a special welcome for the sick (PCS, 135).
- For the Kyrie, the deacon or priest may use the tropes that refer to healing.
- On Sundays (except during Advent and Lent), the Gloria should be sung or said.
- The Opening Prayer may be from the Sunday or one for the sick as found in the PCS (#136).
- The readings are for the day.
- The homily should relate the readings to healing and God's mercy.
- On Sundays the profession of faith follows the homily after which the litany of the sick (PCS, 138) is said. This litany replaces the General Intercessions.

After the litany, the congregation is invited to be seated. The priest then goes to each sick person and lays his hands upon his or her head. During this time the congregation is invited to sing a hymn. After the laying on of hands, the priest says the prayer of thanksgiving over the oil of the sick (PCS, 140). He then anoints each person on the forehead and the hands using the sacramental formula. During this time a hymn may be sung or instrumental music may be played. At the conclusion of the Anointing, the priest should wash his hands and sing or say the prayer after Anointing (PCS, 142). Since there are a variety of illnesses represented, he may use one of the general prayers.

During the Liturgy of the Eucharist, the gifts may be brought forward by family members or caregivers. Both the prayer over the gifts and the preface are taken from *Pastoral Care of the Sick*. These prayers are also found in the Sacramentary. There are special embolisms, which are provided for Eucharistic Prayers 1, 2, and 3 (PCS, 145).

These should be photocopied and put in the Sacramentary at the proper place in the Eucharistic Prayer.

Mass continues as usual. The Prayer after Communion as well as the final extended blessing may be taken from *Pastoral Care of the Sick*.

## ANOINTING OUTSIDE OF MASS FOR A GROUP WITH A PRIEST PRESIDING

Essentially, this follows the same format as the Anointing within Mass with the omission of the Eucharistic Prayer and Communion. Although provisions are made for Holy Communion to be given, if this is done in the parish church, it would be more proper to celebrate Mass. However, if the priest is presiding at a nursing home or assisted living facility where the celebration of Mass would not be feasible, he may bring Eucharist for distribution, in which case a table with candles and a corporal should be prepared.

### Order of Service

Introductory Rites are as usual with the greeting as provided for in the ritual. The priest may sprinkle the assembly with holy water and then offer the brief instruction (PCS, 117). There are several options for the Penitential Rite, including the celebration of the sacrament of Penance. However, since this is a service for a group of persons, the sacrament of Penance should not be offered at this time.

Following the Penitential Rite, the readings are given. Here the priest has wide latitude as to the choice. He may use one of the readings provided or he may use the readings of the day. After the proclamation of the Gospel, the priest may give a brief homily.

In place of the General Intercessions, the litany of the sick is said. After the litany, the priest lays his hands on the head of the sick person. A hymn may be sung or instrumental music played to accompany this action. The prayer over the oil with its response is prayed, after which the sick persons are anointed on their forehead and hands. Music may be used during the Anointing. After Anointing, one of the general prayers or the prayer for those in advanced age is said (PCS,

125). The Lord's Prayer is said by all present, and the service concludes with the blessing and dismissal.

## Healing Service outside of Mass for a Group with a Deacon or Lay Minister Presiding (Nonsacramental)

This is a *nonsacramental* service of healing. It is designed for those whose health is impaired but are not candidates for Anointing. In other words, their illness (either physical, psychological, or spiritual) is not considered life-threatening, but they would still benefit from a liturgical service asking for God's healing and protection. Sample services of this type are found in the *Book of Blessings*.

The format of this ritual is that of a Liturgy of the Word service. The minister begins with the sign of the cross. A greeting follows as well as a brief exhortation inviting those present to be attentive to the Lord's presence. Scriptural readings are read and a Responsorial Psalm may be recited. If the minister so chooses, he or she may offer a brief reflection on the readings. Intercessions for the health of the sick are offered and are concluded with a prayer. The service concludes with the sign of the cross.

There are a variety of services that have options which allow an ordained minister or a non-ordained minister to preside. The *Book of Blessings* has several liturgies prepared: chapter one, section twelve is a ritual for the elderly who are confined to their homes. Chapter two has three categories of blessing pertaining to the sick. The first category is for general illnesses of either adults or children. The second pertains to those who are suffering from addiction or substance abuse. As was noted earlier, some who fall into this category may be candidates for sacramental Anointing. If the minister judges that a person with an addiction could benefit from being anointed (or if the patient asks for Anointing), then arrangements should be made so that a priest may visit and possibly anoint. This particular blessing could ideally be used during a twelve-step meeting by the leader as a way of connecting the counseling with a spiritual dimension. In a similar manner, those who have been victims of crime or oppression, such as domestic violence or spousal abuse, may benefit from the blessing found in section three.

In each of these blessings, the only difference in ritual action between an ordained minister and a non-ordained minister is the gesture during the prayer of blessing and the concluding rite. A priest or deacon says the prayer of blessing with his hands outstretched over the sick persons while a lay ecclesial minister says the blessing with his or her hands joined. A priest or deacon gives the final blessing with the ritual gesture while a lay minister signs himself or herself with the cross while saying the words. In all three blessing rituals, there is opportunity for music to be sung or played at the beginning, as the Responsorial Psalm, and to conclude the service.

## Viaticum

When a faithful Christian has come to the end of his or her life, the transition should be assisted by a celebration. Ideally, the dying person would be surrounded by his or her friends and family who together with the minister pray for a happy death and implore God's mercy. The *Pastoral Care of the Sick* envisions several different scenarios to mark the end of physical life. These are found in Part II of the ritual.

It is important to recognize that while many people still prefer to have a priest perform "last rites," any Catholic Christian may lead the prayers for the dying. As has been noted repeatedly, the sacrament of the sick is for the living, for the seriously ill. Viaticum is for the dying. While a dying person may be anointed, the sacrament that helps him or her to transition to eternal life is the Eucharist. In situations where it is impossible for the priest to attend to someone who is dying (such as might be the case in hospitals or nursing homes), a deacon, a pastoral care minister, or even a member of the family could lead the rites of the dying. If the patient is lucid and is able to take nourishment, a minister could celebrate Viaticum. If the patient is not lucid, the minister could lead those gathered in the prayers of commendation for the dying.

The ritual envisions that Viaticum be received during Mass when feasible. In some cases, a priest may be able to celebrate Mass at the bedside (or in the room) of the dying person. More often than not, however, there may not be enough time to properly celebrate the Mass.

When Viaticum is celebrated during Mass, the baptismal profession of faith follows the homily and the litany replaces the General Intercessions. Prior to administering the Eucharist, the priest has the option of saying one of three introductions (PCS, 193). After the communicant has received Eucharist, the priest adds: "May the Lord Jesus Christ protect you and lead you to eternal life" (PCS, 193). Following the final blessing a priest may add the Apostolic Pardon for the dying (PCS, 195).

When Viaticum is celebrated outside of Mass, a priest, deacon, or lay ecclesial minister may preside. After the usual greeting, the minister places the Blessed Sacrament on a table. (Priests and deacons may sprinkle those present with holy water.) The minister invites those present to be attentive to God's presence and leads them in the Penitential Rite. At the conclusion of the Penitential Rite, a priest may offer the Apostolic Pardon. A very brief reading of scripture is done and may be followed by a brief homily or reflection. The minister then leads the dying person in the baptismal profession of faith which is followed by the litany. The Our Father begins the liturgy of Viaticum and the minister says the following while showing the Eucharist to the assembly (PCS, 207):

*Jesus Christ is the food for our journey; he calls us to the heavenly table.*

or

*This is the bread of life. Taste and see that the Lord is good.*

After giving Communion to the sick person, the minister adds:

*May the Lord Jesus Christ protect you and lead you to eternal life.*

The liturgy concludes with a prayer and blessing. A non-ordained minister signs the cross on himself or herself, while an ordained minister blesses those gathered. If it seems opportune, those who are assembled may give the sign of peace to the sick person (PCS, 211).

## Commendation of the Dying

Chapter eight of *Pastoral Care of the Sick* provides a continuous rite of Penance, Anointing and Viaticum, which a priest may use in emergency situations. In the event that a priest is not available, a deacon or pastoral care minister may also provide solace and comfort to the dying person and his or her family by ministering to them in their time of need. The prayers that are found in chapter six are designed to be used when Penance, Anointing, and Viaticum are not possible or the patient has just received them and the dying process is more protracted. In the commendation of the dying, the minister recites familiar scriptural passages with the patient. Then a longer passage from scripture may be read by one of those present. There are several options to choose from including Psalm 23, 25, or 121. The Litany of the Saints is a reminder to those present that the Church includes those who have gone before us in death and now intercede for us. These holy men and women now await our passage from death to new life in order to welcome us into God's kingdom. Finally, the minister prays one of the prayers of commendation in which the dying person is entrusted to God's mercy and love. If the patient dies while the ritual is proceeding, the minister should begin the prayers for the dead and include a prayer for the decedent's family and friends (PCS, 221–222).

If a minister (priest, deacon, or lay minister) is called to attend to someone who is already dead, the sacraments of Penance, Anointing, or Viaticum are not to be administered. Rather, the prayers found in chapter seven of *Pastoral Care of the Sick* are to be used (PCS, 223). These prayers may be concluded with a gesture of blessing or tracing the sign of the cross on the forehead of the decedent, and a priest or deacon may sprinkle the body with holy water (PCS, 225).

The minister greets those present and then prays the opening prayer. A reading from scripture is proclaimed by one of those present. The minister may then pray a brief form of the Litany of the Saints, adding the concluding prayer. Those gathered then pray the Lord's Prayer and the minister concludes the ceremony with a prayer of commendation.

In short, there is a wealth of liturgical resources found in the current edition of *Pastoral Care of the Sick*. The ritual edition is not just for priests or hospital chaplains. Anyone who is in the position of giving pastoral care to the sick and the dying should have a copy. It would behoove those who are charged with the formation of pastoral ministers in the parish to ensure that each minister receives a simplified version of the rituals of visitation of the sick, Communion to the sick, Viaticum, and the commendation of the dying, if not a copy of the ritual itself. Too often, those who form pastoral ministers feel that they need to reinvent the wheel when it comes to providing resource material. *Pastoral Care of the Sick* is *the* resource that should be used not only by priests, but by all who minister to the sick.

As we conclude this section, a brief word about options. Too often ministers find themselves in a rut when it comes to using ritual. They default to the familiar prayers and phrases instead of exploring some of the material found in the back of the ritual edition. Or they use only option A when there may be choices from B to F. I encourage all ministers to examine the different prayer and scriptural text options that are given throughout the ritual. Don't be afraid to use unfamiliar texts. Very often those texts can provide insight and comfort for a variety of situations, especially those which are most problematic.

## Worksheets for Preparing Liturgies

In this section, sample worksheets are given to assist ministers in preparing the various liturgies found in *Pastoral Care of the Sick.* I have provided some worksheets that the reader may wish to adapt for use in his or her own particular circumstances.

# Visit to an Individual

Date:

Name of the patient:

Address:


Phone number:

Contact person:

Medical notes:



**Expected condition of the patient:**



**Ministry needed:**

❑ Visit only Visit with Communion

❑ Visit with Penance, Anointing, and Communion

❑ Special considerations

❑ Who will visit:

❑ When:

**Pastoral notes for follow-up care after the visit:**



**Visit recorded:**



**Note in Sacramental registry (for Anointing)**

# Visit to a Group of Persons

Date:

Who will visit:

When:

Where:

Names of those to be visited and anticipated condition and room number(s):

**Type of ministry:**

❏ Visit

❏ Visit with Communion

❏ Visit with Penance, Anointing, and Eucharist

**Follow-up care needed:**

**Recorded in sacramental registry:**

# Preparation Checklists

### For an individual visit

- Name of patient and contact information sheet
- Ritual book
- Vestments (if necessary)
- Eucharist (in pyx or vial for Precious Blood)
- [Oil of the Sick]
- Holy water
- Purificator and cotton for cleaning fingers

### Visit to an institution where Mass will be celebrated

- Names of patients who might be present
- Mass kit (bread, wine, sacred vessels, water cruet, dish, purificators, hand towels, corporal, candles, Sacramentary, Lectionary, and pyx for transporting remaining Eucharist)
- Mass vestments (alb, cincture, white chasuble, and stole)
- Ritual book

### For a visit to a nursing home or hospital (larger group)

- Names of those to be visited and room number(s)
- Ritual book
- Vestments
- [Oil of the sick]
- Eucharist in sufficient quantity
- Holy water
- Purificator and cotton for cleaning fingers

### Visit by a deacon or non-ordained minister

- Names of those to be visited
- Ritual book
- Eucharist in pyx
- Corporal
- Vestments (alb or alb and stole for a deacon)
- Holy water
- Votive candles (2)
- Purificator

# Appendix 2:

# Resources for Education and Celebration

This is a brief resource list of some of the materials available for further study.

## CHURCH DOCUMENTATION

*Book of Blessings.* New York: Catholic Book Publishing Co. 1989.

*Pastoral Care of the Sick: Rites of Anointing and Viaticum.* New York: Catholic Book Publishing Co. 1983.

*Pastoral Care of the Sick: Revised Abridged Edition (Bilingual)/Cuidado Pastoral de los Enfermos.* Chicago: Liturgy Training Publications, 2003.

Bishops' Committee on the Liturgy, National Conference of Catholic Bishops. *Study Text 2: Pastoral Care of the Sick and Dying.* Washington, D.C.: Office of Publishing Services, United States Catholic Conference. 1984.

Congregation for the Clergy, et al. *Instruction on Certain Questions Regarding the Collaboration of the Non-Ordained Faithful in the Sacred Ministry of Priests.* Vatican City: Libreria Editrice Vaticana. 1997.

## BOOKS AND ARTICLES

Benedict, Mary Grace. "Open the Sacrament of the Sick to Struggling Alcoholics." *St. Anthony Messenger* 96, no. 10 (March 1989): 37–39.

Carnes, Patrick. *Contrary to Love: Helping the Sexual Addict.* Center City, MN: Hazelden Educational Materials. 1989.

*Catholic Handbook for Visiting the Sick and Homebound 2007.* Introduction by Sister Genevieve Glen, OSB. Chicago: Liturgy Training Publications, 2007. This is an annual publication, revised each year.

Davis, Patricia. "A Parish Celebration of Anointing." *Liturgy* 2 (1981–1982): 33–37.

Davis, Robert C. "Prayers and Liturgy in the Sickroom." *Liturgy* 2 (1981–1982): 59–63.

DeJulio, Robert J. "Is Anointing Really Enough?" *The Priest* 38 (February 1982): 6–7.

Diekmann, Godfrey. "The Laying on of Hands: The Basic Sacramental Rite." *Proceedings of the Catholic Theological Society of America* 29 (June 10–13, 1974): 339–51.

Empereur, James L. *Prophetic Anointing: God's Call to the Sick, the Elderly, and the Dying.* Wilmington: Michael Glazier, Inc., 1982.

Erraught, Joseph. "The Sacraments and the Mentally Ill." *Studies in Pastoral Liturgy II.* Vincent Ryan, ed. Dublin: The Furrow Trust. 1963. pp. 58–60.

Feehan, Marilyn. "A Spirituality of Sickness." *Spiritual Life* 22 (Fall 1976): 179–83.

Gusmer, Charles. *And You Visited Me: Sacramental Ministry to the Sick and Dying.* Collegeville: The Liturgical Press. 1990.

Krantz, Carolyn. "Ritual of Dying in Pastoral Practice." *Modern Liturgy* 11 (March 1984): 2.

Maloof, Patricia. "Sickness and Health in Society." *Concilium* (1991/92): 19–34.

Marchesi, Pierluigi. "The Role of the Church in the Treatment of the Mentally Ill." *Doletium Hominum* 34 (1997): 205–207.

Marin, Ivan. "The Church and AIDS Patients." *Dolentium Hominum* 5 (1990): 242–43.

Marsh, Thomas. "A Theology of Anointing the Sick." *The Furrow* 29 (February 1978): 89–101.

McGuire, Meredith B. *Ritual Healing in Suburban America.* New Brunswick and London: Rutgers University Press. 1988.

McMorrow, Kevin. "Sacrament of the Anointing of the Sick: Historical-Theological Considerations." *The American Ecclesiastical Review.* 169 (October 1975): 507–21.

Melvin, Edward J. "Pastoral Care of Persons Apparently Dead." *Homiletic and Pastoral Review* 84 (May 1984): 45–51.

Meyendorff, Paul. "The Anointing of the Sick: Some Pastoral Considerations." *St. Vladimir Quarterly* 25 (1991): 241–55.

Monge, Miguel Angel. "Integral Care of the Sick: The Role of Spiritual Help." *Dolentium Hominum* 4 (1989): 9–17.

Moynahan, Michael E. "The Sacramentality of Touch." *Modern Liturgy* 5 (April 1978): 28–29.

Notebaart, James. "The Sacrament of Anointing and Total Patient Care." *Homiletic and Pastoral Review* 74 (June 1974): 53–62.

Oates, Wayne E. *The Religious Care of the Psychiatric Patient.* Louisville, KY: Westminster/John Knox Press. 1978.

O'Connell, Matthew J., translator. *Temple of the Holy Spirit: Sickness and Death of the Christian in the Liturgy. The Twenty-first Liturgical Conference Saint-Serge.* New York: Pueblo Publishing Company. 1983.

O'Riordan, Sean. "The Healing Ministry of the Church." *The Furrow* 33 (May 1982): 292–96.

Power, David N. "The Sacrament of Anointing: Open Questions." In Mary Collins and David N. Power, eds. *Concilium: The Pastoral Care of the Sick.* London: SCM Press. 1991/2.

Rhys, John H. W. "Ministers of Healing and Pastoral Care." *Liturgy* 2 (1981–1982): 75–77.

Rosario, Priamo Tejeda. "The Doctor and the Priest at the Service of Life." *Dolentium Hominum* 10 (1995): 122–23.

Sosa, Juan J. "Illness and Healing in Hispanic Communities." *Liturgy* 2 (1981–1982): 65–67.

Talley, Thomas. "Healing: Sacrament or Charism?" *Worship* 46 (1972): 518–27.

Telthorst, James T. "Anointing of the Sick: Community Celebration." *Health Progress* 65 (December 1984): 40–43.

Welbers, Thomas. "The Rituals of Christian Dying: Viaticum and Commendation." *Modern Liturgy* 11/2 (March 1984): 7.

Whalen, William J. "What Different Christian Churches Believe about Anointing of the Sick." *U.S. Catholic* 44 (November 1979): 33–35.

Ziegler, John J. *Let Them Anoint the Sick.* Collegeville: The Liturgical Press. 1987.

# Appendix 3:

# Musical Resources

Here are some hymns that may be used during an Anointing Mass or service with the sick. It is always advisable to use music found in the parish musical resource because this music is more likely to be familiar to the congregation. Some common publications are listed below.

## RESOURCES

*Flor Y Canto.* Portland, OR: OCP Publications. 1989.

*Gather Comprehensive* (G). Chicago, IL: GIA Publications, Inc. 1994.

*Journeysongs* (J). Portland, OR: OCP Publications. 1994.

*Lead Me, Guide Me.* Chicago, IL: GIA Publications, Inc. 1987.

*Worship, Third Edition* (W). Chicago, IL: GIA Publications, Inc. 1986.

## Suggested Hymns from the Resources

Amazing Grace (W, J, G)
Be Not Afraid (J, G)
Come to Me (J, G)
Eye Has Not Seen (G)
Healer of Our Every Ill (G)
I Heard the Voice of Jesus Say (W, J, G)
Jerusalem, My Happy Home (W, J, G)
Just a Closer Walk with Thee (J)
Nade Te Turbe / Nothing Can Trouble (Taizé)
On Eagle's Wings (J, G)
Precious Lord, Take My Hand (J G)
There Is a Balm in Gilead (W, J, G)

There's a Wideness in God's Mercy (W, J, G)
Yes, I Shall Arise (J)
You Are Mine (G)
You Are Near (J, G)
With a Shepherd's Care (Chepponis)

You are also invited to consult the indexes of the publications listed above for further musical suggestions.

# Appendix 4

# Bibliography

## SOURCES

Abbott, Walter M., general ed. *The Documents of Vatican II.* New York: The America Press. 1966.

*Book of Blessings.* New York: Catholic Book Publishing, Co. 1989.

*Code of Canon Law, Latin-English Edition.* Translation under the auspices of the Canon Law Society of America. Washington, D.C.: Canon Law Society of America, 1983.

*Code of Canons of the Eastern Churches, Latin-English Edition.* Translation under the Auspices of the Canon Law Society of America. Washington, D.C.: Canon Law Society of America. 1990.

*Pastoral Care of the Sick: Rites of Anointing and Viaticum.* New York: Catholic Book Publishing Co. 1983.

## Ecclesial Texts

1983. Bishop's Committee on the Liturgy. *Newsletter.* Volume XV. (March–April 1979).

——. *Study Text II: Anointing and Pastoral Care of the Sick. Commentary on the Rite for the Anointing and Pastoral Care of the Sick.* Washington D.C.: Publications Office, United States Catholic Conference. 1973.

The Christian Medical Commission. *Healing and Wholeness: The Churches' Role in Health.* Geneva: World Council of Churches. 1990.

Congregation for the Clergy, et al. *Instruction on Certain Questions Regarding the Collaboration of the Non-Ordained Faithful in the Sacred Ministry of Priests.* Vatican City: Libreria Editrice Vaticana. 1997.

Congregation for the Doctrine of the Faith. *Letter to the Bishops of the Catholic Church on the Pastoral Care of Homosexual Persons.* October 1, 1986. Washington, D.C.: United States Catholic Conference. 1986.

——. *Persona Humana.* December 29, 1975 *(Declaration on Certain Questions Concerning Sexual Ethics).* Washington, D.C.: United States Catholic Conference. 1976.

International Commission on English in the Liturgy. *Emendations in the Liturgical Books Following upon the New Code of Canon Law.* Washington, D.C.: ICEL. 1984.

——. *The Rites of the Catholic Church as Revised by Decree of the Second Vatican Ecumenical Council and Published by Authority of Pope Paul VI. Study Edition.* New York: Pueblo Publishing Co. 1976, 1983.

Lettre pastorale des évêques de la partie francophone de Belgique. "L'Onction des Malades," *La Documentation Catholique* (1er Janvier 1978): 20–22.

National Conference of Catholic Bishops. "Always Our Children: A Pastoral Message to Parents of Homosexual Children and Suggestions for Pastoral Ministers." *Origins* 28 (July 2, 1998): 97, 99–102.

——. *Called to Compassion and Responsibility: A Response to the HIV/AIDS Crisis.* Washington D.C.: United States Catholic Conference. 1989.

——. "Sacraments with Persons with Disabilities." *Origins* 25 (June 29, 1995): 105, 107–10.

——. "The Many Faces of AIDS: A Gospel Response." *Origins* 17 (December 24, 1987): 481, 483–89.

——. *New Slavery, New Freedom: A Pastoral Message on Substance Abuse.* Washington, D.C.: United States Catholic Conference, Inc. 1990.

Pontifical Council for the Family. *From Despair to Hope: Family and Drug Addiction.* Vatican City. 1992.

——. *The Truth and Meaning of Human Sexuality: Guidelines for Education within the Family.* Città del Vaticano: Libreria Editrice Vaticana. 1995.

Pope John Paul II. "Anointing of the Sick." *The Pope Speaks* 37 (1992).

——. "Christ Came to Share Our Afflictions," (The Holy Father's message for the Sixth World Day of the Sick to be celebrated on 11 February 1998), *L'Osservatore Romano Weekly Edition in English.* N. 29 (1500) 16 July 1997: 1, 4.

——. "Defending Human Dignity." *The Pope Speaks* 32 (1987).

——. "Drug Addiction and Alcoholism Frustrate the Person's very Capacity for Communion and Self-Giving." *Dolentium Hominum* 19: 8–9.

——. "The Ethics of the AIDS Crisis." *The Pope Speaks* 36 (1991).

——. "The Image of God in People with Mental Illnesses." *Origins CNS Documentary Service.* Vol. 26, No. 30. January 16, 1997: 495–97.

——. "Of Suffering Humanity." *The Pope Speaks* 30 (1985).

——. *On the Christian Meaning of Human Suffering (Salvifici Doloris).* Apostolic Letter. February 11, 1984. Washington, D.C.: Office of Publishing Services, United States Catholic Conference. 1984.

——. *Reconciliation and Penance.* In *The Pope Speaks* 30 (1985).

——. *Redemptor Hominis.* Encyclical. March 4, 1979. Milano: Scuole Grafiche Pavoniane. 1979.

——. "The Value of Each Person." *The Pope Speaks* 31 (1986).

Pope Paul VI. "Leprosy in Our Time: Homily of Pope Paul VI during Mass for World Leprosy Day (January 29, 1978)." *The Pope Speaks* 23 (1978).

——. "The Value of Christian Suffering: Homily of Pope Paul VI at a Jubilee Mass for the Sick." *The Pope Speaks* 20 (1975).

## Books and Articles

American Psychiatric Association. *Diagnostic and Statistical Manual of Mental Disorders.* Fourth Edition. DSM-IV. Washington, DC: American Psychiatric Association. 1994.

Angelini, Fiorenzo. "Depression: A Problem of Contemporary Man." *Dolentium Hominum* 1 (1986): 58–59.

———. "Indispensable Principles for Health Policy and Care." *Dolentium Hominum* 8 (1993): 14–15.

———. "To Serve the Sick." *Dolentium Hominum* 8 (1993): 58–61.

———. "What Does the Church Expect from Us as Persons Consecrated to Hospital Care?" *Dolentium Hominum* 8 (1993): 63–66.

Anonymous. *Meditations for the Twelve Steps: A Spiritual Journey.* San Diego: RPI Publishers, Inc. 1993.

Antonelli, Ferruccio. "Drug Addiction and Inner Suffering." *Dolentium Hominum* 7 (1992): 205–206.

Ashley, Benedict M., and Kevin D. O'Rourke. *Health Care Ethics: A Theological Analysis.* Fourth Edition. Washington, D.C.: Georgetown University Press. 1997.

Auer, Johann, and Joseph Ratzinger. *I Sacramenti della Chiesa.* Translated by Carlo Molari. Assisi: Cittadella Editrice. 1989.

Autton, Norman. *The Pastoral Care of the Mentally Ill.* London: SPCK. 1963.

Avalos, Hector. *Illness and Health Care in the Ancient Near East: The Role of the Temple in Greece, Mesopotamia, and Israel.* Atlanta, GA: Scholars Press. 1995.

Axelrod, Julius. "Mental Illness, Drugs, and Neurotransmitters." *Dolentium Hominum* 22 (1993): 76–80.

Bednarski, Gloriana. "Catechesis For the Elderly: The Anointing of the Sick." *The Living Light* 11, no. 2 (Summer 1974): 205–16.

Becker, Russell J. "Sin, Illness, and Guilt." In *Religion and Medicine: Essays on Meaning, Values, and Health,* ed. David Belgum. pp. 236–44. Ames, IA: Iowa State University Press. 1967.

Belgum, David. "Patient or Penitent." In *Religion and Medicine: Essays on Meaning, Values, and Health,* ed. David Belgum. pp. 207–15. Ames, IA: Iowa State University Press. 1967.

———, ed. *Religion and Medicine: Essays on Meaning, Values, and Health.* Ames, IA: Iowa State University Press. 1967.

Benedict, Mary Grace. "Open the Sacrament of the Sick to Struggling Alcoholics." *St. Anthony Messenger* 96, no. 10 (March 1989): 37–39.

Botte, Bernard. "L'onction des malades." *La Maison-Dieu* 15 (1948): 91–107.

Bouscaren, T. Lincoln, and Adam C. Ellis. *Canon Law: A Text and Commentary.* Third Revised Edition. Milwaukee: The Bruce Publishing Company. 1957.

Boylan, Anthony. "Why Do We Anoint the Sick?" *Priests & People* 6 (November 1992): 405–408.

Brown, Peter. *Society and the Holy in Late Antiquity.* Berkeley/Los Angeles: University of California Press. (date unavailable).

Brown, Raymond E., Joseph A. Fitzmyer, Roland E. Murphy, eds. *The New Jerome Biblical Commentary.* Englewood Cliffs, NJ: Prentice-Hall. 1968, 1990.

Browning, Robert L., and Roy A. Reed. *The Sacraments in Religious Education and Liturgy: An Ecumenical Model.* Birmingham, AL: Religious Education Press. 1985.

Brzana, Stanislao J. *Remains of Sin and Extreme Unction According to Theologians After Trent.* (Dissertation) Romae: Officium Libri Catholici-Catholic Book Agency. 1953.

Bugnini, Annibale. *The Reform of the Liturgy 1948–1975.* Translated by Matthew J. O'Connell. Collegeville, MN: The Liturgical Press. 1990.

Carnes, Patrick. *Contrary to Love: Helping the Sexual Addict.* Center City, MN: Hazelden Educational Materials. 1989.

Casera, Domenico. "Ethical-Pastoral Aspects of Caring for the Mentally Ill." *Dolentium Hominum* 6 (1991): 276–78.

Casey, Juliana. *Food for the Journey: Theological Foundations of the Catholic Healthcare Ministry.* St. Louis: The Catholic Health Association of the United States. 1991.

Catalonian-Balearic Society for Palliative Care. "The Rights of the Terminally Ill Person." *Dolentium Hominum* 8 (1993): 26–32.

Cazzullo, Carlo Lorenzo. "The Acceptance of Mental Illness." *Dolentium Hominum* 34 (1997): 81–85.

Cazzullo, Carlo Lorenzo, and Costanza Gala. "Psychological and Neuropsychiatric Aspects of AIDS." *Dolentium Hominum* 13 (1990): 142–47.

Champlin, Joseph. *Healing in the Catholic Church: Mending Wounded Hearts and Bodies.* Huntington, IN: Our Sunday Visitor, Inc. 1985.

Chappel, John N. "The Use of Alcoholics Anonymous and Narcotics Anonymous by the Physician in Treating Drug and Alcohol Addiction." In *Comprehensive Handbook of Drug and Alcohol Addiction.* Ed. Norman S. Miller, 1079–88. New York/Basel/Hong Kong: Marcel Dekker, Inc. 1991.

Chavasse, Antoine. *Étude sur l'onction des infirmes dans l'église latine du IIIe au XIe Siècle. Tome I Du IIIe siècle à la réforme carolingienne.* (thèse de doctorat). Lyon: La Faculté de Théologie de Lyon. 1942.

——. "Prières pour les malades et onction sacramentelle," in *L'Église En Prière.* Ed. A. G. Martimort, 580–94. Paris: Desclée & Cie, Éditeurs. 1961.

Cheriavely, John F. "25th Year of the Rite of Anointing of the Sick: Challenges and Perspectives." *Questions Liturgiques: Studies in Liturgy* 78 (1997): 164–75.

Christian Medical Commission. *Healing and Wholeness: The Churches' Role in Health.* Geneva: World Council of Churches. 1990.

Ciarrochi, Joseph W. *A Minister's Handbook of Mental Disorders.* Mahwah, NJ: Paulist Press. 1993.

Clebsch, William A., and Charles R. Jaekle. *Pastoral Care in Historical Perspective.* New York: Jason Aronson. 1975.

Clinebell, Howard. *Basic Types of Pastoral Care & Counseling: Resources for the Ministry of Healing and Growth* (Revised and Enlarged). Nashville: Abingdon Press. 1984.

——. *Understanding and Counseling Persons with Alcohol, Drug, and Behavioral Addictions.* (Revised and Enlarged). Nashville: Abingdon Press. 1968, 1984, 1998.

Coan, Richard W. *Hero, Artist, Sage, or Saint? A Survey of Views on What Is Variously Called Mental Health, Normality, Maturity, Self-Actualization, and Human Fulfillment.* New York: Columbia University Press. 1977.

Coleman, Gerald D. *Homosexuality: Catholic Teaching and Pastoral Practice.* New York/Mahwah: Paulist Press. 1995.

——. "Turning Gays 'Straight'?" *Church* 7 (Spring 1991): 44–46.

Collins, Mary, and David N. Power, eds. *Concilium: The Pastoral Care of the Sick.* London: SCM Press. 1991/2.

Collopy, Bartholomew J. "Theology and the Darkness of Death," *Theological Studies* 39 (March 1978): 22–54.

Colt, George Howe. "Were You Born That Way?" *Life* (1998): 39–49.

Coriden, James A., Thomas J. Green, and Donald E. Heintschel, eds. *The Code of Canon Law: A Text and Commentary.* New York/Mahwah: Paulist Press. 1985.

Costello, Timothy W., and Joseph T. Costello. *Abnormal Psychology (HarperCollins College Outline).* 2nd Edition. New York: HarperCollins Publishers, Inc. 1992.

Cothenet, Edouard. "Healing as a Sign of the Kingdom, and the Anointing of the Sick." In *Temple of the Holy Spirit.* Translated by Matthew J. O'Connell, 33–51. New York: Pueblo Publishing Company. 1983.

Cuschieri, Andrew. *Anointing of the Sick: A Theological and Canonical Study.* Lanham, MD: University Press of America, Inc. 1993.

Dackis, Charles A., and Mark S. Gold. "Inpatient Treatment of Drug and Alcohol Addiction." In *Comprehensive Handbook of Drug and Alcohol Addiction.* Ed. Norman S. Miller, 1233–43. New York/Basel/Hong Kong: Marcel Dekker, Inc. 1991.

Davis, Patricia. "A Parish Celebration of Anointing." *Liturgy* 2 (1981–1982): 33–37.

Davis, Robert C. "Prayers and Liturgy in the Sickroom." *Liturgy* 2 (1981–1982): 59–63.

Diekmann, Godfrey. "The Laying on of Hands: The Basic Sacramental Rite." *Proceedings of the Catholic Theological Society of America* 29 (June 10–13, 1974): 339–51.

Di Menna, Renato. "Caring for the Sick Is a Way of Announcing the Kingdom." *Dolentium Hominum* 1 (1986): 13–16.

Dobbelstein, Herman. *Psychiatry for Priests.* Translated by Meyrick Booth. Cork, Ireland: The Mercier Press. 1953.

Dorff, Elliot N. "The Jewish Tradition." In *Caring and Curing.* Ronald L. Numbers and Darrel W. Amundsen, eds. Baltimore/London: The Johns Hopkins University Press. 1986, 1998.

Dougherty, Kenneth F. "Battle of the Bottle." *The Priest* 28 (July–August 1972): 21–27.

Dubarle, André-Marie. "Sickness and Death in the Old Testament." In *Temple of the Holy Spirit.* Translated by Matthew J. O'Connell, 53–64. New York: Pueblo Publishing Company. 1983.

Dudley, Martin, and Geoffrey Rowell, eds. *The Oil of Gladness: Anointing in the Christian Tradition.* Collegeville, MN: The Liturgical Press. 1993.

Empereur, James L. *Prophetic Anointing: God's Call to the Sick, the Elderly, and the Dying.* Vol. 7 of *Message of the Sacraments,* Monika K. Hellwig, ed. Wilmington, DE: Michael Glazier, Inc. 1982.

——. "Rite On: Anointing," *Modern Liturgy* 5 (April 1978): 15.

Erraught, Joseph. "The Sacraments and the Mentally Ill." *Studies in Pastoral Liturgy II.* Vincent Ryan, ed. Dublin: The Furrow Trust. 1963. pp. 58–60.

Escobedo, Francisco. "The Human Mind, Cultures, and Mental Illnesses." *Dolentium Hominum* 6 (1991): 237–40.

Fagiolo, Vincenzo. "The Care of the Sick According to Canonical Legislation." *Dolentium Hominum* 4 (1989): 5–8.

Farraher, Joseph. "How Often May a Sick Person Be Anointed?" *Homiletic and Pastoral Review* 85 (July 1985): 73.

Favazza, Joseph A. *The Order of Penitents: Historical Roots and Pastoral Future.* Collegeville, MN: The Liturgical Press. 1988.

Feldman, David M. *Health and Medicine in the Jewish Tradition: L'Hayyim — To Life.* New York: Crossroad Publishing Company. 1986.

Fellows, Bill. "Toward a Sacramentality of Sickness." *Modern Liturgy* 19 (October 1992): 16–17.

Finch, Mary Ann. "Healing Through Anointing," *Modern Liturgy* 5 (April 1978): 8–10.

Flipot, Geneviève. "Illness and Healing in the Charismatic Renewal." *Lumen Vitae* 41 (1986): 74–85.

Foley, Edward, ed. *Developmental Disabilities and Sacramental Access: New Paradigms for Sacramental Encounters.* Collegeville, MN: The Liturgical Press. 1994.

Füredi, Janos. "Integrated Therapies for Schizophrenic Patients and Their Families." *Dolentium Hominum* 34 (1997): 183–85.

Glen, M. Jennifer. "A Bibliography on Ministries to the Sick." *Liturgy* 2 (1981–1982): 78–80.

———. "Sickness and Symbol: The Promise of the Future." *Worship* 54 (September 1980): 397–411.

Goodwin, Frederick K. "Alcohol, Drugs, and Mental Illness." *Dolentium Hominum* 7 (1992): 172–78.

———. "The Illness of the Soul: Mood Disorders and Their Biological Aspects." *Dolentium Hominum* 6 (1991): 111–14.

Greshake, Gisbert. "Extreme Unction or Anointing of the Sick? A Plea for Discrimination." *Review for Religious* 45 (May–June 1986): 435–52.

———. "Towards a Theology of Dying," *Concilium* 94. New York: Herder and Herder. 1974.

Gusmer, Charles W. *And You Visited Me: Sacramental Ministry to the Sick and Dying.* Collegeville: The Liturgical Press. 1990.

———. "Anointing of the Sick in the Church of England." *Worship* 45 (May 1971): 262–72.

———. "Ecumenical Perspective." *National Bulletin on Liturgy* 10 (January–February 1977).

———. "Healing: Charism & Sacrament," *Church* 2 (Summer 1986): 16–22.

———. "I Was Sick and You Visited Me: The Revised Rites for the Sick," *Worship* 48 (November 1974): 516–25.

———. "Liturgical Traditions of Christian Illness: Rites of the Sick," *Worship* 46 (November 1972): 528–43.

———. *The Ministry of Healing in the Church of England an Ecumenical-Liturgical Study.* Great Wakering, Essex: Mayhew-McCrimmon. 1974.

Gutierrez, Carlos G. Alvarez. *El Sentido Teologico de la Uncion de los Enfermos en La Teologia Contemporanea* (1940–1980). Bogota: Typis Pontificiae Universitatis Xaverianae. 1982.

Hall, Christine. "The Use of the Holy Oils in the Orthodox Churches of the Byzantine Tradition." In Martin Dudley and Geoffrey Rowell, eds. *The Oil of Gladness: Anointing in the Christian Tradition.* London: SPCK. 1993.

Halligan, Nicholas. *The Administration of the Sacraments.* Cork: The Mercier Press. 1963.

———. *The Ministry of the Celebration of the Sacraments: Sacraments of Reconciliation. Volume II: Penance, Anointing of the Sick.* New York: Alba House. 1973.

———. *The Sacraments and Their Celebration.* New York: Alba House. 1986.

Häring, Bernard. *The Healing Mission of the Church in the Coming Decades.* Washington, D.C.: Center for Applied Research in the Apostolate. 1982.

Harrington, Daniel. "Is Anyone among You Sick? New Testament Foundations for Anointing the Sick." *Emmanuel* 101 (September 1995): 412–17.

Harrison, Patricia Ann, et al. "Drug and Alcohol Addiction Treatment Outcome." In *Comprehesive Handbook of Drug and Alcohol Addiction.* Ed. Norman S. Miller, 1163–97. New York/Basel/Hong Kong: Marcel Dekker, Inc. 1991.

Harvey, John F. "Sexual Abstinence for the Homosexual Person." *Fellowship of Catholic Scholars Newsletter* 15 (1992): 20–21.

———. *The Homosexual Person: New Thinking in Pastoral Care.* San Francisco: Ignatius Press. 1987.

———. *The Truth about Homosexuality: The Cry of the Faithful.* San Francisco: Ignatius Press. 1996.

Hoyman, Howard S. "The Spiritual Dimension of Man's Health in Today's World." In *Religion and Medicine: Essays on Meaning, Values, and Health.* Ed. David Belgum, 186–203. Ames, IA: Iowa State University Press. 1967.

Huels, John M. *The Pastoral Companion: A Canon Law Handbook for Catholic Ministry.* New Series, Second Edition, Revised, Updated and Expanded. Quincy, IL: Franciscan Press. 1995.

———. "'Use of Reason' and Reception of Sacraments by the Mentally Handicapped." *The Jurist* 44 (1984): 209–19.

Itoua, Hervé. "Pastoral Care and the Spirituality of the Mentally Ill." *Dolentium Hominum* 34 (1997): 208–16.

Jackson, Gordon E. "The Problem of Guilt." In *Religion and Medicine: Essays on Meaning, Values, and Health.* Ed. David Belgum, 216–35. Ames, IA: Iowa State University Press. 1967.

Johnson, Paul E. "Religious Psychology and Health." In *Religion and Medicine: Essays On Meaning, Values, and Health.* Ed. David Belgum, 33–44. Ames, IA: Iowa State University Press. 1967.

Kennedy, Dennis. "The Sacrament of Anointing and the Disabled." *Liturgy* 2 (1981–1982): 12–17.

Kilker, Adrian Jerome. *Extreme Unction: A Canonical Treatise Containing also a Consideration of the Dogmatic, Historical and Liturgical Aspects of the Sacrament.* St. Louis, MO: B. Herder Book Co. 1927.

Kryger, Henry S. *The Doctrine of the Effects of Extreme Unction in Its Historical Development* (Dissertation). The CUA Studies in Sacred Theology (Second Series), No. 33. Washington, D.C.: The Catholic University of America Press. 1949.

Kübler-Ross, Elisabeth. *On Death and Dying.* New York: Macmillan. 1969.

Lader, Malcom. "Abnormalities of the Mind in Schizophrenia." *Dolentium Hominum* 34 (1997): 121–24.

Larson-Miller, Lizette. "Women and the Anointing of the Sick." *Coptic Church Review* 12 (Summer 1991): 37–48.

Lawler, Philip F. "The U.S. Bishops and the Gay Agenda," *The Catholic World Report* (November 1997): 32–36.

Lehmann, Karl. "Pastoral Care Based on Hope." *Dolentium Hominum* 5 (1990): 207–13.

Le Trocquer, René. "Anthropologie de l'âme et du corps devant la mort." *La Maison-Dieu* 44 (1955): 5–28.

Linn, Matthew & Dennis. *Deliverance Prayer: Experiential, Psychological and Theological Approaches.* New York: Paulist Press. 1981.

Lisitsin, Yuri. "Alcoholism: Sociocultural Aspects and Spirituality." *Dolentium Hominum* 7 (1992): 154–56.

Marsh, Thomas. "A Theology of Anointing the Sick," *The Furrow* 29 (February 1978): 89–101.

——. "Guided Reading Programme: The Sacrament of the Anointing of the Sick," *The Furrow* 33 (May 1982): 297–99.

Martimort, Aimé Georges. Ed. *The Church at Prayer: An Introduction to the Liturgy, New Edition. Volume III: The Sacraments.* Translated by Matthew J. O'Connell. Collegeville, MN: The Liturgical Press. 1988.

——. "Comment meurt un chrétien." *La Maison-Dieu* 44 (1955): 5–28.

——. "Le nouveau rituel des malades." *La Documentation Catholique* 70 (4 février 1973): 103–104.

——. *The Signs of the New Covenant.* Revised Second Edition. Collegeville, MN: The Liturgical Press. 1963.

May, Gerald G. *Care of Mind, Care of Spirit: A Psychiatrist Explores Spiritual Direction.* New York: HarperCollins Publishers. 1982, 1992.

McCormick, Patrick. *Sin as Addiction.* Mahwah, NJ: Paulist Press. 1989.

McCormick, Richard A. *Health and Medicine in the Catholic Tradition: Tradition in Transition.* New York: Crossroad Publishing Company. 1987.

McDonald, Patrick J. "The Life of the Community and Anointing for Death." *Spiritual Life* 40 (Winter 1994): 211–19.

McGuire, Meredith B. *Ritual Healing in Suburban America.* New Brunswick and London: Rutgers University Press. 1988.

McIntyre, Marie, and Edmund C. Curley. "How Do We Think about Anointing of the Sick?" *Religion Teacher's Journal* 8 (January 1975): 22–23.

McIvor, Dermot. "The Care of the Sick in the Roman Ritual." In *Studies in Pastoral Liturgy.* Volume Two. Ed., Vincent Ryan, 39–51. Dublin: The Furrow Trust. 1963.

Mélia, Elie. "The Sacrament of the Anointing of the Sick: Its Historical Development and Current Practice." In *Temple of the Holy Spirit.* Translated by Matthew J. O'Connell, 127–60. New York: Pueblo Publishing Company. 1983.

Meltzer, Herbert Y. "Recovery from Schizophrenia: New Advances in Pharmacological Treatments." *Dolentium Hominum* 6 (1991): 139–43.

Melvin, Edward J. "Pastoral Care of Persons Apparently Dead," *Homiletic and Pastoral Review* 84 (May 1984): 45–51.

Meyendorff, Paul. "The Anointing of the Sick: Some Pastoral Considerations." *St. Vladimir Quarterly* 25 (1991): 241–55.

Meyer, Roger E. "The Concept of Disease in Alcoholism and Drug Addiction." *Dolentium Hominum* 7 (1992): 113–21.

Miffleton, Jack. "Surprise: Childhood Illness—A Time for Family Ministry," *Modern Liturgy* 5 (April 1978): 23.

Moynahan, Michael E. "The Sacramentality of Touch," *Modern Liturgy* 5 (April 1978): 28–29.

Murphy, Thomas. "Pastoral Care of Parish Communities." *Origins* 24 (April 20, 1995): 755–64.

Murray, Placid. "The Liturgical History of Extreme Unction." In *Studies in Pastoral Liturgy*. Volume Two. Ed. Vincent Ryan, 18–38. Dublin: The Furrow Trust. 1963.

Myss, Caroline, and C. Norman Shealy. *The Creation of Health: The Emotional, Psychological, and Spiritual Responses That Promote Health and Healing.* New York: Three Rivers Press. 1988, 1993.

Nakken, Craig. *The Addictive Personality: Understanding the Addictive Process and Compulsive Behavior.* 2nd Edition. Center City, MN: Hazelden. 1988, 1996.

Nolan, Keiran. "The Sacrament of Anointing and Total Patient Care," *Homiletic and Pastoral Review* 74 (June 1974): 53–62.

Notebaart, James. "The Sacrament of the Anointing of the Sick," *Modern Liturgy* 5 (April 1978): 4, 16.

Oates, Wayne E. *The Religious Care of the Psychiatric Patient.* Louisville, KY: Westminster/John Knox Press. 1978.

Obinna, Anthony J. V. "Catholic Healing in an African Context." *Liturgy* 2 (1981–1982): 69–74.

O'Connell, Matthew J., translator. *Temple of the Holy Spirit: Sickness and Death of the Christian in the Liturgy. The Twenty-First Liturgical Conference Saint-Serge.* New York: Pueblo Publishing Company. 1983.

Onians, Richard Broxton. *The Origins of European Thought about the Body, the Mind, the Soul, the World, Time, and Fate: New Interpretations of Greek, Roman and Kindred Evidence, also Some Basic Jewish and Christian Beliefs.* Cambridge: University Press. 1951.

O'Riordan, Seán. "The Healing Ministry of the Church," *The Furrow* 33 (May 1982): 292–96.

Palmer, Paul F. ed. *Sacraments and Forgiveness: History and Doctrinal Development of Penance, Extreme Unction and Indulgences.* London: Darton, Longman & Todd. 1959.

——. "The Purpose of Anointing the Sick: A Reappraisal," *Theological Studies* 19 (September 1958): 309–44.

——. "Who Can Anoint the Sick?" *Worship* 48 (January 1974): 81–92.

Pickett, R. Colin. *Mental Affliction and Church Law: An Historical Synopsis of Roman and Ecclesiastical Law and a Canonical Commentary.* Ottawa, Ontario: The University of Ottawa Press. 1952.

Pilch, John J. "Sickness and Healing in Luke-Acts." In Jerome H. Neyrey, ed. *The Social World of Luke-Acts: Models for Interpretation.* 181–209. Peabody, MA: Hendrickson Publishers. 1991.

Porter, H. B. "The Origin of the Medieval Rite for Anointing the Sick or Dying," *The Journal of Theological Studies* 7 (October 1956): 211–25.

——. "The Rites for the Dying in the Early Middle Ages, I: St. Theodulf of Orleans," *The Journal of Theological Studies* 10 (April 1959): 43–62.

——. "The Rites for the Dying in the Early Middle Ages, II: The Legendary Sacramentary of Rheims," *The Journal of Theological Studies* 10 (October 1959): 299–307.

Power, David N. "All Things Made New." *Liturgy* 2 (1981–1982): 7–11.

——. "Let the Sick Man Call." *The Heythrop Journal* 19/2 (July 1978): 256–70.

——. "The Sacrament of Anointing: Open Questions." In Mary Collins and David N. Power, eds. *Concilium: The Pastoral Care of the Sick.* London: SCM Press. 1991/2.

Rahman, Fazlur. *Health and Medicine in the Islamic Tradition: Change and Identity.* New York: Crossroad Publishing Company. 1989.

Rahner, Karl. *The Church and the Sacraments.* Translated by W. J. O'Hara. New York: Herder and Herder. 1963, 1968.

——. "Guilt and Its Remission: The Borderland between Theology and Psychotherapy," *Theological Investigations. Volume II Man in the Church.* Translated by Karl-H. Kruger. London: Darton, Longman & Todd. 1963, 1967: 265–81.

——. "The Saving Force and Healing Power of Faith," *Theological Investigations. Volume V Later Writings.* Translated by Karl-H. Kruger. London: Darton, Longman & Todd. 1966, 1969: 460–67.

——. "Proving Oneself in Time of Sickness," *Theological Investigations. Volume VII Further Theology of the Spiritual Life I.* Translated by David Bourke. New York: Herder and Herder. 1971: 275–84.

——. "The Liberty of the Sick, Theologically Considered," *Theological Investigations. Volume XVII Jesus, Man, and the Church.* Translated by Margaret Kohl. New York: Crossroad. 1981: 100–13.

——. "Why Does God Allow Us to Suffer?" *Theological Investigations. Volume XIX Faith and Ministry.* Translated by Edward Quinn. New York: Crossroad. 1983: 194–208.

Rahner, Karl, and Herbert Vorgrimler. "Death." In *Concise Theological Dictionary,* 2nd Edition. London: Burns & Oates. 1965, 1983.

Renati, Charles George. *The Recipient of Extreme Unction* (Dissertation). Washington, D.C.: The Catholic University of America Press. 1961.

Rhys, John H. W. "Ministers of Healing and Pastoral Care." *Liturgy* 2 (1981–1982): 75–77.

Richards, John. *But Deliver Us from Evil: An Introduction to the Demonic Dimension in Pastoral Care.* New York: The Seabury Press. 1974.

Rosario, Priamo Tejeda. "The Doctor and the Priest at the Service of Life." *Dolentium Hominum* 10 (1995): 122–23.

Rossbach, Mary Lee. "Anointing if for the Sick, Not for Everyone over 65." *St. Anthony Messenger* 86 (June 1978): 24–26.

Roth, Gottfried. "The Brain and Pastoral Medicine." *Dolentium Hominum* 6 (1991): 149–51.

Ryn, Zdzislaw Jan. "The Christian Meaning of Suffering: John Paul II and the Sick." *Dolentium Hominum* 10 (1995): 31–36.

St. Romain, Philip. *Becoming a New Person: Twelve Steps to Christian Growth.* Liguori, Missouri: Liguori Publications. 1984.

Salachas, Dimitri. "The Health of the Body and of the Soul in the Byzantine Liturgy." *Dolentium Hominum* 5 (1990): 61–62.

Schaef, Anne Wilson. *Beyond Therapy, Beyond Science: A New Model for Healing the Whole Person.* New York: HarperSanFrancisco. 1992.

——. *When Society becomes An Addict.* San Francisco: Harper & Row, Publishers. 1987.

Schmemann, Alexander. *Sacraments and Orthodoxy.* New York: Herder and Herder. 1965.

Seybold, Klaus, and Ulrich B. Mueller. *Sickness and Healing.* Translated by Douglas W. Stott. Nashville: Abingdon. 1981.

Sheehy, Gerard, et al., eds. *The Canon Law: Letter & Spirit: A Practical Guide to the Code of Canon Law.* London: Geoffrey Chapman. 1995.

Shorter, Aylward. *Jesus and the Witchdoctor: An Approach to Healing and Wholeness.* London: Geoffrey Chapman. 1985.

Statkus, Francis J. *The Minister of the Last Sacraments.* (Dissertation). Washington D.C.: The Catholic University of America Press. 1951.

Sullivan, Lawrence E., ed. *Healing and Restoring: Health and Medicine in the World's Religious Traditions.* New York: MacMillan Publishing Company. 1989.

Telthorst, James T. "Anointing of the Sick: Community Celebration," *Health Progress* 65 (December 1984): 40–43.

Torrey, E. Fuller, et al. *Schizophrenia and Manic-Depressive Disorder: The Biological Roots of Mental Illness as Revealed by the Landmark Study of Identical Twins.* New York: BasicBooks. 1994.

Totman, Richard. *Social Causes of Illness.* 2nd Edition. London: Souvenir Press (E & A), Ltd. 1979, 1987.

Van den Berg, J. H. *The Psychology of the Sickbed.* Pittsburgh: The Duquesne University Press. 1966.

Verheul, Ambroise. "The Paschal Character of the Sacrament of the Sick: Exegesis of James 5:14–15 and the New Rite for the Sacrament of the Sick." In *Temple of the Holy Spirit.* Translated by Matthew J. O'Connell, 247–57. New York: Pueblo Publishing Company. 1983.

Wicks, Jared. "Applied Theology at the Deathbed: Luther and the Late-Medieval Tradition of the *Ars moriendi.*" *Gregorianum* 79, 2 (1998): 345–68.

Wicks, Robert J., Richard D. Parsons, and Donald Capps, eds. *Clinical Handbook of Pastoral Counseling, Volume I. Expanded Edition.* New York: Paulist Press. 1993.

Woestman, William H. *Sacraments: Initiation, Penance, Anointing of the Sick. Commentary on Canons 840–1007.* Ottawa: Faculty of Canon Law, Saint Paul University. 1992, 1996.

Wolff, Hans Walter. *Anthropology of the Old Testament.* Translated by Margaret Kohl. London: SCM Press LTD. 1974.

Worgul, George S. *From Magic to Metaphor: A Validation of Christian Sacraments.* New York/Ramsey: Paulist Press. 1980.

World Health Organization. *The ICD-10 Classification of Mental and Behavioural Disorders: Clinical Descriptions and Diagnostic Guidelines.* Geneva: World Health Organization. 1992.

——. *The ICD-10 Classification of Mental and Behavioural Disorders: Diagnostic Criteria for Research.* Geneva: World Health Organization. 1993.

Ziegler, John J. *Let Them Anoint the Sick.* Collegeville, MN: The Liturgical Press. 1987.

——. "Who Can Anoint the Sick?" *Worship* 61 (January 1987): 25–44.

# Index

# About the Liturgical Institute

The Liturgical Institute, founded in 2000 by His Eminence Francis Cardinal George of Chicago, offers a variety of options for education in Liturgical Studies. A unified, rites-based core curriculum constitutes the foundation of the program, providing integrated and balanced studies toward the advancement of the renewal promoted by the Second Vatican Council. The musical, artistic, and architectural dimensions of worship are given particular emphasis in the curriculum. Institute students are encouraged to participate in its "liturgical heart" of daily Mass and Morning and Evening Prayer. The academic program of the Institute serves a diverse, international student population—laity, religious, and clergy—who are preparing for service in parishes, dioceses, and religious communities. Personalized mentoring is provided in view of each student's ministerial and professional goals. The Institute is housed on the campus of the University of St. Mary of the Lake/Mundelein Seminary, which offers the largest priestly formation program in the United States and is the center of the permanent diaconate and lay ministry training programs of the Archdiocese of Chicago. In addition, the University has the distinction of being the first chartered institution of higher learning in Chicago (1844), and one of only seven pontifical faculties in North America.

For more information about the Liturgical Institute and its programs, contact: usml.edu/liturgicalinstitute. Phone: 847-837-4542. E-mail: litinst@usml.edu.

*Msgr. Reynold Hillenbrand*
*1904-1979*

Monsignor Reynold Hillenbrand, ordained a priest by Cardinal George Mundelein in 1929, was Rector of St. Mary of the Lake Seminary from 1936 to 1944.

He was a leading figure in the liturgical and social action movement in the United States during the 1930s and worked to promote active, intelligent, and informed participation in the Church's liturgy.

He believed that a reconstruction of society would occur as a result of the renewal of the Christian spirit, whose source and center is the liturgy.

Hillenbrand taught that, since the ultimate purpose of Catholic action is to Christianize society, the renewal of the liturgy must undoubtedly play the key role in achieving this goal.

**Hillenbrand Books**™ strives to reflect the spirit of Monsignor Reynold Hillenbrand's pioneering work by making available innovative and scholarly resources that advance the liturgical and sacramental life of the Church.